Since when h
Mose hadn't s
being—a man
not his.

"It pays to know your business," she said quietly.

He looked over and gave her another one of those lopsided grins that caused a funny little curl in the pit of her stomach.

"That's what my daddy always says."

Before she could stop herself, she said, "I'm sure you know your business inside and out."

His head turned in her direction just enough for her to see his brows appear above the frames of his sunglasses.

"You mean the business of training horses?"

"Is there another business you're in?" she asked primly.

The corners of his mouth twitched with humor. "Not the sort that makes money. As for training horses, there's always more to learn. Horses are complex creatures. Sort of like women. You can never be sure about what they're thinking or what they might do next."

"I'm sure you're an expert at both."

As soon as the comment slipped out of her, she very nearly slapped her hand over her mouth. Why had she said such a thing to him? And where had she found the gumption to speak her thoughts out loud?

Dear Reader,

When shy Bonnie Hollister is sent by her father, Hadley, down to Three Rivers Ranch in Arizona, her only plan is to research the history of her late great-grandfather. The last thing she's expecting is to meet a young horse trainer with a sexy grin and a glint in his eye aimed straight at her.

Bonnie rarely dates, and certainly not a flamboyant cowboy, who looks like he just stepped through the swinging doors of an 1880s' saloon! But Mose Martel is unlike any man she's ever met, and before she knows what's happening, the two of them are riding across the desert range together!

One look at blond-haired, blue-eyed Bonnie is all it takes for Mose to start hankering to get closer to the pretty ranching heiress. But he's just plain ole Mose. He doesn't have anything to offer Bonnie. Or does he?

I hope you'll travel back to Three Rivers Ranch with me to see how Bonnie learns she's definitely woman enough for a man like Mose. And he discovers the forever kind of love he feels for Bonnie is all she'll ever need.

God bless the trails you ride,

Stella

CHRISTMAS ON THE RANGE

STELLA BAGWELL

SPECIAL EDITION

If you purchased this book without a cover you should be aware that this book is stolen property. It was reported as "unsold and destroyed" to the publisher, and neither the author nor the publisher has received any payment for this "stripped book."

Harlequin
SPECIAL EDITION™

ISBN-13: 978-1-335-18012-4

Christmas on the Range

Copyright © 2025 by Stella Bagwell

All rights reserved. No part of this book may be used or reproduced in any manner whatsoever without written permission.

Without limiting the author's and publisher's exclusive rights, any unauthorized use of this publication to train generative artificial intelligence (AI) technologies is expressly prohibited.

This is a work of fiction. Names, characters, places and incidents are either the product of the author's imagination or are used fictitiously. Any resemblance to actual persons, living or dead, businesses, companies, events or locales is entirely coincidental.

For questions and comments about the quality of this book, please contact us at CustomerService@Harlequin.com.

TM and ® are trademarks of Harlequin Enterprises ULC.

 Harlequin Enterprises ULC
22 Adelaide St. West, 41st Floor
Toronto, Ontario M5H 4E3, Canada
www.Harlequin.com

Printed in Lithuania

After writing more than one hundred books for Harlequin, **Stella Bagwell** still finds writing about two people discovering everlasting love very rewarding. She loves all things Western and has been married to her own real cowboy for fifty-one years. Living on the south Texas coast, she also enjoys being outdoors and helping her husband care for the animals on the small ranch they call home. The couple has one son, who teaches high school mathematics and coaches football and powerlifting.

Books by Stella Bagwell

Harlequin Special Edition

Men of the West

Her Kind of Doctor
The Arizona Lawman
Her Man on Three Rivers Ranch
A Ranger for Christmas
His Texas Runaway
Home to Blue Stallion Ranch
The Rancher's Best Gift
Her Man Behind the Badge
His Forever Texas Rose
The Baby That Binds Them
Sleigh Ride with the Rancher
The Wrangler Rides Again
The Other Hollister Man
Rancher to the Rescue
The Cowboy's Road Trip
Her Forgotten Cowboy
A Cowboy to Remember
Stone Creek Sheriff
Christmas on the Range

Visit the Author Profile page
at Harlequin.com for more titles.

To my brave and beautiful sister-in-law, Denise.
Love you!

Chapter One

Bonnie Hollister had lived on a ranch for all of her twenty-seven years, yet she could truthfully say she'd never laid eyes on a cowboy like the one striding across the small airport lobby and straight at her.

Who *was* he?

Rising from the short couch, she stood and waited for him to reach her. As soon as he was standing in front of her, he pushed the broad brim of his gray felt Stetson slightly back on his forehead. The adjustment gave her a full view of a pair of rich, golden-brown eyes framed by dark brows and lashes.

"Are you Ms. Hollister?" he asked.

His raspy voice had a slight twang to it, but that was only one of the unique things about the man, Bonnie decided. His worn jeans were stuffed into a pair of tall cowboy boots. The vamps were scarred brown leather, while the shafts were decorated with colorful inlays in the design of a thunderbird. His Western shirt was faded red, with white piping edging the pointed yokes and pearl snaps fastening the placket and wide cuffs. On anyone else, the flamboyant colored work gear would've looked totally out of place, but on this man, it somehow managed to look perfectly natural.

Moments ago, when she stepped off the small commuter plane, her blond hair had been whipped around by the Arizona wind. Now, as she met the cowboy's twinkling gaze, she self-consciously tried to smooth the loose waves back from her face.

"I'm Bonnie Hollister," she said, then asked, "Are you here to drive me to Three Rivers Ranch?"

As she'd watched him walk across the lobby, she'd thought his features had been chiseled from a piece of brown rock. But the lopsided grin now twisting his lips proved otherwise. He was all flesh and blood. And definitely all man.

From the corner of her eye, she glanced at his left hand and wasn't surprised to see his ring finger was bare. He hardly presented himself as a married man. But even if he didn't have a wife, he might have a special girlfriend, she thought, then quickly asked herself why his marital status should be any of her business.

"At your service, ma'am." He extended his hand to her. "I'm Mose Martel. Horse trainer for the Hollisters on Three Rivers Ranch."

Bonnie reached to shake his outstretched hand. It was a big warm hand with thick pads of calluses on his palm and the insides of his fingers. This wasn't a man who sat around talking about being a cowboy, she realized. He *was* one.

Once he released his hold on her, she awkwardly clasped her hands together. "Nice to meet you, Mr. Martel. I appreciate you going to the trouble of driving into town to give me a lift. I understand the ranch is some thirty or forty minutes away."

He grinned again, and Bonnie wondered if the heat and sudden change in altitude had done something to her knees. They were suddenly feeling a little wobbly.

"Depends on the driver. I tend to take it easy. No sense in shaking up the truck unnecessarily. Or my passenger," he added with a playful wink.

He was already shaking her up, she thought. And she wasn't at all sure she liked the feeling. "You needn't take it easy on my account. I'm accustomed to traveling rough roads."

If anything, her remark only deepened the grin on his face and Bonnie wondered why she was finding it such a struggle to look away from him. Sure, he was good-looking. But she wasn't in the market for romance. Not since her one and only attempt at true love had turned out be worse than humiliating.

"That's good to know," he said, then asked, "You have a bunch of bags?"

"A few." She gestured across the lobby to a baggage carrier loaded with her three suitcases.

"Great. I'll load everything for you. And then we'll be on our way."

"Thank you, Mr. Martel," she said primly.

"You're mighty welcome. Except, if it's all the same to you, I'd rather you call me Mose. You're making me feel old with the mister business."

For the past few years, Bonnie had been telling herself she wasn't ready to be involved with another man. And so far she'd stuck to her vow. The last thing she needed to do now was give this flirty cowboy any encouragement. Yet she couldn't stop herself from giving him a faint smile. "Well, I wouldn't want to be guilty of making you feel *old*, so Mose it will be."

"Thanks. Now you just stay put here in the cool 'til I take care of your bags," he told her.

As Bonnie watched him gather her luggage from the carrier and head out the main entrance of the terminal, she wondered if the other men working on Three Rivers Ranch were anything like Mose Martel. The tall, rugged cowboy was oozing masculinity. From his long-legged stride to his broad shoulders and lean waist, he was far too much man for her, she thought ruefully.

But then, Bonnie hadn't come to Arizona looking for a man. She was here to find answers about her late great-grandfather, not swoon over a cute cowboy with a cockeyed grin.

Moments later, as the two of them walked across the parking lot toward a white truck with the Three R brand emblazoned on the door, Bonnie glanced up at the vibrant blue sky. Even though it had been cold this morning in Utah, she'd expected to land in much warmer weather, so she'd donned a sundress and covered it with a heavy denim jacket. Now the Arizona sun was beaming down, making her feel the need to shed the jacket.

She said, "It's the first of December. I was expecting Arizona to be having mild weather, but nothing like this. Is this normal for the Wickenburg area at this time of year?"

"As long as I've been living here, the winters have been mild. And that's been two and a half years." He glanced over at her. "I'm originally from the Texas Panhandle. Hereford to be exact."

"Do you like living here?" she asked.

He opened the passenger door of the truck and as he slipped a hand beneath her elbow to assist her into the cab, Bonnie caught the faint scent of horses, leather and saddle soap emanating off him. She'd never considered those particular scents as an aphrodisiac, but the blended smells seemed to have a direct line to her libido. Or was it his nearness that was making her senses go haywire?

Bonnie silently groaned. Her twin sister, Beatrice, would laugh herself silly at the idea. According to her, Bonnie the wallflower, didn't possess a libido in the first place.

He said, "Oh sure. I like it fine. It's my home now. I wouldn't leave for anything." With his hand resting on the edge of the doorframe, he looked up at her. "Where are you from, Ms. Hollister? Here in Arizona?"

"Call me Bonnie. And I live in Utah. When I boarded the plane it was cold and threatening snow."

He gave her another grin. "Lucky you, Bonnie, to leave that kind of weather behind."

He shut the door, then skirted the front of the truck and climbed into the driver's seat. Since the cab was spacious, she hadn't expected his presence to fill up every spare inch, or suck out all the oxygen. But it was definitely doing both.

She removed her jacket and placed it across her lap. "I didn't expect the sun to feel quite this warm here."

His gaze traveled over her bare arms and shoulders exposed by her sundress. "I'd suggest you still cover up while you're outdoors, even when it's hot out. You could get a sunburn and you wouldn't want to be nursing one of those while visiting your relatives."

She supposed it was perfectly normal for him to assume she was related to the Arizona Hollisters. And she was, of course, but it wasn't as if they were close relations—they were distant cousins. What wasn't perfectly normal, she thought, was the way his brown eyes twinkled whenever they looked at her and how something about him was shooting all sorts of naughty thoughts through her head.

He started the engine and quickly drove out of the parking lot and through the exit gates of the airport property.

Because she couldn't think of any safe subject to talk about, she decided to continue with the weather. "Presently, there's a few inches of snow covering the ground on Stone Creek Ranch," she told him. "That's my family's ranch. Sometimes we even have blizzards. I doubt that ever happens around here."

"If you saw a snowflake around here, even in the dead of winter it would be a miracle. So no use hoping for a white Christmas on Three Rivers Ranch. Now, back in Hereford, we had some humdinger blizzards. I don't miss them. It's hell—I mean, *heck*, on the livestock. Uh, excuse me, Bonnie. I don't talk with ladies like you very often, so I'm not in the habit of minding my manners."

Ladies like her? What kind of women did this guy associate with? The type that didn't blush over crude words or behavior? No. Somehow he didn't seem the low-class sort.

"Don't worry, Mose. I have five brothers. I won't faint if I hear a few curse words from time to time."

"Whoa, five brothers! That's a passel. Are they around your age?"

She shook her head and wondered what was coming over her. It wasn't like her to talk about her personal life with a man she'd only just met.

"All my brothers are older than me. Plus I have an older sister, Grace. She's a medical doctor. And I have a twin sister, Beatrice. We're the babies of the family."

He darted her a curious glance. "You have a twin sister? Are you identical?"

"Yes, as far as our looks go. We have totally different personalities." She turned her gaze toward the passenger window and thought about Beatrice way up in Burley, Idaho. Her and her husband, Kipp, were dealing with snow on their cattle ranch. Bonnie had talked to her twin early this morning before she'd caught the commuter plane to Wickenburg. Beatrice had been bubbling with excitement and kept insisting this trip was going to change Bonnie's life. She hadn't bothered to ask Beatrice if the change would be for the better or worse. Her twin saw everything through a romantic glow.

He said, "I went to school with boys who were twins. The jealousy between them was so fierce it was impossible to be friends with either of them. I often wonder if they finally matured enough to go their separate ways."

She watched him reach for a pair of aviator sunglasses on the dash and slip them onto his face. Now that they were headed in an easterly direction, the sun wasn't glaring directly off the windshield, but it was still incredibly bright.

"My twin and I have always loved each other and been the

best of friends. Last year, she married a rancher up in Idaho. I miss her, but we talk most every day. And I'm happy for her because she's happy."

"So, are you married?"

She'd not expected the blunt question and for a moment it jarred her.

"Uh—no," she said stiffly. "Are you?"

The question caused him to laugh and she wondered if he considered being married a joke.

"No. And I doubt I ever will be. It's just not my nature to be a husband."

For some reason, his comment hit her like a rock. "I guess it's just not my nature to be a wife," she replied.

He shot her another toothy grin and she found herself sucking in a deep, bracing breath.

"That's not to say I have anything against having a night out with a pretty lady," he went on. "What about you? I'll bet you have all kinds of men begging for dates."

She stiffened at his comment. There was no way he could know she purposely kept her dates as little more than friendly outings—when she went out at all. "I'm not a socializer," she said briskly. "I get more out of staying home and studying the global cattle markets."

One of his brows appeared above the rim of his sunglasses. "Well, to each his own. That's what I always say."

No shaming or preaching. No comments about how she was wasting her young years or how she was too pretty to hide herself at home. She ought to feel relieved. Instead, she was close to bursting into tears. Because something about Mose Martel was making her feel like a coward.

Turning her attention to the passenger window, she stared out at the passing landscape. Now that they were traveling away from town, the countryside was open desert with low mountains in the nearby distance. Tall saguaro cacti dotted the land, along with cholla, mesquite and low thorny shrubs she couldn't identify. Slabs of rocks appeared here and there, while in a few spots, some sort of tiny wildflowers were blooming red.

The scenery was beautiful, but she could hardly relax and enjoy the sights. Not with Mose sitting only inches away. Why, oh why, couldn't she be flirtatious and witty like Beatrice? Why had she made a point to let this man know she had no interest in dating? Because she'd been afraid he might ask her out?

Don't be a fool, Bonnie. This man doesn't need or want a boring woman like you.

The mocking voice was still sounding off in her head when he suddenly spoke.

"You must be interested in cattle. Or, at least, marketing them."

Her cheeks grew ridiculously warm. "Naturally. My family runs a cattle-and-sheep ranch. I like to learn as much as I can about the business."

"Planning to run a ranch of your own someday?"

She turned her head in his direction and found he was looking straight at her. And to her surprise, there was no flirty grin or any kind of amusement on his face.

"I'm already part owner of a ranch," she said. "All of us eight siblings own a piece of Stone Creek Ranch. That's the way our parents wanted things. I do all the ranch's bookkeeping and run my father's office. While I'm down here, my parents will be sharing the responsibilities of my job."

"I see. And your brothers? They live and work on the ranch?"

"All except for Hunter and Flint. Hunter is the oldest of all of us, he owns and operates a rodeo company, the Flying H. He's on the road for most of the year. Flint now lives in Idaho on the Bell Ranch with his fiancée."

A mile or two passed in silence before he asked, "Is Stone Creek as big a ranch as Three Rivers?"

"I've never seen Three Rivers before, but two of my brothers have, and they've told me our ranch is nothing close to the size of this one."

He looked thoughtful and she wondered what was going through his mind. Probably curious as to why she'd made the long trip down here, she thought.

"You know Maureen and Gil and their family well?" he asked.

"Fairly well. A couple of years ago, some of the family traveled up to Idaho to attend Bea's wedding," she said. "Actually, Maureen had told me she'd be the one picking me up at the airport. She must have had something else to do."

He laughed, as if the very idea was ridiculous. "Maureen rarely has time to stop for any reason. I've never known any woman who works as hard as she does. Most of her day is spent in the saddle. When it comes to overseeing the cattle, she's very hands-on."

"She's very beautiful, too," Bonnie remarked.

"Yeah. I told Gil if he wasn't around, I'd be chasing after her."

She darted a glance at him. "And what did he say to that?"

Chuckling again, he shrugged his right shoulder. "He laughed. Gil knows Maureen is crazy about him."

Before she could stop herself, she said, "You must be attracted to older women."

This time he did more than chuckle, he laughed outright. "When a woman is beautiful, a man doesn't let thirty years stand in the way. Not a man like me, anyway."

Turning her face toward the window, she rolled her eyes. Oh, if only she had some of Beatrice's quips to throw at this man.

Unable to hold back a sigh, she asked, "How much longer until we get to the ranch?"

"I'd say about twenty minutes," he answered. "Why? You want me to speed up? Or shut up?"

Pinching the bridge of her nose, she released a silent sigh. Here she was, sitting next to one hot, sexy cowboy. She had a wonderful opportunity to make friends with him and learn more about him as a person. Instead, a cautious voice inside was shouting at her to stare out the passenger window and not allow herself to be charmed by his good looks and warm smile.

"I'm fine, Mose. I was just curious."

"It won't be long before we turn off the highway, but the road from there to the ranch house is a long, rough one. The trip is worth it, though."

She wanted to ask him why he'd left Texas and moved here to Three Rivers Ranch, but she kept the question to herself. She didn't want to give him the impression she was personally interested in him. Because she wasn't. She wasn't interested in any man. Especially one like this flamboyant cowboy. The only kind of man she felt comfortable dating was the quiet, introverted sort. The type who'd be satisfied with a simple kiss on the cheek.

After that, he went silent, and for the next several miles, the only sounds to be heard were the whirr of the air conditioner and hum of tires on the hot asphalt. Ahead of them, heat waves shimmered across the highway and disappeared into the thick clumps of chaparral and stands of Joshua trees.

Bonnie was thinking how wild and rugged the land was compared to that of her family ranch when Mose slowed the truck and turned right onto a graveled dirt road. After what felt like several miles, he gestured to a turnoff with a fancy iron entrance arched above a wide cattle guard.

"Bar X Ranch," Bonnie read aloud. "You know these folks?"

"Maureen's youngest son, Joseph and his wife, Tessa, own and operate the Bar X."

"If I'm remembering right, Joe is a deputy sheriff for Yavapai County," she said.

"Right. They have three kids. Little Joe, Spring, and Gilbert. Sam Lemans is foreman of the ranch. He also happens to be Holt's father-in-law. Well, stepfather-in law to be exact. He married Isabelle's mother. I guess you know Holt is one of Maureen's sons and Isabelle is his wife. Holt runs the horse division on Three Rivers Ranch."

She glanced at him. "I knew Holt was a middle son of Maureen's and he was married to Isabelle. But I've not met either of them. I only knew they deal in horses."

He flashed a grin at her. "I'd say they have the best horses in the whole Southwest. But then, I'm a little biased." As they drew even with the entrance, he inclined his head toward the house situated on a rise. "Too bad it's not springtime. Tessa has a bunch of irises growing in the front yard and they're really pretty when they bloom. Her late father, Ray, used to be the sheriff for Yavapai County. I think he planted them years ago for his wife."

As he eased the truck onward, Bonnie tried to keep track of the information Mose had given her. "So, is Tessa's mother still living?" she asked.

"No. But Ray's wife wasn't Tessa's mother. Tessa was the result of an affair. Both women have passed on."

She frowned at him. "To have only been here for two-plus years, you sure do know a lot about the family."

He shrugged. "I'm really not one to go looking for gossip, but I don't mind listening if people want to tell me their stories. Actually, Joe himself told me about the situation with his wife's parentage. He said it was a big shock to the locals when the truth finally came out, but now everyone is happy Tessa turned out to be Ray's daughter. From what I gather, he was a beloved man."

Unable to keep the sarcasm from her voice, she said, "Really? A man, a sheriff at that, who cheated on his wife and fathered a child with his mistress was beloved?"

The faint tightening of his jaw told Bonnie he didn't appreciate her judgmental reaction. But Mose couldn't know that only weeks ago, she'd learned her Grandfather Lionel had been a lying adulterer, who'd also kept a mistress while he was married to Bonnie's grandmother. The revelation was still a raw wound. But she was hardly going to reveal something so personal to this man. And even if she did try to explain, he probably wouldn't understand her feelings anyway.

He said, "People have shortcomings, you know. It's called being human."

She suppressed another sigh. "I don't know anything about the man or the situation. I shouldn't have said what I did. I guess all the traveling today is wearing on me."

Who was she kidding? The traveling hadn't gotten to her, but Mose Martel certainly had, and the longer she was in his company, the more she felt like a fool.

They reached a fork in the road and he slowed the truck to make a sharp left turn. Soon after, the truck rattled over a steel cattle guard spanning a gap between tall, barbed-wire fences.

"We're on Three Rivers Ranch now," he announced. "You'll be there soon."

Mose's prediction of *soon* turned out to be another ten minutes of rough dirt road over rugged desert land scattered with several types of cacti, sage and more thick stands of thorny chaparral.

Throughout the remainder of the drive, Mose only spoke occasionally, and that was to point out a few distant landmarks. Bonnie had thought she'd welcome the silence. But by the time they topped a tall mesa and the ranch headquarters came into view on the distant valley floor, she decided she missed the sound of his voice and being connected to him with conversation.

As the truck descended the rise, she leaned slightly forward and peered through the windshield at an enormous white three-story house and a ranch yard equipped with a network of numerous barns, buildings and corrals.

"Oh my! This is—amazing!"

He glanced over at her. "I was kinda dumbstruck when I first saw the place, too. It's definitely massive."

"Our ranch in Utah is fairly large, but this looks— There's no comparison."

"I've been told that Three Rivers has been in existence since 1846. It's had plenty of time to grow into something big."

"Nearly two centuries," she said thoughtfully. "Some ranches are lucky to survive fifty years. Three Rivers has obviously survived and thrived. It's clear someone knows what they're doing."

"Hmm. Someone who studies the global cattle markets—like you."

Was he making fun of her? If he was, she didn't care. She had more important things to think about than a horse trainer who thought he was God's gift to women.

She shook her head a little at the thought, surprised at herself. Since when had she become so judgmental? Mose hadn't stepped out of line. He was just being—a man. And that was her problem, not his.

You think Mose is struck on himself? No, Bonnie, you need a dose of reality. You've spent less than an hour in the man's company and you're the one who's already struck—by him.

Was that true? Was she looking for reasons to think less of him because she was embarrassed by her attraction? She sure hoped that wasn't it.

"It pays to know your business," she said quietly.

He looked over and gave her another one of those lopsided grins that caused a funny little curl in the pit of her stomach.

"That's what my daddy always says."

Before she could stop herself, she said, "I'm sure you know your business inside and out."

His head turned in her direction just enough for her to see his brows appear above the frames of his sunglasses.

"You mean the business of training horses?"

"Is there another business you're in?" she asked primly.

The corners of his mouth twitched with humor. "Not the sort that makes money. As for training horses, there's always more to learn. Horses are complex creatures. Sort of like women. You can never be sure about what they're thinking or what they might do next."

"I'm sure you're an expert at both."

As soon as the comment slipped out of her, she very nearly slapped her hand over her mouth. Why had she said such a thing to him? And where had she found the gumption to speak her thoughts out loud?

Thankfully, his easy laugh said he wasn't the least bit offended by her remark. And why would he be? He had confidence stamped all over him.

He said, "Let's just say I'm still learning about both."

And having a grand time in the process, no doubt. Which only reinforced the need for her to keep an impersonal distance from this hunk of cowboy. It was safer that way.

Safe, yes. But so very dull.

Chapter Two

Mose wasn't sorry for the hour he'd spent in Bonnie Hollister's company, but he wished he could start over again. Maybe if he'd had the opportunity of a redo, he could make a better impression on the beautiful blonde. Perhaps if he'd been a bit more subtle and more of a gentleman, she might've warmed up to him. As it stood, he was all too aware that he'd lost his chance. But that was probably for the best. Bonnie was a ranching heiress. And long ago, he'd made a vow to avoid wealthy women.

"Here we are. You've reached your destination," he said as he braked the truck to a halt on the circular drive in front of the ranch house. "And I see Maureen coming down the porch steps. Better brace yourself for a big bear hug."

She glanced over at him as she unfastened her seat belt. "It's good to be here. Thank you for the lift, Mose."

At least she was calling him by his first name. That had to be a start, he thought hopefully.

Start of what, Mose? Don't be a fool! You've gone down that path before and you ended up the loser. Remember?

Shutting off the mocking voice in his head, Mose quickly climbed from the truck and went around to the passenger door to help Bonnie down. By the time she was standing next to him, Maureen was hurrying across the graveled driveway with a bright smile on her face.

"Bonnie! Welcome to Three Rivers!" Once she was within arm's length, she pulled Bonnie into a fierce hug. "I've been looking forward to this day for weeks!"

Mose noticed the smile Bonnie gave Maureen was just as shy as the one she'd given him at the airport. So maybe her reserved attitude wasn't aimed solely at him.

She said, "Thank you, Maureen. It's good to finally be here."

Stepping back, Maureen gave Bonnie's appearance a quick study, then turned a coy smile at Mose. "Doesn't she look lovely, Mose?"

"As lovely as a June morning, I'd say."

"You'd say right, Mose." Maureen winked at him. "She didn't give you any trouble on the way home, did she?"

He glanced at Bonnie, then back to Maureen. "Depends on what you call trouble. She's not too talkative, but I figure you'll loosen her up."

Laughing, Maureen patted Bonnie's arm. "Forgive us, Bonnie. We're only teasing. When I get around Mose, he brings out the worst in me."

Bonnie's blue gaze traveled back and forth between him and Maureen. She didn't appear to be amused, but that hardly surprised him. He'd already realized she was the serious sort. Just another good reason to keep his distance. He wasn't into *serious*. Not where women were concerned.

"Dang, I must be slipping. I thought I brought out the best in you, Maureen," he joked, then turned and opened the back door on the truck. "If you two want to go on in the house, I'll carry Bonnie's bags in."

"Thank you, Mose. You're a good man," Maureen told him, then, looping an arm through Bonnie's, urged her toward the house.

"Tell that to Holt," Mose called after her. "He might need to know I'm worth keeping."

Maureen's laughter drifted back to him and Mose smiled to himself as he lifted Bonnie's three bags out of the back seat.

Since Mose had come to work on Three Rivers Ranch, he'd become more than a name on an employee roster. The Hollisters had gathered him into their family fold and given him the close bonds he'd been missing after his parents had split. Now he couldn't imagine himself living away from them, or this ranch.

When he entered the huge three-story house, he found Maureen and Bonnie in the formal living room. The long, rectangular space was furnished with heavy leather-and-wood furniture done in dark brown. Cowhide rugs were scattered over the polished hardwood floor, while photos and paintings of different areas of the ranch were displayed on the tongue-and-groove walls. Presently, there was a huge beautifully decorated Christmas tree in one corner of the room, opposite an enormous fireplace, while pots of fresh poinsettias were sitting on various tables.

Mose wouldn't describe the room as lavish, but it did give off a vibe of old money. And he couldn't help but wonder what Bonnie thought of it. When they'd topped the mesa and first spotted the ranch house, she'd seemed awestruck, and now as she glanced around the room, he noticed the same wonder on her face.

"Oh, Maureen, the Christmas tree is gorgeous!" she exclaimed. "Did you decorate it yourself?"

"I'm afraid Jazelle, our housekeeper, did most of the work on this tree. There's a bigger one in the den and most of the family had a hand in decorating it," Maureen told her. "That's where we exchange our gifts. But we still have lots of decorating outside to do. A couple of hands are going to start putting up lights on the house today. And I always make sure the barns are adorned with red ribbons and evergreen boughs, but that isn't yet done, either. We've been trying to round up the late-born calves so everyone in the cattle division has been super busy."

"Everyone back home is very busy, too. Mom is just now beginning to get the house ready for the holiday." She continued to stare at her surroundings. "This room—it's incredible. There are so many similarities to our ranch house in Utah."

"Yes, Gil and I noticed the same thing when we visited Stone Creek. We thought it rather eerie," Maureen commented.

A perplexed look on her face, Bonnie said, "I don't understand. Grandfather Lionel was never here."

"Not unless he was posing as someone else," Maureen answered.

Bonnie shook her head with disbelief. "Considering the bad feelings, I doubt he ever came near Three Rivers Ranch. But the similarities of the two houses make this one feel like home."

Bad feelings. From what Mose could pick up, a split had taken place in the family many years ago but had obviously been mended between the current branches of Hollisters. Mose was surprised to find himself intrigued about the history of this ranching dynasty. Usually, the past didn't interest him. A man couldn't go back and change anything. Better to Look Toward the Future had always been his motto. However Bonnie was making him wonder about her past life—though that was less interest in her grandfather and more curiosity over why she wasn't married or engaged.

Maureen gave Bonnie's slender shoulders a one-armed hug. "Aww, Bonnie, this *is* your home. For as long as you'd like. Now, let's go up to the second floor, and I'll show you the room Gil and I thought you might enjoy."

Thinking the women had probably forgotten him, Mose cleared his throat. "Maureen, where would you like for me to put Bonnie's bags?"

Both women looked at him and Maureen said, "Oh sorry, Mose. We have you hung up and you're needing to get back to the horse barn. You go on. Bonnie and I can manage to get the bags upstairs."

"I'm not in that big of a hurry," he told Maureen. "Just show me the way."

Maureen directed them out of the room. With a suitcase in each hand and a duffle jammed under one arm, Mose followed them down a long hallway.

They passed several doors before Maureen gestured to one on their left.

"This is the office Gil and I use for ranching business," Maureen said to Bonnie. "Not that we do that much paperwork these days. As manager of the ranch, Blake has his own offices next to the cattle barn. He has a full-time secretary, and last year, he hired an assistant for her. And most of her job is to handle the data involving the horse division. Which Mose can tell you consists of a mountain of forms and veterinarian details."

"It's a mess of paperwork, all right," Mose agreed. "And Holt sends three-fourths of it to Blake's office."

Maureen chuckled. "Holt's never been one to follow the rules and Blake is easygoing enough to put up with his brother's lax behavior."

Bonnie said, "I know what that's like. Jack had rather be out on his horse, herding cattle, instead of in the office with Dad. But he does what's needed so that Dad isn't overloaded with work."

Maureen glanced over her shoulder at Mose. "Jack is Bonnie's second to the oldest brother," she explained. "He co-manages Stone Creek Ranch with his father. He's the first one of the Utah Hollisters that we met. Back then, none of us knew we were actually related."

"Are you telling me a whopper, Maureen?" Mose asked.

"Cross my heart, it's the truth. Neither family knew the other existed," Maureen told him. "It's a long, complicated story. Maybe you can get Bonnie to tell you about it while she's here."

While she's here. Just how long was the blue-eyed blonde planning to stay on Three Rivers, Mose wondered. That was something he'd really like to know. But he couldn't think of a way of asking the question that wouldn't show his hand as to how interested he was in the answer. Besides, he'd already decided she was off-limits as a potential girlfriend. Still, she could be a beautiful friend, he thought.

When they reached the staircase leading up to the second and third floors, the two women climbed the stairs side by side, while Mose followed with the bags.

"The children's combination playroom/nursery is on the third floor, so you shouldn't hear a whole lot of noise from the kids," Maureen explained to Bonnie. "Tallulah Garroway is our nanny. She's married to Jim. He's an assistant to Mose and the other two horse trainers."

"We couldn't run the horse barn without Jim," Mose spoke up. "He's a special guy."

"Jim and Tallulah had a son born last year. We call him Little James and he's a cutie. Now Tallulah is expecting again. The baby is due this spring, right around roundup time," Maureen said.

"In case you didn't know," Mose said to Bonnie, "the Hollisters have lots of kids. So do the people who work for them."

Glancing over her shoulder, Maureen leveled a pointed look at him. "Except for you, Mose. But one of these days that's going to change. When it does, I'm sure you're going to be a doting father. So you might as well get ready for the job."

Mose let out a short laugh. "Maureen, training a yearling to lead is my kind of job. And the way I see things, a young horse is far easier to teach than a kid."

Chuckling, Maureen said, "You know, Mose, you're probably right."

They reached the landing to the second floor, where evergreen boughs and red ribbons were laced through the whole width of the balustrade. Mose had been inside the ranch house on many occasions but had never had a reason to visit the upstairs. The interior of the house was just as beautiful up here as it was on the ground floor, but the carved wood hand railings and polished parquet floor couldn't hold his attention. Not with Bonnie walking slightly ahead of him. He couldn't keep his gaze off her shapely backside and the way the skirt of her dress swayed with the movement of her hips and brushed her slender legs.

Like Maureen had said, Bonnie was lovely. Far lovelier than any woman he'd ever dated. Another sign that she was far beyond him, Mose thought.

"Here we are." Maureen opened the door and motioned for Bonnie and Mose to proceed her into the room.

Once inside, Bonnie walked straight to a set of wide, paned windows and peered out at the view. "Oh, this is wonderful! I can see a portion of the ranch yard from here."

Mose gently placed the bags on the floor at the end of the queen-size four-poster bed, then glanced over to Bonnie. She was staring out the window with a smile of sheer pleasure on her face. Was she really that much of a ranching girl that the sight of cows and horses stirring up clouds of dust filled her with joy? She seemed so feminine and proper it was hard to imagine her stepping around piles of manure or wiping gritty dust from her face. She was a paradox, he decided. One that he'd very much like to unravel.

"I thought you'd enjoy seeing some of the goings-on down at the ranch yard," Maureen told her.

"I'll enjoy it very much, Maureen. Thank you for your thoughtfulness."

Turning, she began a slow survey of the room, and when her gaze eventually landed on Mose, the realization struck him that he needed to be on his way. He'd delivered her bags. There wasn't any reason for him to be loitering around in her bedroom.

He was on the verge of opening his mouth to excuse himself, when Maureen suddenly spoke.

"This was once Camille's bedroom, mine and my late first husband Joel's youngest child. She lives down at Red Bluff now. That's our second ranch located down by Dragoon," she explained. "Her husband, Matthew, manages it for us."

"If I remember correctly, Camille runs her own diner," Bonnie said. "While you and your family were visiting during Bea's wedding, I heard Blake mention Matthew. At first, I thought he was talking about a brother and then I figured out the man was Blake's brother-in-law."

Maureen chuckled. "That's right, Matthew is brother-in-law to my four sons, but they are more like brothers. You see, for many years, he was our ranch foreman here on Three Rivers. But after he and Camille got married, they made their home on Red Bluff. That marriage caused us to lose an excellent foreman and a great ranch hand along with him, since TooTall stayed on as Matt's right-hand man. Those two were nearly impossible to replace. It's hard to find a good man nowadays."

Mose made a production of clearing his throat. "Uh—you found me, Maureen. That wasn't so hard."

Maureen looked over at him and winked. "I'll give Holt the credit of finding you. Anyway, you're the best, Mose."

"Yeah. Me and about twenty other men on the roster," Mose joked, then glanced at Bonnie. "She wants all of us hands to think we're the best. Instead of holding a whip over our head, she uses psychological tactics to keep us working hard."

Laughing, Maureen said smugly, "It works, too. Doesn't it?"

"Sure does," he answered. "And speaking of work, if you ladies will excuse me, I need to get back to the horse barn."

He started toward the door and was more than surprised when Bonnie suddenly intercepted him in the middle of the room.

She said, "Thank you, Mose, for the lift from the airport and helping me with the bags. It was nice of you."

Smiling gently, she offered him her hand, and as he closed his hand around her fragile fingers, a strange little pang struck the middle of his chest.

"You're more than welcome, Bonnie. I hope you enjoy your stay on Three Rivers."

"I'm sure I will."

He held her hand for a moment longer. "Uh—maybe we'll meet again before you go back to Utah."

She held his gaze for a split second before awkwardly glancing away.

"Perhaps," she murmured.

He wasn't sure if it was his suggestion that they might meet again that was making her uncomfortable, or the fact that he was still holding her hand. Yet it took another beat before he could make himself let go. Today would most likely be the last time he saw Bonnie Hollister close-up, and he wasn't ready for their time together to end.

But it had to. Releasing his hold on her hand, he tipped his hat to both women and exited the bedroom. On his way out of the house, he told himself it was probably for the best he wouldn't see her again. Even if she'd take a second look at him, it would be pointless to strike up any kind of relationship with her.

But as soon as he climbed into the work truck, the lingering scent of her perfume enveloped his senses and he realized it was going to be damned hard to forget she was staying on the ranch. And even harder to forget that she was a Hollister.

Nearly an hour later, Bonnie was hanging up the last of her clothing when a light knock sounded on the door.

Turning away from the closet, she called, "Come in."

The door opened partially and a pretty blond-haired woman stuck her head through the open gap. With a cheery smile on her face, she asked, "Am I interrupting?"

"Not at all. Please, come in."

Stepping into the bedroom, she quickly introduced herself. "I'm Jazelle, the housekeeper, maid and general helper around here. I thought I'd say hello and see if you'd like to go down to the kitchen and have a cup of coffee or something?"

Somewhere in her late twenties, the woman had thick blond hair wound into a messy bun atop her head. Dressed casually in jeans and a blue button-down shirt, she was tall and shapely, and Bonnie's instant impression was that she was as genuine and down-to-earth as her employers.

"Coffee sounds wonderful." Bonnie walked over and extended her hand to the woman. "Nice to meet you, Jazelle. Maureen says this house wouldn't run without you," she added with a smile.

"Maureen exaggerates." She shook Bonnie's hand, then gestured to the bags lying on top of the queen-size bed. "Do you need help finding a place for your things? Or is there anything else you'd like in the bathroom? When Maureen told me you'd be using this room, I went through and refreshed everything, but if there's anything in particular you'd like, just let me know."

Bonnie's gaze made an appreciative sweep of the beautiful room that was furnished with cherrywood furniture and yellow-and-blue bedcovers. Cowhide rugs were at the sides and the foot of the bed and also in front of a winged, leather armchair positioned near the windows. And when she'd peeked into the bathroom, she'd seen that it was beautifully appointed and also well stocked.

"Everything is just lovely, Jazelle. I feel very spoiled. This room is fit for a princess," she said, then added with a little laugh, "At least, a ranching princess."

"Well, a ranching princess is what Camille was, and still is, as far as that goes." She gestured to the sunny yellow curtains. "Maureen decided to leave things as her daughter left them."

"The yellow is bright and cheery. And the room doesn't need a thing," she assured the housekeeper. "I've already unpacked everything. So I'm ready to go downstairs."

"Great. If we're lucky, Sophia might be pulling fresh cookies out of the oven right about now."

On the way out of the bedroom, Bonnie said, "Maureen explained that Sophia and her grandmother, Reeva, cook for the ranch house, but there's a separate cook for the men's bunkhouse, right?"

"Right. Reeva has been with the family for years and years—since she was a young woman. She's seventy-six now. Sophia moved here about four years ago so she could work alongside her grandmother. A few months after she got here, she married Colt Crawford. He's one of Holt's horse trainers."

"Oh, then I guess he works with Mose Martel," Bonnie commented as they began to descend the staircase.

Jazelle glanced over at her. "You've met Mose?"

Bonnie inwardly groaned. She hadn't really intended to bring up Mose's name. Yet for some unexplainable reason, it just popped out of her before she could stop it.

"Uh—yes. He picked me up at the airport."

"Oh boy, I imagine he treated you to a little flirting during the drive out here. He likes the girls," Jazelle added with coy grin.

To hear that Mose liked girls was hardly a surprise. But all in all, he'd not done any outright flirting. She supposed he'd made a few remarks that could've been considered suggestive, but for the most part, he'd behaved like any typical man.

Typical man! Hah! Bonnie, you know darn well there's not one typical thing about Mose. He's one of a kind. And just the kind you need to forget.

Fighting against the inner voice, Bonnie said, "Actually, Mose didn't do much flirting. I guess I'm not his type."

Jazelle shot her an impish smile. "I wouldn't take bets on that. You look to me like you'd be everyone's type. To be honest, I'm surprised you're not married," she said, then quickly added, "Sorry, Bonnie. I'm getting too personal and we've only just met. Just tell me to shut up when I get to rattling about things I shouldn't."

Bonnie did her best to sound casual. "You're not offending me. As for me being married, I just haven't found the right man yet."

They reached the bottom of the stairs and Jazelle directed her to the left, where they continued down a long hallway with doors branching off both sides. As they walked, Bonnie could smell lemon wax. The familiar scent brought on a pang of homesickness. Which was ridiculous. She'd not even been gone from Stone Creek for one whole day yet. And it wasn't as though she'd never been away from the ranch before. In years past, she and Beatrice had taken a few short vacations together. But this visit to Three Rivers Ranch was all about family relations. And this house was an eerie reminder of the old adage that blood was thicker than water.

"Believe me, Bonnie, I used to say the same thing. Until I met Connor. I honestly didn't think I'd ever be married. You see, I'd had my son Raine nearly eleven years ago while I was still single. His father turned out to be—well, to put it nicely, not a family man. So I was really wary of the whole love-and-marriage thing."

"But you're happily married now?" Bonnie asked, even though the question was unnecessary. The dreamy smile on Jazelle's face, and the way she fiddled with her wedding ring as if it made her happy just to remember it was there, said everything.

"Very happily. Along with Raine, we have a four-year-old daughter, Madison. She's upstairs with Tallulah right now."

"You're obviously a blessed woman, Jazelle."

Her sigh was a sound of contentment. "Truthfully, Bonnie, my blessings began when the Hollisters first took me in all those years ago and gave me a job. But I don't need to sing their praises to you. You're a Hollister."

Bonnie smiled at her. "From a different branch of the tree. But I like to think we're a generous and helpful bunch, too."

Jazelle gestured to the left side of the hallway. "The den is in there. As family gatherings go, that's where just about everything takes place. But you'll soon learn your way around the house. And just in case you're wondering, Blake and his family use the third floor. Chandler, the veterinarian of the bunch and second oldest, lives with his wife and kids on the second floor on the opposite end of the house from you. But the kids are all over the place. That is, until someone corrals them," she added with a laugh.

Bonnie said, "Presently, there's only one child living in the ranch house on Stone Creek. That's my brother Cordell's little daughter, Bridget. My other siblings who have children live in their own houses, so I'm not around them as much."

"I only hope you like kids," Jazelle commented with a little laugh, "because there are plenty of them around here."

"No worries. I adore children."

Near the end of the hallway, they made a right turn into a connecting hallway. After traveling a few feet more, they reached a pair of swinging doors.

"Here we are at the kitchen," Jazelle announced as she held one of the louvered doors open for Bonnie to pass through.

The moment Bonnie entered the long room, she was met with the delicious aroma of baking yeast bread and something like simmering peppers and tomatoes. A young, dark-haired woman dressed in jeans and a white shirt covered with a bib apron was tending to something cooking on an enormous gas range. Obviously, she had to be Sophia, Bonnie decided. A few steps away, a very slender woman with a long salt-and-pepper-colored braid hanging against her back was standing at a work island in the middle of the room.

As Bonnie and Jazelle moved into the room, Reeva paused and looked up from the carrots she'd been scraping.

"You two come and meet Bonnie," Jazelle told them.

The two women dropped what they were doing to join them. After quick introductions were made, Reeva said, "Welcome to Three Rivers Ranch, Bonnie. If you're anything like this bunch of Hollisters, you're going to like it here."

Jazelle had told her a few minutes ago that Reeva was

seventy-six, but judging by the older woman's smooth complexion and straight posture, Bonnie would've guessed her to be at least ten years younger.

"I'm sure I'll like it just fine," Bonnie told her.

"Probably not as much as we'll like having you here," Sophia added, then turned and hurried over to the coffee machine. "Maureen filled a couple of thermoses before she left the house earlier and drained the coffeepot. I'll make some fresh."

Jazelle sniffed the air. "I smell Reeva's cinnamon rolls. Are they ready to eat?"

Reeva shook her head. "No. They're not ready. And even if they were, I wouldn't let you have any. It's getting too close to dinner for that."

Groaning, Jazelle looked at Bonnie and made a palms-up gesture. "Reeva is a tough bird with a hard heart," she joked.

The older woman stepped forward and gave Bonnie a welcoming hug. "It's good that you've come to stay awhile, Bonnie. We need a new face around here. Especially one as pretty as yours."

Warmed by the woman's greeting, Bonnie hugged her back. "Thank you, Reeva. And I promise not to call you a tough bird."

Reeva chuckled. "I've been called worse."

Sophia left the coffee machine to join the group. "I'm so excited you're here, Bonnie. We can't wait to hear all about your life back in Utah. I hope you're going to be with us for Christmas?"

A little overwhelmed by their warm reception, Bonnie shook her head. "I'm afraid all of you are going to be disappointed if you're expecting an exciting story from me. I lead a pretty dull life. As for being here for Christmas, I'm not sure about that yet. I might get my work on our family tree finished before then."

"Oh no!" Sophia exclaimed. "Just work at a snail's pace, so you won't finish as quickly. That should keep you here for the holiday. As for you living a dull life, I don't believe it. Not with your looks. I'll bet you're engaged. Right?"

Engaged? She'd have to strain to remember the last date she'd been on. "No," Bonnie told her.

"In that case, *I'm* betting you have a steady boyfriend," Jazelle commented with a coy grin.

"No, I date occasionally, but mostly they're just casual outings," Bonnie said.

Sophia and Jazelle exchanged looks of disbelief, while Reeva frowned at her granddaughter and the housekeeper.

"You two need to mind your own business," Reeva said sharply. "Bonnie didn't travel all the way down here from Utah to have her love life picked over by a pair of nosy women."

"Oh Gran, we're not nosey. We're just interested, that's all," Sophia insisted as she moved over to a cabinet and placed four coffee cups on a plastic tray.

Reeva snorted. "There are other things in life besides men."

There certainly were other things in life, Bonnie thought. So why was Mose Martel consuming her thoughts? It was ridiculous.

"It's okay, Reeva. I don't mind the questions," Bonnie assured the older woman. "I'd feel kind of awful if Jazelle and Sophia didn't want to talk to me."

"Hah! No chance of that happening." Sophia cast Bonnie a playful grin. "But we'll try to be more tactful about the subjects we bring up. Right, Jazelle?"

"Right. I'll try to think before I speak. Something Connor says I should do more often."

"Oh no," Bonnie said. "The last thing I want is for you two to think you need to walk on eggshells around me. When I'm around, I want all of you to just be yourselves. Okay?"

Jazelle stepped over and gave Bonnie's shoulders a one-armed hug. "Definitely, okay," she said.

With the coffee poured, Sophia carried it over to a booth-style table situated on the same wall and a few feet down from the cookstove.

"Come on, everyone. The coffee is ready," Sophia announced before getting a little salad plate from the fridge. "And since Gran won't allow us to dig into the cinnamon rolls, we can gnaw on celery and carrot sticks."

"Oh yummy. I'd pick celery over a cinnamon roll any day," Jazelle said with playful sarcasm. "But I know you're trying to get pregnant, Sophia, so you need to eat healthy."

A wan smile crossed Sophia's face. "That's why I made decaffeinated coffee. I hope you don't mind, Bonnie."

"I don't mind at all," Bonnie told her, then asked, "Do you have any other children?"

"No. Not yet. But not for lack of trying," she said. "Colt and I really want a big family."

A sad shadow crossed Bonnie's thoughts as she stirred cream into her coffee. From the time she'd been a small girl, she'd dreamed about being a mother. Claire, her mother, had given birth to eight children and raised them all with a firm but loving hand. Maybe Bonnie was setting her sights high to think she could be as good a mother as Claire. But she longed for the chance to try.

"I've heard this Hollister family has three sets of twins," Bonnie remarked. "And I'm a twin. Multiple births must run in the family."

Reeva chuckled. "When Kate brings up the subject of having another baby, Blake runs backward. After having two sets of twins, he says he doesn't know if he'd be up to fathering a third set."

"And Maureen's oldest daughter, Vivian, and her husband, Sawyer, are talking about having another baby. I'll bet anything she'll have twins again," Jazelle said, then sighed. "Which would be a nice thing, if you ask me. Their daughter, Hannah, is eighteen now and will be heading off to college this fall. Two babies to go with little Jacob and Johnny would be so nice."

Babies and men. Love and marriage. When those subjects came up in the conversation, they always pertained to someone else, not Bonnie. Usually, she didn't let the fact that she was single bother her. After all, she was still young with plenty of time to have a family. But something about these two happily married women underscored Bonnie's awareness of her own single existence. And the image of Mose's handsome face floating around in her head didn't help matters.

Bonnie's thoughts were interrupted as Sophia reached across the tabletop and patted her hand.

"Who knows, Bonnie, being a Hollister, you might have twins of your own someday," she said. "That would be great, right?"

Bonnie did her best to smile, but inside she was fighting hard not to burst into tears. These women had no way of knowing that for years, she'd not wanted to socialize. She'd wanted to hide herself away on the family ranch, away from any chance of being humiliated or hurt by a man. It wasn't until three years ago, when her sister-in-law Vanessa came into the family, that Bonnie finally began to emerge from her cocoon. But she still wasn't ready to spread her wings into a full-grown butterfly.

"Having twins would be special," Bonnie finally replied. "After I've let myself fall in love and get married."

Sophia and Jazelle exchanged looks of disbelief before they both burst out laughing.

Bonnie turned a blank look at Reeva, who was sitting next to her. "Did I say something funny?" Bonnie asked the older woman.

Reeva gave her a gentle smile. "Bonnie, I think these two are just surprised that you think a woman *lets* herself fall in love. It just happens, whether you want it to or not."

Nodding in agreement, Sophia said, "And if it doesn't *just happen*, then it's probably as worthless as a three-dollar bill."

Just happen? If that was the case, she might as well get ready to live single for the rest of her life, Bonnie decided. Because when she met a man *nothing* had ever even come close to happening.

Well, not counting Mose Martel, she thought helplessly. But her reaction to the flamboyant horse trainer hadn't been romantic; it had been carnal and downright wicked. Even now, just thinking about the gleam in his brown eyes made her cheeks burn.

"Bonnie, you have a lost look on your face," Jazelle said. "I hope we haven't hurt your feelings?"

Bonnie glanced across the table at the two women and desperately wished she could be more like them—confident and unafraid. Even more, she wished she'd had the courage to tell Mose she'd like to see him again. Instead, she'd allowed him to walk away thinking she was a snob. That was the only thing hurting her feelings. But she couldn't admit to these three women how, after one keen look, she'd developed a crush on Mose Martel. She couldn't even tell herself such a thing.

Bonnie conjured up another smile. "Not a chance. I was just thinking how glad I am to be here."

Lifting her cup high, Sophia said, "Let's have a coffee toast to Bonnie's arrival."

"Yes, let's," Jazelle seconded the suggestion.

As the four women clinked their cups together, Bonnie realized she was truly glad to be here on this beautiful ranch, making new friends. And she wasn't about to allow a silly preoccupation over Mose ruin her stay. After all, he couldn't break her heart, she assured herself. She'd never let him get that close.

Chapter Three

By late afternoon the next day, Mose reached the conclusion that something was wrong with him. The only problem was figuring out what exactly had gone awry. True, it had been another exceptionally warm day and he'd already put ten head of young horses through a rigorous training session. And then there was all that beer he'd consumed last night at the Fandango club. Even so, it hadn't been enough alcohol to make him feel like he'd been walloped in the head. But that was exactly how he felt. Not that he had the time to dwell on that as he handed the reins of his mount over to the groom who worked as Mose's personal assistant.

"Finished with this one, Mose?"

Mose nodded at Dex, a young wrangler with a mop of black curls hanging out from beneath his straw hat and a wide grin on his face.

"Finished," Mose told him. "Better give him a long cooldown before you put in the bath stock."

"I'll put him on the walker at a slow speed before I give him a shower." He leveled a concerned look at Mose. "I think you're the one who needs a cooldown. You look beat."

"I haven't stopped since this morning." He pushed up the cuff of his denim shirt and glanced at his watch. "Damn, it's nearly three. I didn't realize so much time had passed."

"You want another one saddled?" Dex asked.

Mose held up two fingers. "Two more. Arrowhead, the sorrel gelding, and Blue Beads, the black filly. Once I finish with them, I'll head to the yearling pen. There are three or four of them that still don't want to lead willingly."

Dex rolled his eyes. "We only just started on them, Mose. It takes time for the juveniles to digest what a halter and lead rope are all about."

Mose slanted the cowboy a wry glance. "This isn't my first rodeo, Dex. I know a little about yearlings."

Dex grimaced before wiping the back of his hand across his mouth. "Well, sometimes a man needs to be reminded of things."

"Yeah. Like his work," Mose said with a chuckle. "So get going."

Dex led the horse away and Mose crossed the dusty training arena and entered the barn. As he strode down a long alleyway between rows of horse stalls, the sounds of piped Christmas music, nickering horses and barn workers calling to each other, were added to the whirring overhead fans needed to keep the barn at a bearable temperature. It all added up to a pleasant, familiar hum.

Beyond the stalls, next to a huge tack room, Mose stepped through the open doorway of Holt Hollister's office.

The manager of Three Rivers Ranch's horse division was sitting behind a desk piled with papers and other debris, like a broken bit and two pair of leather reins. Empty coffee cups littered the spaces between a computer tower and a mouse pad. At the moment, the muscular man with rusty-brown hair topped with a black Stetson was talking in a rather heated tone to someone on the phone.

Mose tried to ignore the one-sided conversation as he pulled open the door on a mini fridge and rifled through the bottles of sodas and sports drinks. However, it was hard to dismiss the curse words Holt was throwing at the person on the opposite end of the line.

"No use looking for a beer, Mose. I drank the last one."

Holt's voice pulled Mose's head out of the fridge and he quickly glanced over at his boss. He'd put the phone aside and was leaned back in the leather executive chair, a piece of furniture that looked completely out of place in this former feed room, with walls and floors made of rough two-by-eight boards that had long ago turned to a muted gray color. The large wooden desk had at one time been a nice piece of oak furniture, but now it was scarred and losing its varnish. A row of metal filing cabinets lined one wall, while a green leather couch and a table with a coffee brewer sat against the opposite wall. Fluorescent lighting hung from the rafters to illuminate the desk area. The shadowy back side of the room held several saddles stacked on wooden racks and saddle blankets piled on the floor in one corner. A stranger would never guess a multimillion-dollar horse business was operated from this room. But in spite of the big bucks, Holt was a down-to-earth man and working out of the barn was all he wanted or needed.

Pulling out a bottle of soda, Mose shut the fridge and walked over to one of the wooden chairs in front of Holt's desk. He twisted the cap off the bottle and took a long swallow before he sank onto the hard seat.

"You can't fool me. You never have beer in that fridge," he said as he crossed his ankles out in front of him. "Besides, everyone knows you're a bourbon-and-cola man."

"Hah! I used to belt them down. But that was before Isabelle and I got married. Now she makes sure I don't enjoy more than two a day. A man in my business needs more, but I abide by her rules. I want to keep my beautiful wife happy," he said with a grin.

And he obviously did a good job of it, Mose thought. Anyone who happened to see Holt and Isabelle together could clearly see the couple were deeply in love. Holt was married to a lovely blonde, who also trained horses on their personal ranch, the Blue Stallion. The couple had three young sons all under the age of six, Carter, Axel and Weston. Mose could admit there'd been occasions when he'd envied his boss's family.

Surely a man with a loving wife and children felt fulfilled in a way that Mose had never experienced. But on the other hand, marriage and family meant having a mountain of responsibilities resting on his shoulders. With that in mind, Mose figured he'd be better off just taking care of himself. Besides, getting seriously involved with a woman was a huge risk. He'd already taken one chance on a woman and lost. Why would he be fool enough to take another?

Wouldn't Bonnie Hollister be worth the risk?

Frustrated with the voice in his head, Mose took another long swig of the soda before glancing over at Holt. "So, I guess you made the comment about the beer 'cause you heard I had plenty last night at the Fandango," he said flatly.

One of Holt's brows arched upward. "No. I didn't hear anything about you overindulging. But I did hear you were dancing with every available female in the club. After yesterday, I wouldn't have figured you'd have enough energy to dance half the night. Dex said you went through fifteen mounts. He was worn-out just saddling them."

"Hell! That's what me and the guys go out to the Fandango for. To meet girls and dance and have a good time so we can blow off steam after a hard day's work. You surely remember those days," Mose said.

Holt chuckled. "I'm only thirty-nine years old, Mose. Not ninety. I remember."

Mose shrugged before removing his hat and swiping a

hand across his sweaty forehead. "I guess I did go a little overboard with the dancing. Put all the extra exercise and the beer together and I'm feeling the aftereffects today."

He wasn't about to tell Holt he'd been doing all that dancing in hopes he'd find at least one woman with enough charm to push Bonnie Hollister out of his mind. But he'd not found any who'd been close to interesting enough to make him forget the pretty blonde with the shy smile.

Seeming to take pity on him, Holt said, "You've already put in a long day. Go ahead and wind things up here at the barn. Start fresh in the morning."

"Thanks, Holt, but Dex is saddling a couple more mounts for me and I want to do a little work with some of the yearlings. Besides, Colt is still working in the round pen this evening. I can't let him outdo me," he joked.

"Well, I don't know if Colt mentioned it or not, but I sent Luke over to California to check out a few horses for sale that have just come off Los Alamitos race track. Some are fillies, so they might be good breeding prospects. Luke will know."

Luke Crawford was Colt's older brother and the head horse trainer at Three Rivers. He and Holt often shared responsibilities. However, this bit of news surprised Mose.

"Racing stock? You're not planning to get into racing, are you? I realize we're close to a major track here in Arizona, but that's a whole other ballgame."

Leaning back in his chair, Holt folded his arms against his chest. "No racing. Too risky. Besides, we're not set up here at Three Rivers for that sort of training. And you might be a tad large to do any jockeying," he joked.

"Yeah, none of your horse trainers weigh 115 or under," Mose said wryly. "But seriously, if it's something you're interested in, all you need to get started is a galloping track, a few training gates and a couple of jockeys. It would be easy enough for you to get set up in the business."

Shaking his head, Holt said, "You sound like you'd like for us to jump into such a venture."

"Not necessarily. I just meant that if it's a part of your dreams, go for it." Mose's mother had tried to instill in him and his older brother the drive to always go after their dreams. Life was too short, she'd say. *Don't let your dreams die; go after them.* Regrettably, his mother had been forced to tell many of her dreams goodbye.

"Well, racing isn't my thing, but I do want some horses with speed in their DNA. That's what ropers and barrel racers are looking for—horses with speed plus a good brain. I'm counting on you and Colt to help them along with the good brain, but you can't do much about the speed if they aren't born with it."

Mose drained the last of his drink and rose to his feet. "No. We're not miracle workers. Just close to it," he joked.

Holt chuckled and Mose turned to leave the office, then stopped in his tracks as he spotted Bonnie standing in the middle of the open doorway.

"Excuse me," she said. "Am I interrupting?"

For a second, Mose couldn't make his mouth work. Finally, he said, "Hello, Bonnie. Uh—you're not interrupting. Come in. I mean, this is Holt's office, but he won't mind."

Mose glanced over to see Holt had already spotted Bonnie and had risen from the chair.

"Bonnie, how nice to see you. Come have a seat," Holt invited.

She stepped into the room and Mose felt as though he was seeing a dream right before his eyes. Today she was dressed in jeans that clung to her hips and long shapely legs. A pink-flowered Western shirt was tucked into her slender waist, while a denim jacket was thrown over one arm. Her clothing didn't necessarily surprise him, nor her brown suede boots with scarred toes. No, it was the hat pulled down on her forehead that caught his attention. The buckskin-colored felt was battered and bent in several places on the crown and brim, while a speckled gray-and-white guinea feather was stuck in the band on the left side. It was a hat Mose would wear, but he'd not pictured such well-used headgear for a ranching heiress like Bonnie.

"Thanks, but I don't want to take up your time," she said. "Maureen said if I came down here to the horse barn, someone would find me a mount to take a short ride. But I don't want to interrupt anyone's work. If one of the wranglers will show me a horse I can borrow, I'll handle the saddling."

Holt waved a dismissive hand through the air. "Bonnie, you'll not be a bother to anyone. Mose is right here. He'll be glad to find you a mount and saddle it for you. Won't you, Mose?"

Glad? He'd give his eyeteeth, Mose thought. "Well, sure I'd be happy to," he told Holt before slanting a questioning look at Bonnie. "Unless you'd rather have one of the other wranglers help you."

One of her delicate brows very nearly disappeared beneath the brim of her overworn hat.

"Not at all. I'd be very grateful for your help, Mose."

Holt gazed perceptively at the two of them. "Mose can show you the cattle trails leading away from the barns. Were you planning on staying out long?"

"Not too long. Thirty or forty-five minutes. Why? Will the horse need to be put up before then?" she asked.

Mose answered, before Holt could. "No. Ride as long as you'd like. It's just that we like to know when a rider is expected back, just in case there's an accident or something and we need to go searching."

"Oh. I understand," she said. "I should have known."

Holt spoke up, "Maybe no one in the family has mentioned it to you before. Mom doesn't talk much about the incident. But several years ago, we found our dad, Joel, not too far away from the ranch yard with his boot hanging in the stirrup. He'd been dragged for miles."

Bonnie expression turned contrite. "I'm so sorry, Holt. I knew your father had been killed, but I had no idea he'd been found in those conditions. I can see why you try to keep tabs on the riders."

Holt said, "We don't mean to be overanxious. We only want to make sure all riders, including the ranch hands, get back to the ranch safely."

"I understand," Bonnie said just as Holt's cell phone began to ring.

"Excuse me," he said, then picking up the phone, waved the two of them off.

Once Mose and Bonnie stepped out of the office, he said, "It's really nice to see you again, Bonnie."

She looked up at him and smiled, and the sight lifted his spirits.

"Thank you, Mose. It's nice seeing you, too. I honestly didn't know who I'd find here at the horse barn. Maureen told me just to show up and tell someone what I wanted."

"Then, I'm glad you found me." He gestured on down the barn to the exit. "The horses are this way."

They began walking, and as she matched his strides, Mose picked up the faint scent of her perfume, while from the corner of his eye, he could see her long blond hair swaying gently against her back. The waves were thick and shiny and he wondered if the strands would feel as silky as they looked.

"Do you keep certain horses here at the barn just for riding?" she asked.

Her voice jerked him out of his wandering thoughts. "Only the ponies Holt has for the kids. Otherwise, if anyone wants to ride for leisure, we pull a horse from the remuda after the hands have picked their day mounts."

She glanced over at him. "Oh. So I'll be riding a working horse."

They passed through a door to the outside, and once Mose secured it behind them, he said, "Don't worry. They're all nice and obedient. Holt won't allow any outlaws to be a part of the remuda. I'm sure your father is the same way."

A faint smile touched her lips. "Actually, we don't have what you'd call a large herd of horses on Stone Creek Ranch, but the ones we have are good ones. And Cord is always looking to add more to our little remuda. Dad says Cord is a little horse crazy. One more is never enough."

Her sharing so much without being prodded put a grin on his face. "Sounds exactly like Holt," he said.

Nodding, she said, "Strange, isn't it, that distant cousins who grew up completely separately could be so similar in personalities."

"You make it sound as though your brother is like Holt in more ways than a love of horses."

She let out a soft laugh and Mose thought how the sound was like the merry tinkle of a Christmas bell.

"For sure. Cord has always been the rowdy one of the family. Up until he married Maggie, he made a career out of dating pretty women, if you know what I mean," she said, then quickly glanced away and muttered, "I'm talking too much."

"I'm pretty sure neither Holt nor Cord would mind hearing you call them *rounders*." He placed a hand beneath her elbow and turned her in an easterly direction. "We need to go this way. The horses are a little farther away—in a small paddock."

Frowning, she paused and glanced back at the barn. "Oh, I'm putting you to so much trouble, making you go all the way out to the paddock and then take the horse back to the barn to saddle it."

"No trouble at all. We do it every day," he said, then gave her a sheepish grin. "At least, the ranch hands do it every day. Us trainers have grooms to saddle everything for us."

She looked at him and Mose could see her eyes narrow skeptically as they scanned his face.

"You know, I'm not sure I'm understanding any of this. You're one of Holt's horse trainers and therefore a very busy man. Right?"

"Yep. Sunup to sundown at a minimum, but often times, I put in longer days. Especially if foaling season is going on."

"Then, how is it that you were the one who drove all the way into Wickenburg, a nearly forty-minute trip each way, to pick me up? And now, here you are breaking up your workday to find me a saddle horse. Aren't there any less-important men around this ranch that can assist me?"

She looked so adorable during her little speech that all Mose wanted to do was pull her right into his arms and kiss her bow-shaped lips.

Chuckling, he urged her forward. "Sorry, Bonnie, there are no *less-important* men on Three Rivers. We're all equal here. Every man has an essential job. As for me collecting you at the airport and finding you a saddle horse—well, let's just say you lucked out."

Groaning, she rolled her eyes and muttered, "I should've seen that coming."

"I'm teasing, Bonnie." He glanced over at her. "Do you ever tease anyone?"

"Not really. I'm not good at it or making jokes."

He gently squeezed her elbow. "You know, while you're here on Three Rivers, you might just learn how."

"I came here to the ranch to learn a few things, but none of them have anything to do with joking or having fun," she said to Mose.

However, it was becoming obvious she was learning about him, and by all accounts, he couldn't be more opposite from her if he tried.

Opposites attract, Bonnie. Like steel to magnet. Once the two clamp together, it's damned hard to pry them apart.

Doing her best to ignore the ridiculous voice drifting through her head, she lifted her chin and peered ahead. If she had any sense at all, she'd be regretting this chance meeting with Mose. But she had to be honest with herself. Seeing him again was a sweet pleasure. And there just wasn't any way she could look in his brown eyes and keep a cool demeanor.

"Aww. That's a shame, Bonnie. A pretty woman like you needs to laugh more often."

She cast him a coy glance. "How do you know I don't do my fair share of laughing?"

"Your lips tell me," he answered. "They're just not turned up enough at the corners."

She had not expected that, and for a moment, she was too caught off guard to speak. After clearing her throat, she said, "I'll try to do some nightly exercises to correct the problem."

From the corner of her eye, she saw his brows shoot straight up and she suddenly realized how suggestive her comment must have sounded to him.

Her cheeks burning, she quickly added, "Facial exercises, that is."

He chuckled, but didn't say more on the subject, and Bonnie was relieved. She didn't know what it was about this man, but she said things to him she'd never say to anyone back in Utah. Which only proved that when she was in his presence, she needed to have her guard up.

A minute later, they reached the horse paddock, a stretch of pasture surrounded by a tall rail-board fence. Most of the animals were standing in the raggedy shade of a few scraggly mesquite trees. She supposed there were certain times of the year when the paddock might have grass, but presently it was mostly bare dirt. Bits of alfalfa were scattered around two wooden feed troughs where the animals had been fed earlier this morning.

As Bonnie walked up to the fence and peered through the rails, Mose said, "Take your pick. Personally, I like the sorrel mare with the star in her forehead. Her name is Dinah, but I call her Diva 'cause she knows she's a class act."

Bonnie searched the herd until she spotted the mare. Mose had a good eye for horseflesh. "Dinah is beautiful and carries herself with pride."

He nodded. "I've told Holt she should be a mount for a rodeo queen. She'd look dandy with glitter on her butt and her mane braided. Instead, she herds cows and drags calves to the branding fire. She's an all-out working girl."

Intrigued by his praise for the mare, she looked over at him. "Does she ever have foals?"

"Every other year. Holt believes in giving the working girls in the remuda a little rest between babies."

"From what I've seen in the barn and around the ranch yard, Holt takes excellent care of his horses."

"Which is one of the main reasons I like working for him and the Hollisters. At this ranch, the well-being of the livestock comes first. As it should." He inclined his head in Dinah's direction. "You want to ride her, or one of the others? Trust me, they're all well-mannered."

Trust him? She'd trust his knowledge of horses completely. Anything more, she couldn't say.

Anything more? What makes you think Mose would like anything more from you? He probably has a dozen women just waiting on a call from him.

The annoying voice inside her head frustrated her to no end, and she did her best to shake it away as she looked at him and smiled. "I'd love to ride Dinah and see if she's as classy as you say."

He gave her a playful wink. "You won't be disappointed."

She stood outside the corral fence and waited while he walked into the paddock and stretched out a hand to Dinah. As soon as he called her name, the mare trustingly walked over to him. Bonnie watched closely as he gently slipped the halter over her head and smoothed her forelock with his fingers. The movement caused the muscles in his back and arms to ripple beneath his flowered Western shirt and the sight caused her to wonder how it would feel to be enfolded in those strong arms.

You'll never know, Bonnie. So get the thought out of your head.

Shaking away the spiteful inner voice, Bonnie opened the gate to the paddock and held it wide enough for Mose and Dinah to pass. Once they were through the opening, she carefully closed and secured the latch behind them.

"Thanks for dealing with the gate." He motioned toward the horse barn. "There's another tack room here on the end of the barn. The hands who work the cattle division use it. We'll find a saddle that should come close to fitting you in there."

Bonnie fell in step at his side as he led the mare back toward the barn, which was at least fifty yards away. As they walked, she heard the yips and calls of several cowboys before she spotted a huge cloud of dust coming from the direction of the cattle barns.

"Sounds like the hands are hard at work," she commented.

"Fall branding. They've been rounding up the last of the late-born calves. Do you have those on Stone Creek Ranch?" he asked.

"Oh yes. But none of our roundups would be nearly as large as these on Three Rivers. Do you go on them?"

"No. The horse trainers never get involved with the cattle end of things. Our division basically takes care of itself and the cattle division sticks to its job."

She glanced at him. "Do you like staying in your own lane or would you rather be an all-around hand? Or maybe you're only experienced with horses and not cattle?"

He gave her a lopsided grin. "I've done my share of cowboying. Eating dust, riding fence lines, sweating in the heat, searching for calves in a freezing blizzard. It takes tough men to deal with the work, and I've got nothing but respect for them. But working with the horses is my calling—my love—and I'm good at the job. At least, Holt says I am."

She said, "I've learned that Holt's horses are known for being some of the best all over the West. How does it feel to work for a man with such a reputation?"

He laughed and she thought how she liked the low, husky sound. It was a mixture of pleasure and sultriness that had her imagining how it might feel to have his warm breath brushing the side of her neck, his lips tracking a trail over her cheek. The erotic thought caused her to inwardly shiver.

"No matter if I was working at a county sale barn or training for Holt, I would do my best. That's all a man can ever really do. Right?"

"Yes. My dad often says the same thing. I imagine yours does, too?"

He was silent for a moment and Bonnie was suddenly thinking she probably shouldn't have mentioned his father. Could be he didn't have one. Or he didn't have a relationship with the one he did have. The idea was sad and she desperately hoped she was wrong.

He said, "Dad always does his best."

He didn't say more about his father and Bonnie was happy to drop the subject as they reached the barn.

After tying Dinah's lead rope to a hitching rail beneath an overhang of metal roof, they entered the massive tack room.

The space was illuminated by sunlight streaming through a skylight in the ceiling, revealing countless saddles stacked on wooden racks. Others hung from ropes dangling down from the rafters. Two whole walls were covered with hooks holding all types of bits, bridles and reins. On the opposite wall, an assortment of saddle blankets in various colors and shapes were stacked neatly on deep shelves. Next to the shelves, a cord was stretched several feet off the floor, extending from one corner of the room to the other. The clothesline was of the same sort they used on Stone Creek to hang up sweat-soaked blankets to dry.

"Wow, there's enough tack in here to open up a saddle shop," Bonnie commented. "How do you know where to look for what you want?"

"We always keep things in the same place. That way we can go straight back to whatever it is we need." He walked over to a saddle sitting on a stand at the end of one row. "This is Hannah's saddle. She's Vivian's teenaged daughter. They live up on the Camp Verde Reservation, but she comes down often to visit, so she keeps a saddle here to ride. It should be about your size."

"I'm not particular. I won't mind if the seat is a little too small or large," she told him. "Actually, you don't need to bother with adjusting the stirrups, either. I don't really need them."

He shot her a skeptical look as he carried the saddle over to where she was standing. "You must be an awfully confident rider."

The doubt on his face put an impish smile on hers. "Well, you did say Dinah was a class act."

One of his brows shot up and then he chuckled. "I sure did. It would be embarrassing if she proved me wrong."

She flashed him another smile. "No worries. I understand horses are like children. About the time you brag on them, they immediately misbehave."

Grinning, he swiped a hand across his brow. "Whew. Thanks for letting me off the hook."

She helped him carry the rest of the necessary tack out to the hitching post where Dinah was tethered, then stood to one side while he dealt with the saddling. Bonnie could have easily done the task herself, but she didn't tell him so. For one thing, she got the feeling that he probably wouldn't have allowed her to deal with the job alone. And the other reason was purely selfish on her part. She didn't want to give up his company until she had to. In fact, she wished he was going to accompany her on the ride, but he was obviously busy and she'd never be so forward as to invite him.

Five minutes later, Dinah was ready to go and he led the mare a few steps out in the open before offering her a leg up. She didn't need his assistance to mount the horse, but for once she was going to be a bit like her twin before she'd married Kipp and play helpless when a good-looking man was near.

"How long have you been riding?" he asked as he wrapped a hand around the lower part of her calf and boosted her up into the seat of the saddle.

"Since I was four. My twin and I got into serious trouble

once when we were six years old. We snuck off from the ranch yard and rode up into the mountains by ourselves. Dad was livid and threatened to never let us ride again. But thankfully, after a while, he cooled off."

"I'm assuming you and your sister didn't have any mishaps on your big adventure," he said.

"No. But Bea did break her arm while riding when she was twelve. She thought she could do the hippodrome in a stock saddle. It didn't work, obviously."

"I think I should warn Blake not to have twin girls. He has enough headaches already with two sets of boy twins," he joked, then reached over and gave Dinah's breast collar one last tug to make sure it held in place. "You still planning on a thirty-to-forty-minute ride? I'll remind Holt when I get back to the barn."

"Yes. The sun will be setting soon. And I'm not acquainted with the trails yet. I don't want to get me and Dinah lost in the dark," she told him, then gestured beyond the horse paddock. "Do I just keep riding past the paddock? Or will I run into fences if I go this way?"

"No fences around here. Just keep going past the paddock and you'll see the cattle trails heading south. It's a prettier ride if you go due south." He gave the mare's shoulder an affectionate pat, before giving the toe of Bonnie's boot a friendly little wiggle. "You two have a safe trip."

"Thank you, Mose, for saddling Dinah and—everything."

With a single nod, he lifted a hand in farewell and Bonnie forced herself to put Dinah into forward motion. However, before the mare had traveled more than a few steps, Bonnie desperately wanted to look over her shoulder to see if Mose was watching her go.

She drew in a deep breath and blew it out. It was scary how much she'd wanted to ask him if he'd be around when she returned to the barn. She'd wanted to tell him that she hoped to see him again. But being forward wasn't her style and she'd already taken up too much of his time. Besides, the more she was around him, the more she wanted his company. If she didn't watch herself, she'd soon become infatuated with the Texas horseman. Which would be a surefire way to develop heart trouble.

"What happened to you? Did you stretch out on Holt's couch and take a nap?" Dex asked as Mose walked up to the two young horses tied to a hitching post in the shade of the barn.

Grimacing, Mose said, "Not hardly. When have you ever seen me lying around napping on the job?"

Dex lifted his straw hat and ran a hand across his sweaty forehead. "Never," he answered. "But you were gone a lot longer than I thought you'd be."

Mose's grunt was tinged with humor. "If you want the truth, Dex, for the past half hour I've been with a beautiful young woman. Tall, long blond hair and blue eyes."

"Sure, Mose. In your dreams, maybe."

Mose untethered the filly's reins and backed her away from the hitching post. Deciding he'd not heard enough, Dex followed at Mose's side.

"You're just pulling my leg, aren't you?" Dex asked as he tugged the straw hat down lower on his ears.

Mose chuckled. "Just a little," he admitted. "I *was* with a beautiful blonde. But only because I was available. She didn't come to the barn to see me specifically. She only needed someone to catch a horse for her—to go riding"

"Well, that changes things. Was she a buyer?"

"No. A relative. To the Hollisters."

"Oh. She here to visit for Christmas, or something?"

Mose shrugged as he stopped the filly at the edge of the shade. "*Or something*, I guess. She didn't say. And I haven't asked."

Dex was thoughtful for a long moment. "You went to the airport the other day and picked up someone for Maureen. Was it this woman?"

"It was."

Dex made a rolling motion with one hand. "Well, come on, Mose. Tell me about her. You've been keeping this all to yourself."

Frowning, he turned and after flopping the stirrup onto the seat of the saddle, proceeded to tighten the girth. "Don't start, Dex. Bonnie Hollister is a guest of the family. And I don't want to hear you making any sly innuendos about her. She's not that kind of a girl."

"You mean she's not like that dozen or so girls you danced with last night at the Fandango?" Dex asked slyly.

Mose positioned the stirrup back in place before turning a glare on his friend. "This horse barn is a regular gossip mill," he muttered. "Someone has been doing a hell of a lot of talking around here."

"Yeah, what of it? Since when does it bother you to have the guys mention your—womanizing? What's the matter with you, anyway?"

"I don't womanize. And nothing is wrong with me. Except that I have work to tend to before day's end. And so do you," he snapped. "Maybe you ought to get to it."

Unfazed by Mose's pointed suggestion, Dex chuckled and gave him a little salute. "Right. Off to work. And no more talk about a beautiful blonde."

As Mose watched the groom stride away, he muttered a curse at himself. It wasn't like him to get so curt with Dex. They had a good working relationship. The guy never shirked his work and was always more than happy to take Mose's orders. And as for the teasing about the dancing and dozens of girls, Mose would've normally laughed and let the remark roll off his back. But at the moment, he didn't much feel like laughing. No, his thoughts were too tangled up with Bonnie. Something about being with the pretty blonde for those few minutes had left him feeling a little helpless and a whole lot annoyed with himself.

She'd be returning to the barn in thirty or forty minutes and he wished like hell he could come up with a sensible reason to go back to the remuda paddock and wait for her arrival. But that would be too obvious. Not to mention make him look like an overeager fool.

With a weary sigh, he led Blue Beads into the training arena and easily swung himself up in the saddle. The black filly felt tense beneath him, and he patted her neck and the spot between her ears before he gently nudged her forward. By the time they reached the opposite end of the arena, she was relaxing nicely and Mose was doing his best to follow the filly's example.

After making a couple of circles around the arena, he reined the filly to a stop close to the fence and called to the wrangler. "Hey, Dex, come here."

The wrangler left the horse he'd been showering fastened inside a grooming stock and walked over to Mose.

"You need something?" the young man asked.

"Yeah. In about twenty minutes, I want you to go over to the remuda paddock and wait for Ms. Hollister to return. She'll be coming up the south cattle trail, so you won't be able to miss her."

Dex's jaw dropped. "Me? Why do I need to meet her?"

Mose said, "With her background, I know she's perfectly capable of putting up her horse and saddle herself. But since she's a guest, I figure Holt would want someone around the barn to give her a hand. You're just the man for the job."

Dex's expression suddenly turned skeptical. "And you're not? You're the one who saddled her mount in the first place. Since when have you not wanted to give a pretty woman a helping hand?"

Mose let out a frustrated breath. There was no way he could explain to Dex that being in Bonnie's presence rattled his senses. Oh sure, he wanted like hell to go to the horse paddock and wait for her return. He wanted to see her again, talk with her, and hopefully have that shy smile of hers aimed directly at him.

But that would be too risky to his heart. He'd already made one mistake in believing he could have a wealthy woman in his life. He wasn't going to give himself a chance to make the same blunder a second time.

"After I finish putting Blue Beads through her workout, I still have Arrowhead to put through his paces. I don't have time." Which was true enough, Mose thought.

He knew he wasn't fooling Dex, but thankfully, Dex didn't choose to argue. "Okay," he said with a shrug. "Whatever you say. I'll take good care of Ms. Hollister."

"Listen, Dex, I didn't ask you to take care of Bonnie," he said tersely. "I asked you to take care of her horse and saddle. Got it?"

The wrangler grinned and gave him a thumbs-up. "I got it."

Mose reined the filly away from the fence, and as he trotted her across the plowed dirt to the center of the arena, he pushed hard at Bonnie's image floating through his mind.

She'd probably be leaving Three Rivers in a few days. And for his peace of mind, her departure couldn't come fast enough.

Chapter Four

Later that night in her bedroom, Bonnie sat in a wingback chair near the window and gazed out at the partial view of the ranch yard. From this angle, she could see the lights illuminating a few of the holding pens and a part of the cattle barn. Beyond that massive structure, more yard lamps cast eerie shadows over a section of the horse training arena.

Earlier this evening, when she returned from her ride, she'd hoped to find Mose waiting for her. Instead, a wrangler, who'd introduced himself as Dex, had been there to take Dinah off her hands. Bonnie had to admit she was a bit disappointed over not seeing Mose again. But she'd tried to tell herself it was for the best. Even if Mose did show a spark of interest in her, she could only be his friend.

But how could she be just his friend when his presence didn't conjure up friendly feelings in her? No, her reaction to him was downright sinful in nature.

The ring of her cell phone disrupted her thoughts and she reached across the arm of the chair for it. Seeing the caller was her mother, she instantly pressed the accept button.

"Hi, Mom. Is everything okay?"

The question pulled a chuckle from Claire. "Everything is fine, honey. You think I'd only call if something was wrong? Did you never think I might just want to check up on you?"

Bonnie bit down on her bottom lip, hearing what her mother

wasn't saying—which was that she expected Bonnie was likely already homesick and worrying about everyone back on Stone Creek. True, her father had sent her down here to research his grandfather's life, but Bonnie wasn't totally naive. Her parents were hoping this trip would help to broaden their daughter's world. Not that Bonnie needed to widen her horizons. As far as she was concerned, she liked keeping her life quiet and simple.

Bonnie said, "No, it's not that, Mom. It's just that I've not heard from you since I arrived here two days ago. I thought something urgent might be going on up there."

"Everything is fine, sweetie. Grace and I have been making Christmas plans, and Cord is going to help me decorate the tree tomorrow night," she replied. "Besides, you called your father last night after you got settled, so I knew you were okay."

"It's nice to hear your voice, Mom. It makes me feel like I'm not so far away from all of you."

"Aww, sweetheart, don't tell me you're already getting homesick and pining to come home. You'll be back up here soon enough. Probably in time for Christmas, so while you're there in Arizona you need to enjoy yourself."

Uh-oh. She'd better start choosing her words more carefully, Bonnie thought. "I'm not homesick," Bonnie insisted. "And I am enjoying myself. It's beautiful here and everyone is so nice to me."

Claire sighed with relief. "Good. So tell me what you've been doing so far?"

She'd been thinking about a horseman with the most striking brown eyes she'd ever seen, that's what she'd been doing, Bonnie thought. What would her mother think if she knew her very practical daughter had taken one look at a cowboy and gone a little ditzy?

Doing her best to shake away Mose's image, she said, "Not much anything in the way of gathering information on Parnell Hollister so far, I have to admit. Sorry if anyone was hoping I'd have news by now. Maureen says there's no hurry and we'll start on the project in a few days. I just left her and Gil in the den before I came up here to my room. After being out all day with the men rounding up cattle, she's already talking about starting again before daylight. I don't know where she finds the energy. And frankly, I don't know how she's going to manage to help me do this search of family history, what with her ranch work and Christmas coming."

"Maureen is a hands-on ranch woman, and from the conversations I've had with her, raising cattle and horses is something she's done since she was very young—even before she married Joel, her first husband. So she's seasoned to the job," Claire said. "As for Christmas preparations, I'm sure she'll manage."

"Yes, she's like a whirlwind that never stops. Kind of like you, Mom," Bonnie said affectionately.

Claire laughed softly. "Well, I'm not up on herding cattle like Maureen, but being a mother to you eight children was almost like herding a bunch," Claire joked. "So have you had a chance to do any shopping yet for yourself or Christmas gifts? Or sightseeing around Wickenburg?"

"Not yet. Sophia, she's one of the cooks, is planning for the two of us to make a trip to town soon. She's been telling me about the best places to shop. Especially a certain boutique that's a favorite among the locals."

"That sounds like fun. Is Sophia married? Have children?"

"She's married to one of Holt's horse trainers, but they don't have any children yet. She's about to turn thirty, so she's only three years older than me. All the women on the ranch are so nice and friendly to me. They treat me like family."

"You *are* family, Bonnie."

"Yes. But it's not just the Hollisters who treat me like family. The house staff does, too."

"How many people work in the ranch house?" her mother asked.

"Four. Two cooks, a housekeeper and a nanny."

"Wow! Your father is going to hear about this," Claire said jokingly.

"I realize it sounds extravagant, Mom, but the extra help is definitely needed. The house is huge, and added to the adults, there are seven children living here. Plus, most of the time Jazelle has her two children here with her during the day, even if they don't live here full-time. And Tallulah has a little fourteen-month-old boy and is also expecting another baby in a few months."

"Gracious, the ranch house sounds like a busy place full of kids. Just like Stone Creek used to be," Claire said wistfully.

"Your house will be filled with children again," Bonnie assured her, then mentioned two of her brothers. "Clem and Quint will be having their baby soon. And I expect Bea will get pregnant before too long. And you know how much Willow and Hunter want a child. Just give it time, Mom."

After a slight pause, she said, "You're right. But I didn't hear you mention anything about *you* having a baby—eventually."

"Not without a husband, Mom! And I—" she broke off as Mose's rugged image unexpectedly flashed through her mind "—can't see myself finding a man I'd want to have children with." The words felt strangely like a lie.

Claire groaned. "If you ever fall in love, Bonnie, and I mean real love, not that infatuation you went through in your college days, the babies will naturally follow."

Real love. Bonnie wasn't sure she could ever trust a man enough to believe him whenever he spoke the word *love*.

Holding back a sigh, Bonnie said, "Maybe someday, Mom. Right now, I'm focused on finding the reason Parnell was kicked off the ranch and out of the Hollister will. This has been a long, emotional road for Dad. Getting some answers might help matters, but I fear Dad is going to learn his father and his grandfather were both scoundrels."

"You can't change the past, honey," Claire said ruefully. "All you can do is use it as a learning tool."

No one knew that better than Bonnie. She'd learned her judgment in choosing a boyfriend was terrible. And more recently, she'd learned her grandfather was a liar and a cheat.

A moment of silence passed and then Claire said, "Listen, darling, while you're at Three Rivers, you don't need to spend all your time with your nose stuck in a bunch of stuffy documents or letters. You should make an effort to meet new people and enjoy yourself. Okay?"

It was on the tip of Bonnie's tongue to tell her mother about meeting Mose. But she didn't see much point when nothing could develop between them.

"I will, Mom. I promise."

A couple of minutes later, Claire ended the call and Bonnie walked over to the window and gazed once again at the ranch yard. This afternoon, after Dex had taken Dinah off her hands, she'd considered meandering by the training arena, just to see the men at work with the young horses. But she'd forced herself to walk straight to the house. Not for anything did she want to give Mose the impression she was trying to make a play for him.

Her make a play for a man? The notion was ludicrous. Bonnie had never gone after a man in her life. Even in high school and college, when her friends were agonizing over the right choice of clothing and makeup to help them attract guys, or trying to conjure up ways to *accidently* cross paths with whoever they were crushing on at the moment, Bonnie had chosen to keep to herself and study. That is, until she'd met Ward Lawton.

Good-looking and well on his way to being a member of his father's highly successful farming-equipment business, Ward had been intelligent and nice and most of all, he had seemed to genuinely care for her. When he talked about love and marriage, she'd truly believed he wanted to spend the rest of his life with her. And maybe for a little while, he really had thought Bonnie was his one true love. That is, until he'd met Beatrice.

When her twin informed Bonnie that Ward had secretly made a play for her, Bonnie had been shocked and crushed. And to make the betrayal even more humiliating, he'd told Beatrice that even though Bonnie was equally pretty as her twin, her personality was as dull as dishwater.

Bonnie would be the first to admit that she'd never been the life of the party. Her quiet, reserved disposition had always been glaringly opposite to Beatrice's bubbly personality. Still, she'd been deeply cut to hear that the man she'd been planning to marry thought of her as bland and uninteresting.

But that was all in the past, she thought, as she continued to gaze at the hazy cast of lights over the ranch yard. She'd learned a lot about herself since her college days and she wanted to believe her self-esteem had grown past that insecure period in her life. But had it grown enough to give her the courage to open her heart to the right man?

With a wistful sigh, she turned from the window and, after gathering her nightclothes from the chest of drawers, headed to the bathroom to get ready for bed.

***

The next afternoon, Mose was standing with Colt beneath the overhang of the barn, inspecting the leg on a chestnut filly, when Holt strode up to them.

"Oh heck, Mose. We're in trouble," Colt joked. "The boss has caught us on the ground instead of in our saddles."

Holt chuckled. "I'm sure you two are shaking in your boots."

"Yeah, I usually shake in sixty-degree weather," Mose said with playful sarcasm.

Grinning, Holt crossed his arms across his chest and rocked back on his heels. "Okay, I'm down here to give orders, but not about work. Mom is up to her usual mischief. She's planning a little party tomorrow night and you two are to be there. Luke, Tag and Jim, plus their families will be there, too. Along with all of us Hollisters."

Colt looked surprised, while Mose was inwardly doing fist pumps. Ever since he'd seen Bonnie yesterday at the horse barn, he'd regretted not waiting around to unsaddle Dinah when she returned from her ride. Now he'd been racking his brain, trying to come up with some reason to see her again. Thankfully, Maureen had given him the perfect opportunity.

"Sophia will most likely be cooking for the party," Colt said. "So I'm sure she'll be telling me all about it tonight."

"What is this party? An early Christmas shindig?" Mose asked.

"Let's just call it a pre-Christmas party. To give Bonnie a chance to meet everyone. And get all of us in the holiday spirit, I suppose," Holt said with a grin. "You know Mom. If she doesn't have a reason to throw a party, she'll make one up."

"Well, I'm sure glad Bonnie has come for a visit," Colt spoke up. "Sophia doesn't get away from the ranch that much and it's good she's made a new friend around her own age. I can tell she adores your new cousin."

Mose felt Holt turn an inquisitive eye on him. "What do *you* think about our new cousin, Mose?"

Colt darted a curious look at Mose. "You've already met Bonnie?"

Why did Mose feel like dropping his head and kicking the dirt with the toe of his boot? There wasn't anything shady or inappropriate about his spending a few minutes with Bonnie. Even so, he could feel a tinge of heat collecting in his cheeks.

"Yeah. I drove her home from the airport, and yesterday I saddled a horse for her," he told Colt, then glanced at Holt. "And I think she's a very nice girl."

Too nice for the likes of him, Mose felt like adding, but kept the thought to himself.

"I'm glad to hear Bonnie is fitting in. As for the party, Mom wants us there at seven. Everyone will be gathering on the patio. It might be a bit chilly, but I expect Gil will have a roaring fire going to keep everyone warm." He gestured toward the chestnut standing quietly at Colt's side. "When I walked up, you two were inspecting her left front leg. She having a problem?"

"We're trying to figure it out," Colt said. "Occasionally, she takes a lame step on that foot. But we can't see anything wrong with her foot, ankle, or knee."

Mose added, "We're thinking Chandler ought to have a look and do X-rays."

Chandler was the brother between Holt and Blake. A respected veterinarian, he owned and operated a fairly large animal hospital located on the outskirts of Wickenburg. He also took care of the medical needs of the livestock on the ranch. But with his business in town growing busier every day, and Three Rivers constantly adding more cattle and horses, the man's time and energy were spread thin. Mose had heard Holt and Blake discussing the idea of hiring in a resident veterinarian for the ranch, but so far it was only talk. However, everyone agreed that Chandler desperately needed some of the responsibilities lifted from his shoulders.

Holt said, "I'm sending Luke into town tomorrow to deliver a couple of horses I've sold. I'll have him drop the filly by Chandler's on the way. Let's pray it's not a serious problem. I have a small fortune invested in her. In the meantime, don't ride her."

After Colt assured him the filly would rest in her stall until she visited the vet, Holt left the two men.

As Mose watched their boss enter the horse barn, he said, "You know, Colt, I used to wish I had lots of money. But the longer I'm here on Three Rivers, the more I realize I'm just fine like I am."

Colt grunted with amusement. "Why?"

"The Hollister men carry heavy responsibilities. If they don't make the right choices, they stand to lose thousands," Mose answered. "I couldn't sleep at night with the burden of those kinds of decisions on my shoulders."

Colt chuckled. "A man has to take risks in order to get ahead. As for sleeping, if you had a loving wife snuggled in your arms, you'd forget about losing or making money. Actually, you'd forget about sleeping, too."

Mose leveled a pointed look at his coworker. "I take it that was meant to be advice? That I'd be a lot better off with a woman in my bed?"

Grinning coyly, Colt said, "It wasn't necessarily advice. Just a suggestion."

Mose scowled at him. "Sorry, but I'm perfectly okay just like I am."

With a mocking little laugh, Colt reined the filly in the

direction of the barn. After leading the horse a few steps, he paused and tossed over his shoulder, "One of these days you won't be okay with living alone, Mose. And then I'm going to say I told you so."

"That'll be the day," Mose muttered.

That afternoon, as Sophia drove the two of them into town, Bonnie realized when she'd made the trip from the airport with Mose, she'd missed a big portion of the beautiful desert landscape.

"Until I came down here, I'd never seen a saguaro cactus up close before," Bonnie commented, as she gazed out the passenger window. "Some of them are far taller than I expected them to be. They're really majestic, aren't they?"

"Yes. Were you aware they're protected by law?"

"No," Bonnie answered. "But I can see why. They're so beautiful."

Sophia said, "I didn't know much about them until I moved here from California. Saguaros have to be fifty to seventy-five years old before they grow an arm. Sometimes if the area is really dry it can take up to a hundred years before they develop arms. So if someone is caught damaging one, the person is charged with a felony and does jail time."

"Oh, I had no idea. I have plenty to learn about things down here. It's far different from the area where I live."

Sophia glanced over at her and smiled. "You might enjoy reading about the saguaros. There are lots of Native American myths and legends about them that I think you'd find interesting."

"Yes, I'm sure I would. Thanks for the suggestion. Especially since it looks like I'm going to have a bit more leisure time on the ranch than I first thought. Maureen isn't in any hurry to dig into Parnell's life."

Sophia nodded knowingly. "I'll give you a heads-up, Bonnie. Maureen wants to stretch your stay as long as she possibly can. She likes having you here and I know she wants you around for all the Christmas festivities."

Bonnie frowned at her. "I don't understand. I only see her for a few short minutes in the morning and then in the evening when we all have dinner together. That's the extent of our connection. Why would she care so much about whether I stay or go?"

"Don't try to understand Maureen. It's impossible," Sophia said with a fond smile. "You'll soon learn that she doesn't do things halfway and that includes her relationships with people. She either loves you or she'd rather see your backside going out the door. She happens to love you."

"I'm glad she does," Bonnie said thoughtfully. "But I—"

"You what?" Sophia prompted.

Bonnie made a helpless shrug as her thoughts drifted to Mose. Her preoccupation with the man was beginning to scare her. Even if she went back home to Stone Creek tomorrow, would that erase him from her mind? Somehow she doubted the miles would cure this infatuation that had come over her.

"To tell you the truth, Sophia, I wasn't planning on being at Three Rivers for very long. My family will expect me home for Christmas."

Sophia frowned as she continued to keep her attention focused on the highway. "Are you getting homesick already?"

Bonnie held back a sigh. "No. I'm just a little worried about my parents becoming overloaded with the office work that they're handling for me. I could do some of it remotely on my laptop, but my parents wanted me to have a break from the work on Stone Creek for a while."

Which was true, Bonnie thought. But it wasn't the real reason she was feeling antsy. She couldn't admit to Sophia that after two short encounters with Mose, she'd developed a foolish crush on the man. It was humiliating.

Sophia said, "The way I see things, your parents would've never sent you down here if they were worried about work piling up in the ranch's office. Quit worrying. Tonight is party night. Maureen says Viv and Sawyer are driving down from the reservation to join us, so you'll get to see their twins, Johnny and Jacob. They're about to turn five now."

"Let me see if I have this straight. Viv and Sawyer are park rangers, right?"

"Right," she said, then continued listing the family members who Bonnie would most likely meet tonight. "And, of course, Holt's wife, Isabelle, and their three sons will be coming, too. And just wait 'til you meet Isabelle's mother and stepfather. Gabby and Sam are such an adorable couple. He's probably twenty years older than her and they're as different as can be. He's a wiry old cowboy, while Gabby is an artist. But when you see them together, it's a warm reminder of what true love really is."

True love. There were times Bonnie wondered if the humiliation she'd gone through with Ward had skewed something within her so deeply that she'd never be capable of loving a man.

"I'm looking forward to meeting everyone," Bonnie replied, then couldn't stop herself from asking, "Uh—will any of the ranch hands be coming to the party tonight?"

Sophia cast a cheeky grin in her direction. "Sure. Colt said Holt made a point of inviting him and Luke and Mose and Jim. And they'll be a few more guys from the horse and cattle divisions show up. So," she added with a sly grin, "that means there will be some cute, single cowboys for you to meet."

A flash of heat suddenly stung Bonnie's cheeks. "Actually, I've already met one."

Surprised, Sophia glanced at her. "You have? Who?"

"I told Jazelle about Mose driving me home from the airport. I'm surprised she didn't mention it to you."

"No, Jazelle must be slipping," Sophia said wryly. "I took it for granted that Maureen taxied you home."

Bonnie absently fiddled with the silver-cross pendant nestled in the hollow of her throat. "For some reason, she sent Mose to fetch me instead."

Sophia's expression turned thoughtful. "Mose, eh? So what did you think of him?"

Although Bonnie tried to stop her reaction, a nervous little laugh slipped out of her. "I have to admit he's not like any man I've met before. Actually, he saddled my horse for me yesterday and we chatted for a few minutes. He's nice-looking and likable. And he has a big personality, that's for sure. I can't explain it, but there's something about him that—I—I'm drawn to."

Sophia didn't reply and Bonnie looked over to see she was nodding her head up and down with smug approval.

Seeing where her friend's mind was headed, Bonnie quickly added, "But that doesn't mean anything, Sophia! I like him as a person. Anything else—well, we're total opposites. He's confidant and flamboyant and—I've been described as dull."

"Anyone who called you *dull* is totally wrong. And remember what I said about Gabby and Sam. It's like mixing a hot jalapeño with plain scrambled eggs. You might not think to put them together, but if you do, you find out they're a delicious match."

Bonnie couldn't help but laugh. "You would use food to emphasize your point."

Sophia laughed along with her. "A cook knows all about mixing different flavors."

Yes, but Bonnie couldn't picture herself *mixing* with a man like Mose. Even though she wished she had the courage to try.

Five minutes later, the two women arrived in Wickenburg and Sophia drove straight to the grocery market to gather a few extra things needed for the party. After that chore was completed, Sophia took them to the Cactus and Candles Boutique to search for something to wear to the party.

Inside the quaint little shop filled with Western-themed clothing, accessories and household items, Sophia wrapped a hand around Bonnie's arm and led her straight to a rack of dresses.

"Sophia, I'm all for shopping, but I'm not sure I really need a new dress. I showed you the skirts and dresses I brought with me, just in case I needed something to wear for a special occasion while I was here. What's wrong with wearing one of them?"

"Bonnie, those things are beautiful. But to be honest, they're a bit too fancy. This is an outdoor party. You want to look casual and beautiful at the same time."

Bonnie groaned. "You sound just like Bea. If she was here, she'd be grabbing up something simple but fun that would show a hint of cleavage and leg. To make things look interesting, she'd say."

Sophia laughed under her breath. "That's just the sort of thing we need to find for you. So an unnamed horse trainer will look in your direction."

Rolling her eyes, Bonnie muttered, "I should've never said a word about Mose. Now you're going to be pestering me about him. Which is ridiculous. I'm not looking to catch a boyfriend, or even a date!"

Hangers screeched as Sophia pushed the garments back and forth on the metal rack. "What's your favorite color?"

"Bea says I look good in blue."

Sophia shot her an irritated look. "Forget about what color your twin thinks you should wear. What do *you* like?"

Bonnie smiled guiltily. "I like pink and red. See, I do have a mind of my own, Sophia. But sometimes I don't trust my judgment."

"And you think your twin is always right?"

"Well, everything turned out well for her, so she must have made the right choices," Bonnie admitted.

Sophia curled an arm around Bonnie's shoulders and gave her an encouraging squeeze. "Oh Bonnie. You need to trust in yourself. You're beautiful and intelligent. You can be just as confident and sassy as—well, as me," she added with an impish laugh.

Bonnie laughed along with her. "Okay. Confident and sassy. But even if I find something a little sexy to wear, that doesn't mean I want Mose to look in my direction, or any other man for that matter."

"Hah! I used to have that same mindset. Until I took one look at Colt and my heart turned traitor to my brain." She motioned for Bonnie to dig into the rack of dresses. "Come on. We don't have much time. I need to get back to the ranch to help Gran finish the cooking."

"Okay." Turning her attention to the long rack of dresses, she located the section with options in her size, and she hurriedly scanned through the garments.

"What do you think about this?" Bonnie asked as she held up a dress with a tight-fitting bodice, a low square neckline, long full sleeves and a flared skirt. "If it's chilly on the patio, I have a white lace shawl to throw over my shoulders."

Sophia slanted her a cunning grin. "Bonnie, you are going to be a total knockout in that piece. And I love the tiny red-and-white rose print of the fabric. For a woman who's uncertain of her choices, you didn't waste any time making this one."

"Well, you did say we needed to hurry," Bonnie reminded her.

Sophia said, "Okay, since you made such a quick and perfect choice for yourself, why don't you find something for me? I'm the world's worst at picking out clothing."

They both laughed at that, and as Bonnie helped her friend flip through the dresses, she thought of her twin. If Beatrice could see her now, she'd be happy and smiling. She'd be thrilled to know her reserved sister was planning to wear a revealing dress and she might even find the courage to try and catch the attention of one tall, sexy Texan.

Chapter Five

One of the special perks Mose received for being a horse trainer on Three Rivers Ranch was living rent-free in a house located about a mile from the big ranch house. Nestled on a rise and surrounded by cottonwood, mesquite and Joshua trees, the residence overlooked the desert mountains, while a small river made a meandering curve about fifty yards behind the house. The Hollisters had built the three-bedroom brown stucco a little more than thirty years ago for Maureen's widowed mother, Gwendolyn. Unfortunately, she'd only lived there about ten years before she'd passed away from health issues. Since that time, Maureen had made sure the house was well maintained and nicely furnished.

The stucco was the first nice house Mose had ever lived in. His parents had both worked hard and provided as best as they could for their two sons, but the couple had never been able to scrape up enough money to buy a decent house. The family of four had always lived in apartments or shabby rental houses. After his parents had divorced, their father had moved himself and his two teenaged sons into a tiny apartment in Hereford, Texas, while their mother had gone to live with her parents in Fort Worth. After he'd grown up and moved out, Mose had mostly lived a transient life, moving around the Texas Panhandle area, to wherever he could find steady work breaking horses. And during those days, he'd made his home in everything from camp trailers and apartments to bunkhouses. But now, thanks to the Hollisters and his job here on Three Rivers, he had a real home, one he planned to never leave.

As he backed his truck from beneath a carport attached to the left side of the house, he wondered what Bonnie would think of his little home. Being a Hollister, even an offshoot of this family, she undoubtedly lived in a big fancy ranch house with all the extra comforts. She most likely had closets filled with nice clothes, along with jewelry, expensive perfume and makeup. All the things he thought a woman enjoyed, he figured Bonnie had or could purchase at any given moment. In that aspect, she was just like Nicole, he thought, glumly. But did wealth and material things mean as much to Bonnie as they had to Nicole? He supposed that was the question he should be asking himself.

Bonnie. Bonnie. Bonnie.

The name rolled through his mind like a haunting melody as he drove the truck over the dirt track toward the big ranch house. Ever since Holt had announced Maureen was throwing the little pre-Christmas shindig, he'd not been able to think of much else besides seeing Bonnie again. No one had to tell him he was being a fool. As far as the beautiful blonde was concerned, he realized he was headed down a dead-end street. But he couldn't help it. From the moment he'd walked up to her in the airport lobby, some sort of spell had come over him. What he was feeling was far more than attraction for a pretty girl. It was an obsession to know everything about her, a deep yearning simply to be in her presence. What was the matter with him, anyway?

Just like she's going to give you a chance to get close to her? In that shirt? She probably already views you as some sort of clown.

Muttering a curse at the mocking voice in his head, Mose glanced down at the Western shirt he'd paired with the blue jeans he kept reserved for special occasions. The tiny blue-flowered shirt with solid blue yokes on the front and back, which matched the wide pearl-snapped cuffs, wasn't yet faded. Mostly because the darn thing had cost a mint at the Western store and he'd been taking extra care to launder it in cold water.

Mose favored retro styles, perhaps as a result of him being an old soul at heart. He liked the way cowboys had looked and dressed years ago. He'd also liked their code of morals, especially emphasizing loyalty to family and friends. Maybe his flamboyant shirts and tall fancy boots did make him appear out of place to some folks, but frankly, he didn't care. He wasn't going to change, even to garner Bonnie's attention. He had to be true to himself or he wouldn't be much of a man to her, or anyone.

Before he reached the big three-story house, he spotted a number of vehicles parked along the circle drive and on the side of the dirt road leading down to the ranch yard. Mose drove on past the line of trucks and parked his truck in an out-of-the-way spot not far from the cattle barn.

As he walked the distance back to the house, the smell of mesquite smoke drifted in his direction, along with the muted sounds of Christmas music and peals of laughter. The Hollister family was huge, and from the looks of the gathering, Mose realized that all of them must have turned out to greet Bonnie and enjoy some early holiday cheer. Which most likely meant that he'd be lucky to get to say a quick hello to her before the other guests monopolized her attention.

He was chewing on that disappointing thought when he spotted Colt striding out of the shadows and straight at him.

"Hey, Mose! I wondered when you were finally going to show up," he called to him.

Mose picked up the pace of his steps and met Colt in the middle of the road. "Hey, buddy, looks like there's a big turnout for the party. Am I late?" Mose asked as he glanced at his wristwatch.

"Not at all. I think most of the family wanted to come early and do some extra visiting," Colt explained. "Matthew is presently moving cattle down at Red Bluff, so him and Camille couldn't make the drive up here. But the rest of the family has shown up."

Mose had met Maureen's youngest daughter, Camille, and her husband, Matthew, a couple of times since he'd moved to Three Rivers. As for the others who lived nearby, he knew all of them very well.

"It's a nice evening. A little cool, but nothing the firepit can't overcome," Mose commented as the two men made their way toward the patio at the back of the house.

Strings of twinkling lights had been hung from the roof of the patio and across a section of the yard. At one end of the patio, a Christmas tree had been erected and decorated with rows of silver garland and multitudes of colorful lights. Chatter and laughter mixed with holiday music and carried on the night air. The festive mood lifted Mose's spirits.

"Gil has already built a fire, so no one should get chilled. And Sophia and Reeva have outdone themselves with the food. I'd say I hope you're hungry, but you're always hungry," Colt joked.

Mose usually did have a big appetite. But for some reason, he wasn't all that hungry tonight. Maybe because his thoughts were more on Bonnie than consuming a plate of food. "I'd probably weigh a hundred pounds more than I do now if I was married to a chef."

Colt's chuckle was sly. "The food is just a side benefit. I'd be crazy in love with Sophia even if she couldn't heat a can of soup."

Crazy in love. Colt might as well have spoken the words in a foreign language. Mose had never been *that* much in love. Oh yeah, he'd thought he'd been in love with Nicole, but later, after she'd deserted him—too scared to face a future without her parents' wealth—he'd realized what he'd felt for her had been an appreciation for the idea of having a home and companion, not necessarily love. Not the deep kind that kept two people together until the end of their lives. Now that he was thirty-three, he was beginning to believe he'd never experience the sort of feelings Colt shared with his wife.

Colt nudged Mose into a faster pace. "Come on. Let's go mingle and have a drink before Maureen declares it's time to eat."

When they entered the backyard, a group of kids were racing around the lawn, screeching with playful laughter as one boy tried to avoid being tagged by the bunch chasing after him. Along with the kids, two yellow cur pups were yelping and running along with them.

"Looks like they're having fun," Mose said as he quickly sidestepped one of the dogs, which had come close to dashing between his legs.

"I remember when Luke and I used to chase each other like that," Colt said fondly. "Now I look at these children and wonder if Sophia and I will ever have a brood of our own."

Not long after Mose had come to work for the ranch, Colt had confided in him about Sophia suffering a miscarriage. Mose realized how much his friend wanted children. He also understood the man's worries that his wife might have problems getting pregnant and carrying a child full-term.

"You'll have kids someday," Mose told him with a reassuring grin. "And then you'll be wanting Uncle Mose to babysit and give you some relief."

Colt laughed. "You, babysit? I can just see you changing a dirty diaper."

"Couldn't be any worse than housebreaking a puppy," Mose joked. "I'll never do that again."

"Hey, guys, come on over and join us," Holt called out to them. "Jazelle is making drinks."

While Colt waved a hand of acknowledgment to their boss, Mose discreetly glanced around the patio. The space was packed with people, while to one side, endless dishes of food were displayed buffet-style on a row of portable tables.

Family members and coworkers called out to the two men as they wove their way through the crowd to where a portable bar was set up not far from the firepit, loaded with mesquite logs.

"What will it be for you guys?" Jazelle asked. "I have some palomas already mixed, if you'd like one. And there are plenty of margaritas. Or if you want more Christmas cheer, you can have an eggnog with brandy."

"I'll just play it safe like Holt and have a bourbon and coke," Colt told her.

"I'll take a paloma," Mose said. "You're the only person I know who can make a good one, Jazelle."

She gave him an appreciative smile. "Why, thank you, Mose. But I can't take all the credit. Reeva taught me how to mix them even before I was old enough to drink one myself."

"Hah! Better not let your husband or Joe hear you say that. They might arrest Reeva for contributing to the delinquency of a minor," Colt joked.

Jazelle laughed. "I'm afraid Reeva would be guilty of resisting arrest if Connor and Joe tried such a thing."

She fixed the drinks, and once they had them in hand, the

two men worked their way over to where Holt was sitting at a table with his brothers Blake and Chandler.

"Sit down and join us," Holt said. "Blake was just telling us how he thinks Santa ought to bring another cattle barn to the ranch. I told him we need another horse barn a whole lot more. Don't you guys agree?"

"Oh, for sure," Mose answered. "We especially need a bigger facility for the foaling mares."

Blake chuckled. "You wouldn't be just a bit biased, would you, Mose?"

Mose grinned sheepishly. "Only a little."

"Well, I'm backing Holt and Mose. At times we have mares and babies running out our ears and no place to keep them until the foals are sturdy enough to go out with the herd," Colt said.

"Brother, it sounds like you're outnumbered on this," Chandler told Blake. "And while we're on the subject of a foaling barn, it would be helpful to me if you'd build a treatment room somewhere in the building. With an X-ray machine, especially."

Blake let out a good-natured groan. "I'm being ganged up on. Let me call Tag and some of the cattle hands over here. They'll sing a different tune."

While the brothers carried on a friendly discussion about the barn, Mose took the opportunity to scan the crowd for Bonnie. After two sweeping glances, without catching sight of her, he concluded she must be in the house. But then he spotted her at the shadowy edge of the lawn where the children's gym set and sandbox were located. Several kids were gathered around her and he could only think how perfectly natural she looked as she leaned forward to listen intently to their chatter.

"Uh—excuse me, Colt. I'm going to go say hello to Bonnie," he said in a voice only Colt could hear.

"Right," Colt said with a coy grin. "Make hay while the sun shines."

With drink in hand, Mose slowly worked his way through the crowd, pausing several times to say hello to friends and acquaintances. By the time he reached Bonnie, the children had scattered and she was walking toward the far end of the patio.

Quickening his stride, he crossed the lawn to intercept her. As soon as she spotted his approach, she stopped and gave him a smile and a little wave.

"Hi, Mose!"

He came to a halt a couple of feet in front of her and it was all he could do to keep from reaching for her hands and holding them tight. "Hello, Bonnie. How's your party going so far?"

She laughed lightly. "It's not *my* party. It's an early Christmas celebration. And so far it's a very nice one, don't you think?"

Her voice had a soft, velvety sound to it and just listening to her say anything was a pleasure to his senses. "I confess I've only been here a few short minutes." He held up the drink in his hand. "Colt insisted we go to the bar. Have you had anything to drink yet? Even if she's left the bar, there's a pitcher of margaritas leftover."

"Thank you, I'm fine. I had an eggnog and brandy earlier. And one is about my limit."

She gave him a shy smile and his eyes were drawn to her lips. They were plump and moist, and the dark cherry color of her lipstick matched the roses of her dress. And what a dress, he thought. The top part showed off her tiny waist and the fullness of her breasts, while the neckline was just low enough to tease a man's senses.

"So what happened to all the kiddos?" he asked. "There for a minute, I thought you might need rescuing."

Her smile wide, she shook her head. "These kids are so much fun. Now that I've been here a few days, I'm getting to know them all better. I can even tell Blake's twins apart. But Vivian and Sawyer have their twins here tonight and I can't distinguish between those two at all. They are truly identical."

"That's funny, coming from a twin," he said. "Are you and your sister fully identical?"

"Everyone says so. But when we look at each other, it doesn't exactly feel like we're looking in a mirror. It's hard to explain."

"I'm sure," he said, then grinned. "I can't imagine my parents dealing with two of me at once. I was sort of a rascal."

"Aww, I would've never thought it."

For a girl who'd said she wasn't good at teasing, she was doing a great job of it now, he thought. The notion that she was capable of letting loose made her that much more attractive to him.

"Oh. Guess that rascally part still shows a little, huh?"

She laughed. "Only a little. And by the way, you look very nice tonight. I like your shirt."

Mose made a triumphant fist pump in his mind. "Thanks. You look better than nice tonight, Bonnie. You look lovely."

She glanced down at her red cowboy boots, and Mose figured if they were standing in the light, he'd see a flush of a pink blush on her cheeks. The idea made him wonder how she could be twenty-seven years old and still seem so innocent.

"Thank you, Mose."

He cleared his throat and glanced around at the people

sitting and milling about on the patio. "Uh, have you had a chance to meet everyone yet?"

"Yes. Most of the family arrived early, so I've spoken with all of them," she said, then asked, "Did you see the tables of food? There's enough to feed half the town."

"There's never a shortage at one of Maureen's parties. And the company is pretty nice, too," he added with a wink.

Smiling faintly, she inclined her head toward the group of partygoers. "We should probably join the others, don't you think?"

She wouldn't want to hear what he was actually thinking he'd like to do. Specifically, he wished the two of them could slip off to some shadowy spot and get to know each other in a very personal way. With his arms around her, her lips pressed to his.

The erotic image had him quickly draining the last bit of drink from his glass and wishing he had another. "Sure, we probably should," he answered. "Or everyone will get the idea we're antisocial. Or that we want to be alone together."

The wary look she darted him was accompanied by a nervous little laugh. "That might be a little sudden."

For her, maybe. Not for him, he thought.

With a hand at her back, he urged her forward and they crossed the shadowy lawn until they reached the milling crowd. They were stepping onto the rock floor of the patio when Maureen announced it was time to eat.

Mose was wondering how he could go about suggesting they sit together, when to his surprise, she solved the problem for him.

"Would you like to share a table with me?" she asked with a tentative smile. "That is, if you haven't already promised to sit with your friends."

Was this the way a man felt when he made a gold strike,

Mose wondered. He wasn't sure his boots were still on the ground.

A broad grin on his face, he placed a hand against the small of her back. "I don't need to sit with my friends. I see them every day. I'd consider it a real honor to sit with you," he told her.

"Thank you, Mose. I'm glad you feel that way."

Mose could've told her his feelings were all purely selfish. But he could see she thought he was a nice guy, and he didn't want to give her any reason to think otherwise.

Several eyes turned in her and Mose's direction as the two of them approached the buffet line together. Bonnie supposed they were all wondering what sort of connection had developed between her and the horse trainer. Especially since she'd only been on the ranch for only a few days. But surprisingly tonight, she wasn't feeling shy or concerned about what people were thinking of her. She'd spent too much of her life shrinking into the background and trying to avoid drawing attention to herself. Silly or not, Mose was giving her the courage to step up and be a part of the party.

The moment Gil spotted Bonnie and Mose slipping into place at the back of the line, he motioned to them. "Bonnie, you're the honoree of this fiesta. Come on up here to the front and bring Mose with you. Blake and Kate have already begun filling their plates. You can go after them."

She felt Mose hesitate and glanced up to see an uncertain frown on his face. "You go on, Bonnie. I'm not family. I don't deserve to cut the line."

"I think you do." She clasped her hand around his and urged him forward until they reached the space Gil had made for them between Katherine and himself.

Gil gave Mose's shoulder a friendly slap. "Glad you're here

tonight, Mose," he said. "You can entertain Bonnie with some of your horse experiences."

"The good ones or the bad one?" Mose joked.

Gil chuckled. "I imagine she'd enjoy hearing about both."

Directly in front of Bonnie, Blake's wife looked over her shoulder and gave her an apologetic smile. "Sorry for going ahead, Bonnie. Blake and I haven't eaten all day. We couldn't wait."

"My goodness, you shouldn't be apologizing, Kate. Mose and I weren't expecting Gil to cut the line for us anyway."

Katherine smiled again. "He wants you to feel special. And you, too, Mose."

Bonnie didn't know how she could feel any more special than she did right now. And the feeling had nothing to do with Gil's preferential treatment. No, it was all about Mose being with her, as though he really wanted her company.

"First or last, I don't care," Mose replied to Katherine's remark. "I'm just happy I'm getting to eat."

"Beats the heck out of bunkhouse food, right?" Katherine joked to Mose.

"Yeah. Or my own cooking," he said to her. "I either burn everything or leave it half raw."

Blake and Katherine moved on down the table, and Bonnie picked up a plate for herself, then handed one to Mose. The heavy paper plates were bright red, edged with holly leaves, and matched the plastic glasses and cups.

"Thanks," he told her. "I can't wait to put a steak on this plate. Three Rivers Beef is the most delicious meat you'll ever taste. Uh—but I'll admit I've not tasted your family's beef. It's probably just as good."

"Everyone says our beef is delicious," Bonnie told him. "But I've never tasted anything like what we had for dinner the other night. I think Reeva does something special to the steaks. I've begged her to show me, but she won't reveal her secret."

By the time they made their way to the end of the buffet line, Bonnie's plate was partially filled with sliced brisket and stir-fried vegetables, while Mose's was piled high with steak, potato wedges and bread rolls.

Glancing around the crowded patio she searched for an out-of-the-way place for them to sit. "The cool night air is drawing most of the guests to the firepit," she said. "How about sitting over by the Christmas tree? There's an empty table there and it might be a little quieter. Unless you think it will be too cool."

"It's perfect," he said with a nod. "I imagine enough of the heat from the fire will drift that way to keep it comfortable."

After picking up drinks to go with their dinner, they made their way to the table and Bonnie was pleasantly surprised when he slid next to her on the bench seat instead of across from her.

"I hope you're planning on going back for seconds," he said as he took a moment to eye her plate. "You don't have enough food to feed a baby bird."

She gave him an impish smile. "I'm saving plenty of space for dessert. I have a terrible sweet tooth. What about you?"

With a guilty groan, he patted his flat midsection. "If I didn't ride horses all day long, I'd probably weigh a ton. I love sweets, too. And early every morning, Jazelle brings fresh pastries to Holt's office. My brain has a fight with my stomach to keep from eating one, or two, or three. And it will only get worse as Christmas draws closer. Reeva and Sophia will be sending homemade cookies and candies to the barns."

She took a small bite of the melt-in-your-mouth brisket. After she'd chewed and swallowed, she said, "It's dangerous for me to go into the kitchen now. I can only imagine how tempted I'm going to be when the holiday baking gets in full swing."

"Does your family give many parties on Stone Creek?" he asked curiously.

"Nothing like Maureen and Gil do. The parties we have at home are usually centered around the holidays or a birthday or weddings and anniversaries. Presently Mom is busy decorating the house."

He slanted her a curious glance. "You told me you're the only sibling in your family who doesn't have a spouse or fiancé. Does that bother you?"

His question shocked her a little. Mainly because she didn't figure he cared one way or the other about her marital status. "I think it bothers my parents far more than me. You see, they worry I'm going to turn into an old spinster."

"You have a lot of years to go before you'll be old," he said with a grin and then his expression turned sober as his gaze slowly slipped over her face. "And why would they worry you're going to remain single?"

Bonnie stared down at her plate as a blush stung her cheeks. "Probably because I'm—not outgoing enough to catch a guy's attention."

"You caught mine."

She breathed deeply, in hopes the extra oxygen would slow the rapid thump of her heart. "That's because—you're different."

He smiled as he sliced off a bite of rib eye. "I'm glad you noticed. Because I *am* different. That's the way I want to be. I don't want to be cookie-cutter, or boring."

Then, why was he wasting his time with her, she wondered. Surely he viewed her as a bit boring. Or had she finally met a man who could see past her reserved nature? Could he actually see she had longings for a man's love, the deep desire for a husband and children?

"Being boring is one thing you don't need to worry about," she told him.

"Neither do you. You're not boring. Maybe a bit shy, but that just makes you sweeter and prettier," he said with a somewhat naughty grin.

She was out of her league, she thought, as she struggled to keep her attention focused on her food. Mose was not a typical man. Yes, maybe that's why she was drawn to him. But she wasn't experienced enough to know how to deal with the unexpected things he said, or the sexual magnetism that oozed from him.

After downing several bites of food, she managed to find her voice. "Do you mind if I ask you something personal?"

He arched a dark brow at her. "No. But you do understand that a guy is never completely honest about how much gas mileage his vehicle gets, or his sex life. So you might want to skip those two questions."

Laughter bubbled up in her throat, and when she tried to swallow it down, she ended up coughing instead. "Uh—those questions can wait. I was wondering what made you decide to leave Texas and make your home here in Arizona. I realize you like working for Holt, but I imagine you broke and trained horses back there, also."

He nodded. "I did. I've been riding horses for a living ever since I graduated high school."

"That young? Who taught you the trade? Your father?"

"Only some of it. Dad was a good hand with a horse and he taught me the basics. But I learned most of my training skills from an old rancher who worked on a spread just outside of Canyon. I had a job there during the summer months, helping in the hayfields and building fences. Anyway, Ira trained all the ranch's young horses. By the time I was a teenager, he was in his seventies. He was a full-blood Comanche, and I was mesmerized by the way he could communicate with them through his hands and body movements. He was gentle and soft-spoken, and the only time I ever saw him angry was when a ranch hand mishandled a horse."

She could hear the affection in his voice as he talked about the man. No doubt Ira had ended up being a key factor in the direction of Mose's life. "I imagine Ira has passed on by now," she said.

"Yeah. But actually not that long ago. He lived to be ninety-three and credited his longevity to spending his life on the back of a horse."

Curious, she asked, "Did Ira have a family?"

"A wife. But she died young and he never remarried after that."

"Sounds like Reeva," Bonnie said. "Sophia tells me her grandmother never remarried after her husband died in the Vietnam war."

"Well, when a person loses their one true love, they usually don't look for another," he said. "But obviously Maureen is an exception. From what Holt has told me, his mother was madly in love with Joel, her first husband and father to her six children. She was devastated when he was killed. But a few years later, she fell in love with Gil and you see how much they adore each other."

Nodding, she said thoughtfully, "When Maureen first contacted Dad about the genealogy search, she told him about Joel's death and Gil's return to Three Rivers. At that time, I thought it a little strange that she'd married her late husband's brother. But later, after I heard all the circumstances and met them in person, I realized Maureen and Gil make a perfect pair. And to me, it's even more wonderful that Gil is a Hollister."

Smiling faintly, he reached over and touched a hand to her forearm. "Bonnie, I do believe you're a romantic."

Another flash of heat stung her cheeks. "Maybe. But you still haven't answered my question about leaving Texas."

"Oh well, that was a no-brainer," he said. "When Holt asked me to come to work for him on Three Rivers, it was like a dream come true. I couldn't accept his offer fast enough."

"Had you met Holt before? How did you learn about him and Three Rivers? Or did he find you through a job application?"

A chuckle rumbled in his throat. "Holt doesn't advertise for trainers, or wranglers, or even barn workers. He hires by recommendations from the people he trusts. In my case, I was slightly acquainted with Luke and Colt—see, they're from the Panhandle area, too. They suggested to Holt that I was the third trainer they needed on Three Rivers. Which came as a surprise to me. Until Holt called me, I didn't know they admired my work or that they'd suggested me for the job."

"Oh," she said. "Then, you must have been very surprised when Holt reached out."

He grinned. "Floored. Thrilled and excited. I was pretty much walking on air."

"Hmm. I guess that means there wasn't anyone in Texas you couldn't bear leaving behind." Like a special girlfriend, she thought. The idea disturbed her more than it should have.

"I have family in the Panhandle. My brother, Mitchell, and Dad. See, my parents divorced when Mitch and I were teenagers. Since then Mom moved to Fort Worth and remarried. Dad never wanted to go the marriage route again," he said with a grimace. "But as for anyone else I hated to tell goodbye to, no. There were no strings keeping me there."

His father had obviously given up on marriage. And from the looks of Mose, he wasn't interested in being a husband, either. Because his parents had parted? Or had some woman broken his heart and ruined his idea of living happily ever after? She wanted to ask him. But she'd only met him a few days ago. She had no business asking him such a private question.

"Living near your family must not be important to you."

"Not so important I wanted to give up the opportunity of a lifetime. But don't get me wrong, Bonnie. I enjoy spending time with my brother and Dad. And I try to visit Mom as often as I can. I just don't feel like they need to be in my life on a daily basis. Why do you ask? Do you need to have family around you all the time?"

She forked up a piece of red bell pepper and savored the bite before she answered. "When Beatrice married Kipp and moved to Idaho, I was afraid I couldn't survive without her."

He said, "I've heard twins are more emotionally connected than regular siblings. I can understand if you felt like you were going to lose a part of yourself."

His appreciation of her feelings touched her and she flashed a grateful smile at him. "Well, as you can see, I survived. True, I miss Bea a lot, but I've been making it fine on my own. Which surprised me. I thought I would at least fall into a temporary funk, but I didn't. Funny isn't it, the things we learn about ourselves—whether we want to or not."

"Yeah. I think as the years go by, especially since I moved here on the ranch, I've begun to see myself differently."

From the corner of her eye, Bonnie discreetly scanned his face in the shadowy light. She couldn't guess how he viewed himself when he stood in front of a mirror, but she definitely saw him as an incredibly masculine man. His chiseled lips were squared at the corners with the bottom lip being full and the top somewhat thinner. He had strong, angled jaws and one of those chins that jutted slightly forward as though he dared the world to try and knock him down. Yet it was his amber-brown eyes that demanded attention. Each time she looked at him, she found it very difficult to tear her gaze away from his.

"You see yourself differently now? In what way?" she asked.

He forked a piece of potato into his mouth, and after a quick chew and swallow, he said, "I've finally begun to see myself as worthy as the next man."

Stunned by his response, she didn't say anything. She was too busy wondering how a man like him could've ever thought of himself as less than anyone. He was skilled and talented, healthy and handsome. Not to mention he possessed a charm that made her heart go pitter-patter.

She must have been silent for longer than she thought, because after a moment, he asked, "What's wrong? You've gone quiet all of a sudden."

"If you want the truth, you surprised me. I can't imagine you seeing yourself lesser than the next man."

He shrugged. "My life wasn't always the way it is now. When Mitch and I were growing up, we never had much. Not in the way of material things. Our parents worked hard to provide a home and three square meals for us, but they often struggled. The kids who came from wealthy families often looked down on us."

"Unfortunately, that's just the way some people behave."

"True. Especially kids. But to tell you the truth, that never bothered me or Mitch very much. We were basically happy. Mom and Dad loved us—still do. And that made us richer than many of our friends."

"Of course it did. Money or material things don't make a person valuable in the ways that matter," she said.

"I suppose when I was growing up, I never really thought about being that different than the affluent folks. Until later, when I tried to be a part of a different social circle. It didn't work. And for a while the whole mistake did a number on my psyche. I wouldn't say I grew bitter—more like determined to be true to who I am and proud of myself."

Before she considered her reaction, she reached over and placed a hand on his forearm. Beneath the fabric his flesh was hard and warm, and the pleasure of touching him, instinctively made her want to scoot closer to his side.

"And so you should be proud of yourself. Since I've come here to the ranch, it's become obvious to me that Holt would have only the best men handling his horses. And you're one of them. Surely the trust he puts in you gives you a good feeling about yourself."

"Heck, yeah, it does." He grinned and then his expression slowly turned serious. "Bonnie, you're too nice for me. I hope you realize that."

She shook her head as she felt something very real and strong pass between them. Like a jolt of sweet coffee, the feeling caused her heart to jump into a fast jig. "Maybe we're nice for each other," she said softly. "That's the way I see things."

Chapter Six

He didn't make a reply, and after a moment, she could see her remark had made him uncomfortable. The notion had her pulling her hand away from his arm and returning her attention to her plate.

When another moment passed in silence, she said, "Forgive me, Mose. I guess that sounded a bit too forward. To be honest, I'm not exactly accustomed to being in a man's company—alone and in the shadows. I've probably said things I shouldn't. Anyway, I was just trying to let you know that I like you, that's all."

He placed his fork on a napkin next to his plate, then slowly turned to face her head-on. "Bonnie—I'm the one who's sorry. I didn't go quiet because I was offended at what you said." Shaking his head, he reached for her hands and she gladly gave them to him. "To tell you the truth, I was so touched that I didn't know what to say. See, I'm a little like you. Even though I've dated plenty of women, I don't know anything about being in the company of a woman like you."

His hands were warm, the palms calloused at the base of his fingers. The feel of his skin pressed against hers was enough to send a wave of heat washing through her. "A woman like me?" she asked softly. "Someone who's inexperienced with men?"

Frustration made his groan sound more like a growl. "No,

Bonnie! Someone who is—well, a lady, in every sense of the word."

Her lips parted as she studied the shadows flickering in his eyes. "And you're not used to spending time with ladies?" she asked. "Or, I'm just not your type? I can certainly understand if I'm not."

His frown was tinged with disbelief. "Bonnie, you're exactly my type! I think we're nice for each other, too. It's just that we're—like those different worlds I was talking about earlier."

"Not that different," she countered. "We're both ranching people. We both love horses and riding. We both like living in the country. At least, I think you live in the country."

He smiled and the pleasant expression filled her with joy. He was a generally happy man. That was one of the first things that had drawn her to him. And she wanted him to stay that way. Happy and smiling.

"I live about a mile or so east of here. In a house where Maureen's late mother used to live. It's small, but nice, and it's near the river."

"Oh, is the house anywhere near the cattle trail I rode Dinah over? I crossed a wide creek."

"You were close. The place is about a quarter mile west of where you crossed the creek."

She thought about telling him how much she'd enjoy seeing his home, but she kept the comment to herself. He was probably already thinking she was getting too familiar with him.

You getting familiar with a man? That's hilarious, Bonnie. Holding Mose's hands is probably the most intimate you'll ever be to him. You're too much of a coward to get any closer.

Mentally shaking away the mocking voice in her head, she said, "That area was especially pretty. I imagine you enjoy living there."

"It's great. Sometimes I feel guilty because it's such a plus to be living right here on the ranch and in such a comfortable house. Some of the other single hands who live in town have to make the long drive in and out every day. And others stay in the bunkhouse. Which is certainly okay. They have comfortable beds and a good cook to provide them two square meals a day. But they don't have the space or the privacy that I do."

He was still holding on to her hands. Bonnie didn't want to think about the moment he released her and she no longer felt the firm strength of his fingers wrapped around hers.

"And how did you manage to get the house?" she asked. "If it's as nice as you make it sound, I'm sure some of the other men had their eyes on it, too."

"From what Holt told me, Maureen never allowed any of the ranch hands in the past to live there. I'm not sure why she offered the place to me. I must have looked pitiful," he said with a wry chuckle.

"I suspect she thought you looked responsible."

Smiling faintly, he released his hold on her hands and picked up his fork. "I've never seen you wearing glasses, but I'm wondering if you need a pair," he joked.

She tried to refocus her attention on the scrumptious food, but she might as well have been eating soggy oatmeal. Being close to this man and having him touch her, even in such an innocent way, was playing havoc with her senses. For the past thirty minutes, she'd hardly noticed what she'd been eating or drinking. And she couldn't help but wonder if once the party ended and Mose had gone to his home by the creek, her heart would stop hammering and her mind cease its spinning. At the moment, she doubted she'd ever return to normal.

Mose pointed his fork at her half-eaten meal. "If you're finished pushing that brisket around on your plate, we should check out the desserts. Maybe something sweet will tempt you to eat."

She pulled a playful face at him. "I've already eaten a pile of brisket. I put too much on my plate. But I'll try my best with a bit of dessert. Otherwise, Sophia will be disappointed in me. She made a special dewberry cobbler."

He waggled his brows at her. "I'd be disappointed in myself if I didn't eat some of her cobbler and whatever else is on the dessert table."

After dumping their paper plates in a trash container, Bonnie and Mose made their way back to the buffet tables. At the end of the food line, a ridiculous number of desserts were arranged on a checkered tablecloth, along with a coffee urn and all the fixings.

Bonnie settled for only the cobbler, but Mose was finding it difficult to choose which desserts he wanted. She was urging him to try several, when Colt's brother Luke walked up.

"Try the bread pudding and the frosted brownies," he told Mose. "I'm already back for seconds."

Mose reached over and jabbed his forefinger into the man's flat midsection. "Much more of this and you won't be able to get on a horse," he jokingly warned.

Chuckling, Luke pointed to Mose's plate that was already piled with several desserts. "Neither will you," he said, then gestured to Bonnie's single bowl of cobbler. "We need to use self-discipline like Bonnie. She's the smart one here."

Bonnie smiled at the other man. "Believe me, Luke, the only reason I'm being so restrained is because I'm already stuffed. That's why I'm going light on the desserts. But I am going to get coffee. The night air is getting chillier than I thought it would be."

"Pru and I are sitting at a table not far from the firepit.

You and Mose should come join us. We need the company," he said to Bonnie, then looked over to Mose. "Okay, Mose?"

Mose glanced from Luke to Bonnie. "Wherever you want to sit is fine with me."

Bonnie really wanted the two of them to go back to the private spot where they'd been sitting before, but she didn't want to appear unfriendly. Especially to Mose's friends and coworkers.

"Well, it would give me a chance to visit with Prudence," she said. "I'm sure she has some great stories to tell about her job as a school superintendent."

Luke let out a short laugh. "I don't know about *great*. Most of them are crazy."

Mose said, "Pru tells me that trying to corral Luke is much harder than keeping the students in line."

Luke let out a good-natured groan. "Oh now, Mose, don't try to mislead Bonnie. She'll figure out for herself that you're the rascal around here."

The two men kept up their banter until they reached the table where Prudence was sitting. Bonnie had barely had time to take a seat and say hello to the other woman, when Colt and Sophia dragged up a pair of folding chairs to join the group. After that, the conversation was nonstop as the men swapped stories about horses, while the women chatted together about family and friends and all the things Bonnie should see and do while she was here at Three Rivers.

Eventually, Luke and Prudence announced they needed to fetch their four-year-old son, J.J., from the house, where Jazelle and Tallulah had taken the children to play a few games.

"J.J.'s going to nursery school, so he needs to be home in bed soon," Prudence explained to Bonnie.

Next to her, Mose stood and informed Bonnie that he needed to be going home, also.

"Colt and I are starting some fresh two-year-olds in the morning," he said. "I need to be rested."

Colt chuckled. "Bonnie, you need to understand that Mose is getting old. He has to be in bed at an early hour."

Sophia leveled a playful, but pointed, look at her husband. "Colt, I think you should remember that you and Mose are the same age."

While everyone enjoyed a laugh, Bonnie rose to her feet and placed a hand on his forearm. "I'll walk you to the gate. Just in case you start feeling wobbly from old age," she added teasingly.

Laughing louder, Colt said, "Right, Bonnie! The guy does need help walking at times. If you'll notice he's already getting bowlegged."

Mose waved a dismissive hand at his friend before guiding Bonnie away from the group. As they made their way off the patio, he made a point to seek out Maureen and Gil, who were sitting near the firepit, to say good-night and thank them for the great party.

"We're glad you came, Mose. And glad you enjoyed it," Gil told him.

Maureen's sly smile encompassed Mose and Bonnie. "Bonnie loves to ride horses," she said to Mose. "I imagine she'd like for you to join her some afternoon and show her around the ranch."

Glancing at Mose, Bonnie expected to find a deer-in-the-headlights look on his face. Instead, her heart began to hum at the sight of his agreeable expression.

"Maureen, that's a great idea." Mose darted a quick grin at Bonnie. "Now, if I can just talk Holt into letting me have an hour or two off, we'll hit the trail. Right, Bonnie?"

She was suddenly so thrilled it was hard not to gush. "I'd love to go riding together."

"One thing about it, Bonnie," Gil teased, "if your horse gives you any problems, Mose can help you get him under control."

Maureen shook a playful finger at her husband. "Bonnie won't need any help with her horse. Her father, Hadley, has already told me that she's a first-class horsewoman. All she'll need from Mose is good company and a guide to the trails."

"I'll have to work on the *good* part, Maureen," Mose joked.

Gil winked at Mose. "I wouldn't worry about that, Mose. I expect Bonnie will keep you in line."

With a sheepish grin, Mose clasped his hand beneath Bonnie's elbow and nudged her forward. "I think we'd better go on that one, Gil."

They exchanged goodbyes and soon Bonnie and Mose were walking across the dimly lit lawn. As they strode together, Bonnie was intensely aware of his leg brushing against the skirt of her dress and the warm, firm hold of his hand on the back of her arm.

Since the painful debacle she'd gone through with Ward, Bonnie hadn't wanted to be physically close to a man. She'd endured a few kisses and caresses from some of her dates because she'd wanted to try to feel what she imagined a normal woman would experience. She'd desperately wanted to feel desire. Instead, she'd felt nothing. Until now. Until Mose. Just standing close to him was enough to set her heart to pounding and make her hands itch to touch him. She couldn't explain her reaction to him, much less come up with a sensible reason.

"I've parked way down toward the cattle barn," he told her. "So I need go around to the front gate."

She said, "Okay. There are three yard lamps there, so we shouldn't have any problem seeing."

"You really don't have to go all the way to the gate," he told her. "I can make it fine on my own."

She laughed softly. "Mose, I didn't actually believe Colt when he said you were getting rickety."

He said, "I know. I only meant that you can go back to the party and enjoy sitting by the fire with Maureen and Gil—or something."

"Are you trying to get rid of me?" she asked.

He glanced down at her and though they were passing through a very shadowy portion of the lawn, there was enough light for her to see a lopsided grin on his face.

"No. I'm just giving you a chance to—change your mind."

She glanced up at him. "About spending time with you?"

"Yeah. You have a lot of family here that you want to get to know better. And—"

Before he could finish, she interjected, "I want to get to know you better, too, Mose. Unless— Well, if you're not interested, just tell me. I don't like for people to be pushy and overbearing. I'd hate to think I was doing that to you. Frankly, it would be worse than embarrassing."

He paused and when his hands clasped her shoulders and turned her toward him, her pulse took a wild leap. Good thing they weren't standing beneath a yard lamp, she thought. Otherwise, he'd see the bodice of her dress shaking with every heartbeat.

"Bonnie, you have to be one of the most confusing women I've ever met. I don't understand why you keep offering me the option to end our friendship. Believe me, if I didn't enjoy your company, I wouldn't be here with you right now."

Releasing a long breath, she lifted her gaze to his. "Sorry. I guess it does sound like I'm throwing up red warning signals."

"I'm getting that impression," he said gently.

A rueful sigh passed her lips. "Okay, I think I need to be honest. Then you might understand why I'm being so—wary. I don't date that often, but when I do go on a first date, I never hear from the guy again. I'm too boring, dull, reserved—too *whatever* to hold a man's attention. So if that's what you think of me, too, I figured it would be less painful if you'd come out and tell me now, rather than later."

His eyes searched her face for long moments before he slowly shook his head with dismay. "Tell me, Bonnie, do you think you're boring?"

"Well, I'm far from the life of the party. But I don't think I put people to sleep."

Amusement twisted his features. "No. You don't come anywhere near close to putting me asleep. So let me ask you this—did these one-time daters tell you to your face that you were boring?"

She thought for a long moment. "Now that I think about it, no. I just assumed that was the problem when they never asked for a second date."

"I think it was probably the other way around. They assumed you weren't interested in them."

She gazed down at the toes of her cowboy boots. "I never thought of it like that, Mose. And to be honest, I *wasn't* interested. I guess my indifference showed."

"Poor guys," he murmured. "I'd hate for you to be indifferent to me."

"Are you saying that just to be polite?" she asked.

"I like to think of myself as a nice guy, Bonnie. But I'm not so nice I'd lie just to make someone happy."

"Thank you," she said softly. "I'm going to remember that."

Smiling faintly, he slipped an arm around the back of her waist and urged her forward across the clipped grass. When they reached the gate leading out to the circle driveway, he paused and turned to face her.

"Thanks for walking me to the gate," he told her.

His voice held a husky tone, and the shiver that raced down

her spine had nothing to do with the cool night air. "You're welcome," she murmured.

He reached for her hand and she breathed deeply as he pressed it between the two of his.

"Uh—when would you like to go on a ride?" he asked. "I probably can't shake loose of work until late tomorrow evening. How about the day after tomorrow?"

She could see he was serious and the idea sent a rush of excitement through her. "As far as I know, I should be free," she told him.

"Great. Since it's December and the sunlight is limited let's try to start around two thirty or three. Is that okay with you?"

He could've said midnight and she would have gladly agreed.

Better watch it, Bonnie. You don't want to appear too eager or easy to get.

Doing her best to ignore the ridiculous voice in her head, she said, "Sounds good. I'll get to the barn a little early so I can saddle Dinah and you won't have to tack up two horses. Or will Dinah even be available? Since she's a part of the working remuda, should I—"

"I'll make sure Dinah is there for you," he promised.

She drew in a shaky breath. "Thanks. So, I'll see you then."

He was still holding on to her hand, making it impossible for her to turn and leave. Which hardly mattered. She could have stood there forever, gazing up at him, drawing in his masculine scent and feeling the delicious warmth of his hands spreading through her whole body.

He said, "Before you go, I wanted to say tonight has been—special. I've really enjoyed spending time with you, Bonnie."

She couldn't make anything monumental out of his words,

she quickly told herself. She just couldn't. Otherwise, she'd be leaving Three Rivers Ranch with tears in her heart.

"And eating all that scrumptious food, too, right?" she added with an impish grin. "You must be on sugar overload after all those desserts."

His smile suddenly turned gentle. "You've been the sweetest dessert of the night for me," he murmured, then before she could guess his intentions he lowered his head and placed a kiss on her cheek. "Good night, Bonnie."

For a split second, she forgot to breathe and then she finally pulled in enough air to speak. "Good night, Mose. See you soon."

"Yes, soon."

His gaze continued to scan her face and Bonnie started to get the wild notion that he might actually kiss her. Really kiss her. But then he quickly released his hold on her hand and let himself out of the gate.

As he strode off into the darkness, he didn't glance back at her. But Bonnie continued to stand there by the gate until she could no longer see him.

The next day turned out to be a trying one for Mose. And not just because he was dealing with two-year-old colts who knew how to do little more than follow a lead rope. So far today, he'd been kicked in the shins, bitten on the back of the arm and had come very close to being bucked off. And all of these little mishaps had occurred with only one horse. The other five mounts he'd worked had been just as wild and unruly.

Normally, Mose loved the challenge of teaching young horses. He expected the bites and kicks, the rearing up, running backward, and not to mention, the bucking. The job required his full attention, but it was hard to focus when most of his brain wanted to linger on Bonnie. If he didn't get control of himself, he would be headed toward major trouble. He could see it coming. Like standing on a railroad track and watching a fast-moving train headed straight at him. Any sensible guy would know to jump off the track and away from danger. But Bonnie seemed to make him forget about being sensible.

"Hey, Mose, let's take a break."

Mose reined the sorrel filly he was riding to a stop and turned her toward the sound of Colt's voice. "I could go for that. Let me turn this girl over to Dex. She's had enough for today anyway."

He climbed out of the saddle, and Colt walked along with Mose as he led the horse over to the fence where the wrangler was waiting.

Once Dex was leading the young horse off to the shower stocks, Colt and Mose walked beneath the shedrow of the barn. A minute later, they reached a breezeway that ran between the part of the building where the horses were stalled and the section used for feed storage.

Several motel chairs were lined against one wall, along with an old-fashioned metal soda case. Colt lifted the lid and pulled out a can of cola. He then waited while Mose fished out a bottle of water before he lowered the lid back in place.

The day had warmed considerably, and both men shed their jackets before sinking into a couple of the chairs and crossing their ankles out in front of them.

"Luke and Holt have been gone since early this morning. They must've found a whole herd of horses to look over," Mose remarked.

"Luke said a rancher up by Prescott was supposed to have a bunch of nice yearlings for sale. We both know how Holt is when he sees fresh horses. He kind of goes a little crazy."

Mose guzzled down half of the bottled water. "He can afford them."

"Yeah, but will we survive the extra work?" Colt joked. "You know, Jim is certainly experienced enough to help us train, but he doesn't want to ride these unschooled ponies."

Jim Garroway had been working on Three Rivers Ranch for many years. In the beginning, his job had been a wrangler for Holt. But as Holt was now focusing more on the management side of the horse division, Jim had been assigned to assist Luke.

"Jim likes just being an assistant. And with Tallulah expecting their second baby, he probably doesn't want to risk his neck." Mose glanced across the arena to the adjoining pen where Jim and Luke usually worked. "Now that you've mentioned Jim, it occurs to me that I've not seen him around today. Did he eat and drink too much at the party last night?"

"He took off today to take Tallulah in for a doctor's checkup," Colt told him. "Jim is so overprotective, he doesn't want her driving into town alone."

"I can understand him being protective," Mose said.

Colt took a long swig of his cola. "If Sophia was pregnant, I'd be calling her every half hour and telling her not to do this or that. Which probably wouldn't go over well. Sophia doesn't like me giving her orders."

"Hah! What woman does? When the time comes, you'll just have to back off, Colt, and give her breathing room."

Colt's grimaced. "Don't you mean *if* the time ever comes? I'm beginning to fear Sophia might never get pregnant."

Mose studied his friend's glum expression. "Don't get offended, Colt, but have you ever wondered if the problem might be you? It's not all that uncommon for men to have fertility problems."

The frown on Colt's face deepened. "I'm way ahead of

you, Mose. I recently got checked out by our family physician. Everything tested normal. He says Sophia and I only need to stop obsessing over the problem. And once we quit thinking about it, she'll most likely get pregnant. Tell me, Mose, how the hell are we supposed to *not* think about it?"

Mose couldn't answer Colt's question any more than he could figure out how to quit thinking about Bonnie. Telling himself she was off-limits didn't seem to be working.

"You can't. But you shouldn't worry. I have a little crystal ball in my head. I can see you being a daddy. And sooner than you think."

Colt let out a good-natured groan. "Okay, buddy. I'll try to think positive," he said, then slanted a thoughtful glance at Mose. "So, what did you think of the party last night?"

He was still reliving every minute he'd spent with Bonnie. He'd memorized each lovely feature of her face, the softness he'd felt in her hands, and the sweet fragrance she emitted whenever he was close.

Clearing his throat, he said, "Reeva and Sophia outdid themselves. I ate so much I wasn't even hungry for breakfast this morning."

"I'll let them know you enjoyed the meal. But the food wasn't what I was asking about. I noticed you were monopolizing Bonnie. How did that happen?"

With a grunt, Mose left his chair and, after tossing his empty water bottle in a trash barrel, fished a cola from the soda case. As he popped the lid, he glanced at Colt. "What do you mean, *how did that happen*? It's not like Bonnie and I just met last night. We have a past, you know."

Colt's brows shot straight up. "Man, Mose, I knew you were a fast worker, I just didn't realize how fast. You two were practically clinging to each other last night."

Mose grimaced as he sank back into the chair he'd just vacated. "Clinging? I'd say that was an exaggeration."

Colt chuckled. "Okay, I'll change that to a little handsy."

He didn't reply to Colt's observation. After all, what could he say? He supposed he had held her hands, touched her arm and... Well, he was mighty glad Colt hadn't seen that kiss he'd planted on Bonnie's soft cheek. His friend would automatically assume Mose was falling head over heels for Bonnie.

And would the assumption be wrong? Face it, Mose. You are falling for Bonnie.

Mose silently groaned with frustration. "Is there anything wrong with that?" he practically snapped. "Bonnie is—she's a lovely woman."

Colt eyed him skeptically. "Nothing wrong. So why are you getting your dander up all of a sudden?"

Why was he? Because after he'd gone home last night, he'd not been able to sleep. He'd ended up getting out of bed and wandering through the house, thinking about Bonnie. When he'd impulsively kissed her on the cheek, he'd had a real struggle to stop himself from placing another kiss on her lips.

"My dander isn't up," he argued, then released a heavy sigh. "Actually, Colt, I'm worried."

Colt's brows shot straight up. "About what? Bonnie?" he asked incredulously.

"Hell, yes, about Bonnie. I need to play things smart and stay away from her. As far away as possible. She's not my kind of woman."

Scowling at him, Colt said, "From what I saw last night, you two are perfect for each other. So what's the deal with this 'stay away' plan? You must be having a sunstroke or something."

Mose shook his head. "Colt, think about the situation.

Bonnie is here temporarily. Plus, she's a Hollister. She's out of my league."

Rolling his eyes, Colt said, "Hollisters are just people, Mose. They only difference between us and them is that they have a little more money in their bank accounts than we do."

"Hah! A little? Now you're the one having the heatstroke."

"Look, we're good buddies, and your ideas about women are your business, not mine. All I'm saying is there's no harm in you enjoying Bonnie's company while she's here."

"I hope you're right because we're going riding together tomorrow afternoon."

Colt nodded smugly. "Now you're talking."

Struck with restlessness, Mose stood and walked aimlessly back and forth across the breezeway. "You don't get it, Colt. Bonnie is one of a kind. And I'm afraid—"

"You don't want to get too taken with her," Colt finished, "but you already have. Is that what you're trying to say?"

"Sort of. Damn, Colt, what's the matter with me? She's the love-and-marriage kind. And I'm not. Even if our lives weren't so different, she, uh, needs a man who can give her what she wants out of life."

"Mose, you're only taking the woman on a horseback ride, not proposing marriage," Colt said tersely. "You can do that without going gaga over her."

Pausing, Mose leveled a pointed look at his friend. "You obviously didn't stop yourself from going gaga over Sophia."

Colt grinned guiltily. "After a while I decided I didn't want to stop myself. Going gaga felt pretty damn good. One of these days you'll feel it, too. And you'll be happy you gave in."

"Give in? Don't you mean surrender?" Mose asked sarcastically. "I don't need to wave a white flag to make myself happy. If I was any happier right now, I'd bust!"

Grinning, Colt said, "Yeah, the way you look we'd better get back to work before you explode into pieces."

A cutting reply was on Mose's tongue, when Dex suddenly appeared in the breezeway and waved.

"Hey, you two! Holt and Luke just drove up with a trailer full of horses," he shouted. "They're down at the holding pens right now about to unload. Better get down there!"

Relieved for the distraction, Mose motioned Colt up from the chair. "Come on, buddy. We have new horses!"

And hopefully, he'd have something to push sweet Bonnie out of his mind.

Chapter Seven

Later that afternoon, Maureen found a break in her day to join Bonnie in the ranch-house office. The room was located on the ground floor, and much like her father's office on Stone Creek, the walls were lined with built-in shelves filled with books, photos and sentimental mementos. At the far end of the room, a large oak desk was situated next to a row of paned windows with a lovely view of the desert mountains. Nearby, a smaller desk was equipped with a typist's chair and a laptop computer, currently folded shut.

Yesterday, Jazelle had brought in a couple of poinsettias and a tiny Christmas tree with twinkling lights to brighten the room with holiday cheer. And today, she'd already left a tray of decorated sugar cookies on a table near the window.

Maureen picked up one of the treats and nibbled a bite before she gestured to a row of boxes and containers stacked on the floor at the back of the room.

"These things have been stored away for years," she told Bonnie. "And there's a good chance nothing useful to your investigation is among them. But we have to start somewhere, right?"

Bonnie nodded. "When I was searching for proof of my grandfather's birth, I went through tons of things that had been stored in the attic of our ranch house. Sifting through everything was tedious, but you never know when you might come across a clue."

Standing next to the larger of the desks, Maureen tapped a finger on top of a stack of what appeared to be scrapbooks and photo albums. "These hold old clippings and news articles that will help give you a sense of Three River Ranch's history. Although, Parnell's connection to the ranch ended when he was very young."

Bonnie said, "It's unfortunate that Parnell was killed long before Gil and your late husband were born."

A rueful smile crossed Maureen's face. "The only thing they knew about their great-uncle was that he'd been banished from Three Rivers. Gil and Joel's father, Axel, discouraged his sons from asking questions about Parnell. Clearly he was a sore spot within the family."

Bonnie nodded glumly. "Grandfather Lionel was the same way about his ex-wife—my grandmother. He more or less tried to erase her existence. If you brought up her name around him, he'd bristle. None of us had any idea he was actually trying to hide who he really was."

"Sounds to me like a case of like father, like son. Both men were deceitful." Maureen shook her head. "Sorry, Bonnie. I shouldn't be making such harsh judgments. Especially since I'm not privy to the details of the situation. These men were your grandfather and great-grandfather, and I'm sure they had wonderful traits to them, too."

Bonnie shrugged. "Sugarcoating the circumstances can't change the past, Maureen. Family splits are difficult under any circumstances."

Maureen moved away from the desk and over to the stacked rows of containers. "It would be great if we could find a diary or journal, like your brother Flint found. Being able to read your grandmother's actual words was like finding a gold mine of information. And I don't mean just actual facts, but emotional glimpses into your grandparents' lives. To me, that would be the real treasure."

Bonnie strolled over to Maureen. "This probably won't make sense, but after Grandfather's past came to light, I've had trouble talking with Dad about the whole issue. Discussing it with Mom is easier. Lionel was her father-in-law, not her father. And she never knew Scarlett, her mother-in-law, so learning the truth hasn't affected her as deeply. But Dad—he doesn't let on like the truth about his father has shaken him. But I know better. He admired his father. And how could he not? The man built Stone Creek Ranch from scratch and left the property and all its holdings to Dad. Grandfather was a very young man when he began the venture of building the ranch, and he succeeded. So you're right that there had to be some good traits to him. I have to keep telling myself that, Maureen. But it's—hard."

Maureen wrapped an arm around Bonnie's shoulders and gave her a supportive hug. "I can understand that. Especially the harsh way he treated your grandmother and cheated you all out of having her in your lives."

Bonnie's throat was suddenly tight with emotion. "I keep imagining how it would've been if she'd been living on Stone Creek Ranch with us. I wish things could've been different."

Maureen gave Bonnie's shoulders another squeeze. "Of course you do. But the Hollisters are a strong bunch. We don't let anything get us down. We count our blessings and march forward."

Maureen's strong, yet gentle, words were exactly what Bonnie needed to hear, and she impulsively leaned forward and kissed the woman's cheek.

"I hope it's okay to give my—uh, cousin a kiss on the cheek. Are we cousins, or what?" she asked.

Maureen tapped a thoughtful finger against her temple.

"Well, let's see. Your father and Gil are second cousins. So that makes you and I third cousins, or something like that. But it doesn't really matter, because I've already declared myself your second mother. And I'd be especially hurt if you didn't want to give me a kiss or a hug once in a while."

Her throat thick, the most Bonnie could do was nod and give the woman a tight hug. Finally, after she'd cleared her throat several times, she said, "Thank you, Maureen. I'm glad I'm here. Really, I am."

"Good. Now, let me help you open some of the boxes and I'll let you get to work." She glanced at her watch. "Gil and I have to be ready to leave in an hour for a cattleman's meeting down at Scottsdale."

Bonnie waved her toward the door. "You need to get going, Maureen. I'll handle this."

"There's no hurry, Bonnie. Hadley and Gil aren't expecting you to come up with information about Parnell anytime soon," she said.

"I don't plan on rushing this, Maureen. But I can't stay here on the ranch forever. And I'm sure my family will be expecting me to return home for the holidays," Bonnie told her.

"As far as I'm concerned you can stay here indefinitely. With Vivian and Camille being gone from the house having you around is good for me. As for the holidays, it would be extra nice for you to spend them with us. Don't you think?"

Bonnie gave her a grateful smile. "I feel like being here is good for me, so that goes both ways. And I'll wait and see what my parents think about me staying for the holidays before I make any promises."

"Of course." Maureen gave her a wink, then gesturing down to her dusty jeans and shirt, she started out of the room. "I'd better go get ready."

"You and Gil have a safe trip tonight," Bonnie told her.

"See you tomorrow, sweetie."

Maureen closed the door behind her. Bonnie thoughtfully walked over to the row of windows. Beyond the branches of a cottonwood tree, she could see a portion of the front lawn and a section of the road that led to the ranch yard. And farther still was a ridge of desert mountains dotted with sage, saguaros and Joshua trees.

She'd never expected Three Rivers Ranch to be so beautiful and she'd certainly not anticipated she would fall in love with the place. Her feelings filled her with a tinge of guilt and a bit of shock. She'd always believed there was no place for her like Stone Creek Ranch. Never in a million years would she have imagined herself feeling at home anywhere else.

Since she'd arrived on Three Rivers Ranch, she'd begun to realize she'd clung to her home in Utah because it was isolated and safe. There, she'd not had to face the outside world, where she might risk the chance of meeting a man who could break her spirit the way Ward had broken it all those years ago. Yet the image she had of herself and her future was now beginning to take a subtle shift.

She couldn't exactly determine what was causing the change in her. Whether it was being on this beautiful ranch, meeting new people or the strong attraction she felt for Mose. Or perhaps it was all of those things meshed together that had given her the courage to wear a slightly daring dress and stroll through the shadows with a sexy cowboy. Whatever the case, she hoped this newfound bravery wouldn't waver before she saw Mose again.

The next day, Mose was so busy he'd barely had time to wash the dust from his face before he hurried to the east tack room to saddle the horses for his and Bonnie's ride. To save time, he'd asked Dex to catch Dinah from the remuda paddock and place her in a stall next to Mose's personal horse, Bear.

Now, as he quickly saddled Dinah and tethered her to a nearby hitching post, he realized he was nervous about being with Bonnie again.

The notion had him snorting with self-disgust. Since when had he ever been nervous about having a beautiful woman's company?

Since Nicole made it clear you'd need more than a smile and a decent bank account to hold on to a worthwhile woman. Face it, Mose, you don't have what it takes to make a serious bid for Bonnie.

Shutting out the miserable voice in his head, he fetched Bear from his stall and began the process of saddling the black gelding. He was slipping the bridle onto Bear's head when he heard a footfall behind him. Glancing over his shoulder, he felt a spurt of joy as he spotted her walking toward him.

She was wearing the same old hat she'd worn on her first ride. Because the wind was stiff, she'd pushed the stampede string tight beneath her chin. The hems of her snug-fitting jeans were stuffed into her scarred boots, while the tail of her pink-and-white-striped shirt was tucked into the waistband. The close-fitting garments made it impossible for him not to notice her slender build had plenty of curves in all the right places.

"Hi, Mose!" she called and gave him a little wave. "Looks like I'm late. I was going to saddle Dinah and you've already done it for me."

He turned and greeted her with wide smile. "Hello, Bonnie."

She came to stand next to him. "What is this guy's name? He's beautiful."

"I call him Bear. His registered name is Heza Bear Too. I brought him with me from Texas." He glanced over at her. "Sometimes you get a horse you just can't be without and he's mine."

She gave him another smile and Mose felt like an idiot as his heart kicked into a rapid thump. Five minutes ago, he would've sworn Bonnie couldn't get any more beautiful. But now as his gaze took in the blond hair waved against her back, the full curve of her lips and her clear blue eyes, he had to admit she looked incredible.

"I understand what you're saying. My favorite horse on our ranch is too old to ride now. But I enjoy grooming him and making sure he's healthy and happy."

He nodded. "I'm guessing he'll be on Stone Creek Ranch until he's lives out his last day."

"Oh yes. He'll be buried with all the other special animals we've had down through the years. How old is Bear?"

"Eight. I've had him since he was a yearling, so we've been buddies for a long time." He turned his attention to fastening the girth around the horse's belly, but all the while, he was intensely aware of her subtle fragrance and the fact that she was standing mere inches away from him.

"Did you have property of your own back in Texas with enough space to keep horses?"

Normally, he would've been offended or suspicious if a woman asked him such a question. But he understood Bonnie wasn't digging to find out whether he'd had money then, or now. She was simply curious. And in her case, he hoped that being curious equaled to being interested.

"No. I moved around fairly often—wherever there was a need for a horse trainer. So I never bothered with purchasing a place of my own. I kept Bear at my Dad's place—he lives a few miles from Hereford."

"I see. Is that area of Texas anything like this?"

"The only similarity is the dry heat in the summer." He glanced over at her as he finished tucking the end of the girth in its holder. "There's not as much cacti or thorny vegetation as you have here. Not many trees, either. It's mostly open plains. Where the wind never stops."

"The wind is doing a pretty good job of it here today," she said. "But the sky is clear and I'm amazed at how warm it is. It's a wonderful day for riding, don't you think?"

Rain could have been coming down in sheets and he would consider it a wonderful day for riding with her. "Perfect. I hope you're up to a long trip. There are several places I want to show you."

She smiled at him. "I'm up for it. What about you? Have you been busy since the party?"

He reached up and adjusted the throat latch on Bear's bridle. "I haven't had enough time to draw a good breath. Holt purchased more horses—yearlings—yesterday, so we've been dealing with them."

She chuckled shrewdly. "Oh boy, teenagers. Nothing quite as rowdy as dealing with that age group."

"Are you talking about horses or humans?" he asked wryly.

Her smile was lopsided. "Horses. But my sister-in-law, Vanessa, is a schoolteacher and she'd probably answer 'humans.'"

He smiled back at her, and as his eyes scanned her lovely face, he was suddenly reliving the kiss he'd planted on her cheek. Her soft skin had felt like velvet beneath his lips and now he had to wonder if the rest of her would be as equally smooth to his touch.

"I don't know—my shin is currently black and blue from a kicking yesterday," he told her. "Plus I have perfect teeth marks on the back of my arm. A two-year-old was having a little tantrum."

"Oh my, are you sure you're up to this ride?" she asked.

The genuine concern he heard in her voice put a playful grin on his face. "I'm only teasing, Bonnie. You don't think bruises and bite marks would get me down, do you?"

"Not really. But I wouldn't want to put a strain on you."

It was all Mose could do to keep from bursting out laughing. "Bonnie, you're just too funny and sweet."

A shy smile touched her lips. "I try not to be a sour person."

He stepped away from Bear and collected a pair of leather saddlebags thrown over the hitching post. "I'm taking bottled water with us. In case we get thirsty."

"Now that I think about it, I probably should've brought a jacket with me for later this evening."

He glanced at her shirt. The fabric was too thin to ward off the chilly air that usually drifted in as the sun set. "I have an old jean jacket in the tack room," he told her. "It'll be much too big for you, but if you get cool, it would keep you warm."

"Thanks, Mose. I should've thought about a jacket before I left the house, but I was running late and in a bit of a hurry. I've been busy on the ancestry work."

Mose wanted to ask her how long she expected it would take to finish digging into her past relatives but didn't. He didn't want to appear overly interested. And anyway, she might not yet be able to gauge how long it will take to finish the job.

Resting his forearm on the saddle, he looked at her. "How's that going?"

"At a snail's pace. It's very tedious."

She couldn't know how happy her answer made him. "I want to hear all about it, but we'd better get started on our ride. Let me get the jacket from the tack room and we'll mount up."

"Right," she said, "we don't want to waste the daylight."

Five minutes later they were riding eastward, away from the ranch yard and past the cattle trail that Bonnie had ridden over a few days ago.

"This will take us toward one of the hay meadows," he told her. "On the other side of it, we'll run into some bluffs that overlook the southeast portion of the ranch. There's an easy trail to the top and the view is pretty from there. Unless heights make you nervous."

"Not at all. Bea and I used to ride the mountains on our ranch at home. Years after the excursion we made as six-year-olds," she said with amusement, "and we convinced Dad we could handle the trails. You see, the mountains there are much higher in elevation and home to plenty of black bear and mountain lions."

"Damn, Bonnie! Why would you and your twin want to take that kind of risk? Or maybe I should ask why your father ever allowed you to go on such rides?"

She laughed outright. "Oh Mose, I'm pretty sure you know that bear and mountain lions don't want anything to do with us humans. Not unless you deliberately provoke them. But just in case, Dad always made one of us carry a rifle."

Stunned, he stared at her. "You and Bea know how to handle a rifle?"

"Of course. Dad and our brothers taught us and our older sister, Grace, all the outdoor things we needed to know. Fortunately, all we've ever had to shoot at was a paper target. No bears or mountain lions."

He shook his head and she asked, "What's wrong? You think I'm too ditzy to know how to handle myself in the mountains?"

Frowning, he said, "I don't think you're ditzy, at all. That's the whole thing that bumfuzzles me. You're brainy and beautiful and very—well, feminine. It's hard for me to imagine you doing such outdoor things."

She laughed softly. "Mose, you should know you can't judge a woman by her looks."

He should've learned that lesson with Nicole, he thought. She'd had the glitz and the glam, but not much devotion or loyalty underneath. Now, as he looked at Bonnie's pretty face, he realized there was far more to her than he'd first imagined. And not just because she was a capable ranch woman. She was steadfast and true. And totally unassuming. She was just the kind of woman he'd want by his side, if he wanted one on a permanent basis. But what did he know about being in love or being a husband and father? Next to nothing. That's why he had to think of Bonnie as nothing more than a temporary delight.

Up until now, Bonnie had cautiously ridden her mare a few feet away from Mose's horse. But now as the trail narrowed, she was forced to rein Dinah closer to his side.

"Will Bear mind if I ride abreast of you?" she asked.

"Not at all," he said with a grin. "Texans take most things at an easy pace and Bear is no exception."

As Dinah matched her stride to Bear's, the gelding looked over at the mare, then bobbed his head as if to say he approved. Bonnie and Mose both laughed at the horses.

"I think he likes her," Bonnie said.

"He's fond of Dinah," he told her. "They've known each other for quite some time."

"Oh, so these two have a past?" she asked impishly.

"They do," he said wryly. "But Dinah has no idea that Bear has a roving eye. He also likes a little blonde in the remuda pen."

"The big question is does the little blonde like Bear?" she joked.

He pointed down to the horse's head and spoke in a lowered voice, "Not really. But I don't want him to know it. Bear's feelings are sensitive."

Bonnie laughed outright. "I'll just bet. He sounds like a two-timer to me."

Mose laughed, then after a moment said, "So, tell me about the ancestry search you're doing. Or is *ancestry search* the right words for the job you're doing?"

"I'm not sure there's a label for what I'm trying to do," she admitted. "But whatever you label it, it's gone on for the past few years. Ever since my brother Jack traveled down here to Three Rivers and took a DNA test with Blake. When the results revealed that the families were related, all of us wanted to know when and how. That's when we realized we didn't have proper documentation for Grandfather's birth name or his birthplace."

"Are you saying his birth certificate was lost or misplaced?"

Groaning, she shook her head. "Nothing that simple. We discovered that Grandfather had lied to us about his origins, which created lots of digging to unearth the truth."

His expression curious, he asked, "And did you find the truth of where he was born?"

"Yes and that's what has led me down here to Three Rivers. We discovered Grandfather was Parnell Hollister's son. So I'm here to learn more about him. So far, I know that Parnell was next to the youngest of Joseph Hollister's four children and that something occurred within the family when Parnell was in his early twenties. Joseph disinherited him and banished him from the ranch. We're not exactly sure when this happened, but likely around the mid to late 1930s."

He shook his head. "Man, that would take some deep-rooted anger to banish your own son."

Bonnie sighed. "We can only assume the problems with Parnell must've been serious. Anyway, after he left the ranch no one knows where he went at first. Ultimately we learned that he entered the army and was killed on a Normandy beach during the invasion of WWII. But before that happened, he married an English girl and they had a son together. The boy grew up and eventually became my Grandfather Lionel."

He gazed thoughtfully on up the trail as his fingers absently combed through a hank of Bear's mane. "Obviously, your grandfather isn't living. Otherwise, he could've given you the answers to all these questions."

"Grandfather died a few years ago. Complications of a stroke." Her expression dismal, she shook her head. "But even if he was living, I'm not sure he would have told us anything. He concealed his past for so long. We had no idea, until recently, that Lionel had been born in England, or that he was Parnell's son. Grandfather kept everything a secret from us. Seems he didn't want anyone knowing he was related to these Three Rivers Hollisters. So he—well, he actually lied to us about where he was born and a host of other things. Frankly, Mose, learning the truth about him was shocking."

"I can only imagine. To me it's pretty darn odd," he said. "I mean, it's clear that this generation of Hollisters are responsible and trustworthy. I can't imagine him wanting to keep the connection between the two families secret."

She nodded. "To be honest, Mose, it's embarrassing to learn your relatives were—well, dishonest."

He didn't reply and Bonnie tried to focus on the rugged landscape, the sound of the horses' shoes scraping against an occasional rock and the wind whistling through the sage. But none of those things could tear her thoughts away from Mose sitting tall in the saddle, his big hand loosely holding the reins and his thighs straining against his jeans as he shifted his weight in the stirrups.

As he'd told her earlier, Dinah and Bear were fond of each other and the pair occasionally walked so close together it caused Bonnie's lower leg to brush against Mose's. The contact was electric and like nothing she'd ever experienced before. The intense reaction made her wonder how it might actually feel if he did decide to take her into his arms and kiss her.

No. She very much doubted he wanted to get *that* close to her. True, he'd held her hands and kissed her cheek, but he'd not given her any signals that he wanted to be more intimate with her. And yet she wanted like heck to get next to him.

Then, why don't you show him you want to get closer, Bonnie? The man can't read your mind!

The daring voice was rolling around in her head when he suddenly looked over to her and said, "I don't know how you view the situation, but I figure discovering what started this rift in the family those many years ago will be cathartic for you and all the Hollisters."

She cast him an appreciative smile. Not only for understanding the situation with her relatives but also for distracting her from the erotic thoughts rolling around in her head.

"I've been reading through clippings and articles about the ranch and how it all started. It's mind-boggling to me that Three Rivers Ranch came into existence when Arizona was only a wild territory."

Nodding, he made a sweeping gesture with his arm at the land around them. There were outcroppings of layered rocks, stands of mesquite trees and an occasional saguaro. In some spots, wildflowers bloomed bright orange between clumps of sage and creosote. The scent of sage and grasses drifted on the wind, and high above, turkey vultures circled the blue sky in search of a meal below.

He said, "This land is beautiful, but it can also be very unforgiving. Especially in the dead of summer when triple-digit heat is soaring over the desert. It's hard to imagine the adversities and hardships the first Hollisters must have faced."

"Some of the papers I've been reading talk about Edmond Hollister, the original patriarch of the family, and how he had to deal with bandits and cattle rustlers," Bonnie said. "But for sure, there also had to be illnesses and injuries to contend with. And hardly any medical aid to be found."

"Probably had to settle for home remedies and a lot of prayers. And you might add wildfires and the weather to the list of difficulties," he replied. "Plus, the area must've turned really wild and dangerous when gold was discovered near Wickenburg in 1863. Did you know about that piece of history?"

She nodded. "Sophia and Reeva were telling me all about the Annual Gold Rush Days festival that takes place in town. It sounds like a big celebration that goes on for a few days. From what they said, there's a carnival, and the streets are filled with all kinds of food and game booths. If I am still here in February, I can attend some of the celebrations. But that's a long time away. I'll probably be back in Utah long before then."

"You'd enjoy Gold Rush Days. A big rodeo goes on in town during the festivities," he told her. "Maybe you'll still be here in February. Or maybe you could come back for another visit."

No. Her parents wanted her to have a break from running the office on Stone Creek, but she couldn't keep bouncing back and forth—not when her family was depending on her. Come February, she'd be hundreds of miles away from Mose. The idea filled her with a sadness she'd never expected to feel. Why? Stone Creek was her home, her safe haven. Mose shouldn't be pulling her away from all that.

Forcing a smile on her lips, she shoved at the unsettling thoughts. "Do you go to any of the festivities?" she asked him.

"Sure. Most all of us ranch hands go to the rodeo," he said. "It's a fun time. And the street dance is great."

She arched a curious brow at him. "You like to dance?"

He flashed a grin at her. "To me dancing is as enjoyable as eating a good meal. Haven't you ever heard of the Texas two-step?"

Yes, she could imagine him, holding a woman tight in his arms, and swaying to the music. His shoulder would feel warm and strong beneath her cheek and the whisper of his breath against the side of her hair would cause her eyelids to drift downward and her hand tighten around his.

The sensual image prompted her to draw in a deep breath and blow it out.

"I vaguely recall hearing that phrase," she finally answered. "Honestly, I'm not much into dancing. I can circle the floor without falling on my face, but that's about it."

He shot her a look of disbelief. "I find that hard to believe. Anyone who can ride a horse as well as you would have to be a good dancer."

She shrugged. "Dancing needs practice and I rarely get it. I suppose the last time I danced was at Bea's wedding reception—with my brothers. And that's been two years ago."

He clicked his tongue with disapproval. "I'd never admit such a terrible thing. Before you go back to Utah, we need to do something to remedy that."

Was he hinting that he might take her dancing? Just the thought was enough to make her heart race. And suddenly she was wondering if she was inviting more trouble than she could handle. Just because she found Mose wildly attractive hardly meant she should go on a date with him. In fact, the reckless feelings she had toward him should probably stand as a warning to keep her distance.

But would playing it safe with Mose make her happy?

Since her college days, she'd walked a careful path in order to avoid heartbreak and humiliation. And over the years she'd managed to keep her heart intact. Yet at the same time, she'd been empty and lonely and wishing her life was different. Mose was giving her a chance to make it different, she thought, and something was telling her she'd be a fool not to grab that chance.

She slanted him a playful smile. "Then, all I can say is you'd better have a pair of steel-toed boots to wear."

Laughing, he reached over and gave her hand a little squeeze. "I'm not worried about my toes."

And she wasn't going to worry about getting her heart crushed. Being with Mose felt too good to worry about anything.

"Want to nudge the horses into a long trot?" she asked.

Grinning his approval, he gave her hand another squeeze before he took up Bear's reins. "I thought you'd never ask."

They urged the pair of horses into a fast trot, and as they rode side by side down the trail with the horses snorting and the wind brushing her cheeks, Bonnie felt as if Mose was taking her to the top of the world.

When the two of them finally reached the edge of a hay meadow, they reined their horses to a stop and gazed out at the green field that stretched over a massive number of acres. An irrigation system was currently sprinkling water over a section of the alfalfa already grown to several inches in height.

"Wow! I wouldn't have expected to see a crop at this time of year," she told him.

"In some areas of the state, alfalfa is grown year-round. Here on Three Rivers, the winter months are usually mild enough to produce a good crop," he explained.

She looked over to see him lifting his hat from his head and raking a hand through his dark hair. She'd only seen him without his hat a few times, and on each occasion, she'd noticed his hair was thick and shiny with the kind of loose waves that some women spent hours trying to achieve. She wondered how it would feel to slide her fingers into his hair and feel the texture against her skin. She couldn't help but wonder, too, just how many women had ever been that close to him?

Disturbed by the self-induced questions, she pulled her gaze away from him and back to the green field of alfalfa.

"Where does the water come from?" she asked. "Is there a nearby creek or underground wells?"

"This particular field is irrigated from a deep well. But there are a couple of meadows that rely on river water. That is, while the water is running. By late summer, they're usually dry. Blake tries to get as many cuttings as he can before lack of water becomes a problem."

She said, "Dad recently purchased a large section of land to the west of us that used to be a farm. It was already set up with irrigation systems, so he's been growing as much alfalfa on it as he can. He says the money he saves by not having to buy hay will pay for the property."

"You think it will?"

The question pulled her gaze back to his face, and as she studied his rugged features in the waning sunlight, she felt a hunger well up inside her. It was a feeling she'd never experienced and the depth of it shook her.

She swallowed to clear the thickness from her throat. "I'm certain it will. Since I keep the ranch's books, I deal with the dollar numbers and I can see the profit adding up. Dad likes to be right."

His smile was gentle. "All men like to be right, Bonnie."

Chapter Eight

Ever since they'd started on this ride, Mose had been thinking how much he'd like to pull her down from the saddle and straight into his arms. But there was something about Bonnie that stopped him from reaching for her. She was shy, but not so shy that she avoided the touch of his hand. She was also reserved, but not snobbishly so. No, the thing that was keeping him from planting a hot kiss on her lips was his own fears.

Kissing Bonnie would be addictive. He didn't think he could stop with just one, and where would that lead him? Bonnie wasn't the sort to have casual sex. He wasn't altogether sure that she'd ever had sex. Which meant a few of her kisses would undoubtedly lead him straight to a cold shower.

"Are you getting tired yet?" he asked. "We've ridden a fair distance."

"I'm not tired at all. I feel great."

"Good. See the bluff to our right? That's the one I mentioned to you earlier. It's about a half a mile to the base of it and then we can hit a trail that will take us to the top. Think you can make it all right?"

"Don't worry about me, Mose, I can ride all day long."

Her smug response put a grin on his face. "Maybe Holt should hire you to train his horses."

She laughed. "I said *ride*. Not train. That's your expertise."

"Expertise? Come on, let's get going," he said teasingly, "before you make my head swell too big for my hatband."

A long trot took them to the base of the bluff in quick time, but once they started up the steep trail, the going slowed down to a hard climb. Because the rough terrain demanded most of their attention, very few words passed between them. Every few moments, Mose kept glancing around to make sure she was following safely behind him. And each time, she was right there, sitting in the saddle as though she was born to it.

Most of the girls he'd dated in the past had lived in town and weren't familiar with horses. He'd never had a girlfriend who could ride a gentle horse more than ten minutes, even going at slow walk on a flat surface. Bonnie was all horsewoman and it felt good to share this common interest with her.

When they finally broke over the crest of the rocky cliff, he motioned for her to follow him to an open space where they could tie their horses to the snag of a juniper tree.

"We need to dismount so you can walk up to the edge and look off," he told her.

Her chuckle was calculating. "Look off, or fall off?"

He shook a playful finger at her. "You have a fiendish imagination."

"I watch too many old horror movies. Seems like half of the heroines end up running from a villain until they're dangling from the edge of a cliff, screaming for help."

"I'm perfectly capable of saving screaming heroines," he teased.

He climbed down from the saddle. After tying Bear's reins to the branch of a juniper, he walked around to Dinah's left side and reached his arms up to her.

"Let me help you down," he told her. "Your legs might be a little wobbly."

"Thanks. After that steep climb, I am ready for a little rest."

She dropped the reins onto Dinah's neck and eased her boots out of the stirrups. When she swung her right leg over Dinah's hips, Mose placed his hands on either side of her waist and lifted her weight out of the saddle.

Even after her boots touched the ground, he continued to hold her until she found her footing, and he marveled at the slender curve of her waist under his hands and the warmth of her body seeping into his hands.

"Okay?" he asked.

Turning slightly, she grabbed hold of his upper arm. "Oh, uh, yes. I'm okay. My legs are just a bit shaky."

He continued to hold her for another moment and then she looked up at him with a sheepish expression. "And here I was bragging about riding all day," she said wryly. "I guess I've gotten a little out of shape. Don't tell Maureen. She'll think I'm a wimp."

Instinctively, his hand began to move up and down her back. "Maureen would never think such a thing about you and neither would I. We've ridden a long distance. Actually, we should've dismounted at the hay meadow and rested before we headed up here. But once the sun gets close to the horizon, it sinks really fast and I wanted you to see this."

She tilted her head back and, from beneath the brim of her hat, gazed up at him. There was a slight quiver to her lips, but he wasn't sure if that was because she was tired or if being close to him was affecting her. He knew one thing: Having his hands on her was definitely doing something to him.

"Thanks for being my anchor," she said softly. "I'm fine now. Let's, uh, go have a look off the cliff."

"Sure," he replied. "And you can hang on to my arm if you'd like. The ground is kind of rocky up here."

Smiling now, she wrapped her arm around his. "I'll take you up on that offer."

They walked a forty-foot distance along a dim trail through gnarled juniper trees and tall stands of sage and rock.

"I suspect wildlife such as deer and pronghorns have made these trails, but do the cattle come up here?" she asked.

"Tag, our foreman, has told me the cattle do venture up into these high places. Looking for forage, I suppose."

"Our cattle do, too. Especially in the summer months when the mountain meadows are green," she told him. "But Quint gets testy if too many of them come around. He thinks all the high meadows are for his and Clementine's sheep. Which actually, they are for the sheep herd."

As they walked, her shoulder pressed against his upper arm, while her hand clung to his forearm. The warm contact was playing havoc with his senses and he was finding it a struggle to follow their conversation.

"And how does that work? Do you have fences to separate the sheep from the cattle?"

"Other than the boundary fences, there are only a few cross fences on Stone Creek. The cattle and sheep are mostly separated by a large amount of land. The cattle stay on the east side of the range and the sheep on the west, where it's more mountainous."

He could hear a bit of pride in her voice, making it obvious that she loved her home. And why not? Even if it wasn't as majestic as Three Rivers, he had no doubt it was a prosperous ranch. "Sounds beautiful and interesting. I don't know much about sheep. How did your brother Quint get so involved with them?"

"Grandfather always kept sheep and left a stipulation in his will that sheep would always be on Stone Creek Ranch. And from the time he was a small boy, Quint has been drawn to the animals. He knows all about breeding and caring for them, shearing and keeping them safe from predators. He'd be the first to tell you that his wife knows more about raising sheep than he does. So they make a perfect pair."

He suddenly thought about his parents and the painful marriage they'd tried to hold together. Over the years, Mose had realized that marriage wasn't for everyone. And if a person wasn't cut out to be a spouse, they needed to avoid the union entirely.

"It's nice they can work together and love each other at the same time. They're lucky."

"They realize how blessed they are. Especially now that they have a baby on the way."

Most of his friends had already settled down and started families. But Mose didn't want to think about marriage and babies. Those things would never be on his radar. All he wanted to think about was the pleasure of having Bonnie close to him and the way it made him feel whenever she smiled and touched him.

"Okay, I think this is as far as we should go," he told her as they stopped several steps back from the rock ledge overhanging the bluff. "It might be safe enough to step out on the ledge, but I wouldn't want to chance it."

"Neither would I," she agreed. "It's a long drop down. And it looks like there's a deep arroyo at the bottom. I can see a few patches of water here and there. It must have rained before I arrived here, because I've not seen a drop fall."

"There was a bit of rain maybe three or four weeks ago. I'm surprised it's not dried up yet." He motioned toward the wide-open vista sweeping away from the bluff. "This is what I mainly wanted you to see. Isn't it something?"

She pushed the hat off her head and allowed the stampede string to catch against her throat and anchor the hat against her back. "I'm thoroughly impressed, Mose. It's like a beautiful painting. I never realized desert landscape could look so green. And the black Angus cows dotting the scene makes me wonder again about Edmond Hollister and his wife, Helena. Obviously, the couple had big dreams. But I doubt they could've dreamt that Three Rivers Ranch would someday be one the largest and richest in the state of Arizona."

"A man can dream for the future, but he can't know if his wishes will ever come true," he said gently.

Turning slightly, she looked up at him. As Mose looked into her eyes, it was like he was seeing his own future and it was all wrapped up in her. The thought shook him to the very core of his being.

"That's the first time I've ever heard a tinge of bitterness in your voice, Mose. It's not a good sound on you."

He breathed deeply. "Sorry, Bonnie. I'm not any different from the next fella. I've had a few disappointments and sometimes I can't help but remember."

Her lips tilted into a wan smile as her hand came up to rest in the middle of his chest. "We've all had disappointments. I've come to view mine as learning tools."

Learning tools. Yeah, he believed he'd learned plenty from Nicole. But at this very moment, he couldn't think about the lessons or risks. All he could think about was the warm inviting look in her eyes and the alluring curve of her moist lips.

"Bonnie." He reached out and touched a silky strand of her hair. "I don't think you realize what you do to me."

Confusion filtered into her blue eyes. "What do I do to you? Get on your nerves?"

He groaned and then his hands were on her shoulders, drawing the front of her body next to his.

"Yeah, you get on my nerves, all right. And there's not a one of them that isn't aching to do this."

Her eyes wide, she started to speak, but he only gave her

enough time to murmur his name before he lowered his head and covered her lips with his.

The contact created a groan in her throat, but the small sound was muted by the roar in his ears. Her lips tasted like nothing he'd ever experienced before. And even though he'd planned to keep the kiss quick and simple, his plans went instantly awry as her soft lips urged him to continue.

His senses blurred, he slid his arms around her shoulders and under the barrier of the hat hanging against her back. When he pulled her tight against him, he was instantly aware of her breasts pushing at his chest, her legs pressed against his. She was a delicate dream in his arms and the more he kissed her, the more he wanted the moment to never end.

Seconds ticked away as the heat of their bodies melded together and her arms slid around his neck. It wasn't until he heard her groan a second time that he recognized the kiss was spiraling out of control.

Calling on every ounce of self-control he possessed, he managed to break the union of their lips and lift his head. As he gulped in a huge breath of air, he glanced down to see her face was still tilted upward toward his. Her eyes were closed, the fringe of her long lashes creating dark crescents upon her pale skin. Their kiss had left her lips rosy red and glazed with moisture. The luscious sight made him want to forget all caution and lower his mouth back to hers.

"Bonnie," he whispered her name and touched her cheek with his fingertips. Her eyes slowly fluttered open and he was a little stunned to see the blue orbs were clouded with desire. Even though he'd felt an eager response in her lips, he'd not expected it to affect her this strongly. "I, uh, wasn't planning on that happening."

"What do you mean? You hadn't planned on kissing me? Or hadn't expected to enjoy it?" she asked.

With a slight shake of his head, he rested his hands on the tops of her shoulders. "I didn't think we'd, uh, get that lost. At least, I was lost. I can't speak for you."

Sighing, she nestled her cheek against his shoulder and Mose couldn't resist sliding his fingers into the silky hair at the back of her head.

"I'm still not sure where I am," she murmured. "Except that I'm in your arms."

And that was where he wanted to keep her. The reality of his thoughts frightened him. Especially when he didn't quite understand these feelings that were growing stronger and stronger inside him. On one hand, he wanted to make passionate love to her, while at the same time he wanted to cherish and protect her. How did a man tread such a narrow path, he wondered. Moreover, what did it all mean? That he was losing his head over her? No. He wasn't going to allow himself to fall that hard for the ranching heiress—particularly one who lived so far away from him. She had every reason in the world to walk away from him, and come time, he had no doubt that she would.

But maybe, as long as he remembered that fact and didn't let himself get too attached to something he couldn't keep, he'd be fine. Maybe they could enjoy being together while she was here.

His fingers gently caressed the back of her head, while the lower part of his body was aching from the contact of her warm curves pressing against him. "You're on the ledge of the cliff, remember? Only you're not screaming for help," he added teasingly.

Sighing again, she slowly eased from his embrace and turned her back to him. "To tell you the truth, Mose, that kiss did scare me a little. I'm—and please don't laugh—not accustomed to kissing a man. Not like what just happened with us. I didn't know it could feel so—overwhelming."

He wrapped his hands around the backs of her arms and was surprised to feel a faint tremor pass through her. "I wouldn't ever laugh at your feelings, Bonnie. Or your inexperience. To tell you the truth, it's pretty darn nice not to hear you spouting vulgar comebacks or suggestive propositions to me."

Glancing over her shoulder, she gave him a wobbly smile. "I do try to be a lady. But you're probably thinking I wasn't acting very ladylike a few moments ago."

"Oh Bonnie, don't be silly," he gently admonished, then slowly turned her to face him. "When we kissed—I thought you were being honest and natural."

Her eyes dropped shyly away from his. "I thought you were being honest, too."

Smiling wryly, he said, "Good. Because I was. I don't know where that puts things between us, but I hope—I want to see more of you, Bonnie. And that you'd like to see more of me. I realize your stay here is temporary. But we can make the most of the time before you have to return home."

The look of wonder that filled her eyes caught him by surprise. From the very first day he'd laid eyes on her at the airport, the attraction he'd felt for her had been so strong he figured it had been fairly obvious to her and everyone else around them.

A long breath eased out of her. "I'd like to see more of you, too, Mose. I—just wasn't sure you—well, I wanted to make sure you actually wanted my company. Not just tolerated me because I'm your employers' relative."

Groaning softly, he wrapped his arms around her and pressed a kiss against the side of her hair. "And I didn't want you to think I was being with you just because you're a Hollister," he said gently. "Oh Bonnie, meeting you has been special for me. I hope you'll always remember that much."

"I won't forget anything about you, Mose. Even when I'm five hundred miles away—in black-bear country," she added impishly.

Five hundred miles away. He wasn't going to allow himself to think about the vast distance that would eventually stretch between them. There'd be time enough for that after she was gone.

A crooked grin was all he could manage as he gently set her apart from him. "I'm definitely not going to think about you being in bear country. Even with a rifle."

A tentative smile quivered her lips. "Don't worry. Once I'm back on Stone Creek, I'll be so busy catching up with my office work that I won't have time for horseback rides."

"All the more reason for you to take plenty of rides while you're here." He turned her slightly toward the northwest area of the ranch and pointed to a patch of green woods. "See that wooded area with the fall-colored leaves? The next ride we go on, I'll take you there. Since you're working on Hollister history, I think you'll enjoy visiting the spot. The original ranch house is still there. A three-room cabin, where Edmond and his wife, Helena, lived in the beginning."

She brightened with interest. "Oh, I would love to see it. But I suspect the cabin is probably caving in by now."

His expression turned crafty. "I'm not saying more. I want you to be surprised."

"Okay, I'll wait and see." Turning, she gave one last look off the cliff. "Shadows are creeping across the valley floor. I suppose we should be heading back before dark catches us."

"Right," he said. "We don't want folks back at the ranch worrying we might've run into trouble."

With his hand resting against the small of her back, they

walked over to where the horses were standing quietly tied to the juniper snag.

"I think I'll get the jacket from the back of the saddle. It's already cooling down," she said.

He skirted around Bear's hindquarters and joined her at Dinah's left side. "Here. Let me untie it for you," he told her.

After a few tugs on the saddle strings, he had the jacket in hand, and he shook out the garment, then held it out so that she could slip her arms into the sleeves.

Once he'd lifted the jacket onto her shoulders, he couldn't resist taking hold of the lapels and turning her until she was facing him.

Her eyes twinkled up at him at the same time her palms came to rest against his chest. The touch filled him with such warm pleasure that he couldn't stop himself from lowering his head and brushing his lips against her cheek. "Warm now?" he asked.

"Deliciously warm," she murmured.

He eased his head back just enough to look into her eyes. "I shouldn't kiss you again, Bonnie. But I sure do want to," he whispered.

"And I sure do want you to," she said softly.

Groaning with need, he settled his lips over hers. This time he purposely kept the intimate contact light and brief. But still it was a battle to make himself lift his head and end the embrace.

"As nice as that was, we'd better hit the trail." He reached down and clasped a hand around her ankle. "Come on, I'll give you a lift to the saddle."

Once they were both mounted, Mose led the way down the winding, cliffside trail. By the time they'd reached the bottom and rode west across the open desert range, twilight had fallen and the evening star was rising on the western horizon.

As Mose gazed at the brilliant light, his mother's words drifted through his thoughts.

Make a wish on the evening star, boys, and it will come true someday.

He and Mitch had wished and wished, but none of their childhood desires had ever come true. And now? As he glanced over at Bonnie, he decided he'd be a fool to waste his time longing for something that was as far from his reach as that evening star. But her kisses darned well made him want to try.

The next afternoon found Bonnie in Maureen's office, sitting cross-legged on the floor, slowly sifting through a box of old photographs, when her cell phone rang. Seeing her twin's name pop up on the ID, she quickly set the box aside and punched the accept button.

"Bea! I was about to decide you were sick or something! It's been forever since I've heard from you!" Bonnie exclaimed.

Her sister laughed. "*Forever?* Shame on me! Sorry, sissy. I've been very busy at the boutique. And my evenings have been taken up with helping Kipp feed cattle. Warren, the ranch's foreman, has been down with the flu, so Kipp is trying to make up for his absence. But I should remind you, Bonnie, the phone works two ways. Those gadgets can receive calls or make them."

Smiling, Bonnie rested her back against the carved leg of the big oak desk. "Okay, I apologize for not calling. You're probably not going to believe this, but I've been busy, too."

"Hah! Exactly how busy can you be down there with cooks to prepare your meals and a maid to keep things tidy for you? From what Mom tells me, all you're doing is looking through a bunch of old papers. I can't imagine anything more boring."

"Boring to you, but not to me. It's more than just old papers, Bea. This afternoon I've been going through old photos, which are turning out to be very interesting. But I've been doing other things besides digging up info on our great-grandfather."

Beatrice said, "I'm glad. Unless you tell me you're digging for answers to some other family mystery."

"No. This has been fun stuff," Bonnie assured her. "Maureen and Gil threw a little, early Christmas party, mostly for my benefit, I think. Anyway, it was an outdoor event with lots of food and music. Everything was great. I got to meet a bunch of our newfound relatives. And meet Holt's in-laws, which was a special treat."

"Oh, why were they special?" Beatrice asked curiously.

"Gabby and Sam are just a neat couple. He's in his late seventies and the current foreman of Joe and Tess's ranch, the Bar X. And she's at least twenty years younger, beautiful and a successful artist. I've never seen a couple more in love. Unless it was Maureen and Gil. Well, and Mom and Dad, and you and Kipp, of course."

There was a long pause and then Beatrice said, "Bonnie, you're shocking me! You're rambling. And about being in love, of all things! What's going on with you down there?"

"Don't be silly. I've talked about being in love before. At least, about other people being in love," she swiftly corrected, then drew in a deep breath. "I don't know, Bea, maybe it's all this Arizona sunshine or something, but I just feel different. And—I've gotten acquainted with one of the horse trainers here on the ranch. I guess spending a bit of time with him has made me—well, made me feel like a woman."

There was another pause and then Beatrice said, "You've always been a woman, Bonnie. Albeit a shy one. So, tell me about this horse trainer. What's he like?"

Shy? She'd not felt a bit bashful or reticent when she'd been in Mose's arms, kissing his lips and feeling his hard body pressed to hers. Even now, the memory sent a shaft of pleasure rushing through her.

"His name is Mose Martel and he's thirty-three, single and originally from the Texas Panhandle."

"Hmm. This is interesting, sissy. What about his looks? Average, homely, handsome?"

Bonnie giggled, something she hadn't done since her teenaged years. "He looks like a dream, Bea! He's tall and lean, but strong as a whip. His hair is dark and just long enough to curl at the back of his neck. He has brown eyes that have so many gold flecks around the pupils that they look almost amber in color. And his face is rugged and manly and—well, just right. Oh, and did I tell you he's a flashy dresser? Like the cowboys used to dress years ago with colorful shirts and tall boots."

"And this guy caught your eye? Unbelievable!" After a long pause, Beatrice went on in a firm voice, "I think I'm going to tell Kipp I need to go down to Three Rivers Ranch to check on you. You must be hitting the Christmas eggnog and brandy already! You sound like you've fallen in love! Have you?"

Bonnie lifted her gaze to the row of windows on the opposite side of the office. The evening sun was beginning to sink and cast shadows across the road leading to the ranch yard. Mose would soon be ending his long day at the horse barn and she wished she would be spending the evening with him. But when they'd returned from their ride last night, he'd not mentioned when they might see each other again. And she'd not wanted to press him. He'd kissed her and told her he wanted the two of them to spend more time together. She had to trust that he meant what he said.

"Bea, you're being ridiculous. I only met Mose a few days ago."

"So what? I fell in love with Kipp almost instantly. And look how good we've turned out."

Bonnie couldn't deny that Beatrice and Kipp were the perfect pair and deliriously in love. "I'll admit you two are a great couple and your marriage is as solid as a rock. But you know me, Bea, I'm not impulsive. Especially when it comes to men. So as for me being in love with Mose already—it's a far-fetched notion."

Beatrice's long sigh sounded in Bonnie's ear and she realized there wasn't much she could hide from her twin. She knew Bonnie inside and out.

"Is it really, sissy? I believe I'm hearing genuine affection in your voice when you speak this cowboy's name."

Bonnie's head dropped as she massaged her closed eyes. "Okay, I do have genuine affection for Mose. Maybe I feel even more than fondness for him, but on the other side of the coin, I realize I'd be making a huge mistake to—well, fall in love with him."

"You think you can stop yourself?" Beatrice let out a loud laugh. "Love doesn't work that way, Bonnie!"

Bonnie released a long sigh. "I think I'm beginning to figure that out, Bea. Because the more I'm with Mose, the more these feelings I have for him just come to me out of nowhere. Like I really don't have any control of myself. To tell you the truth, Bea, it's a little scary."

"Yes, but scary in a wonderful way," Beatrice told her. "That's what makes falling in love so magical. It just happens."

Bonnie groaned. "I'm not sure I want my feelings for Mose to go that far, Bea. The time will come for me to leave Three

Rivers and then what? Even now, it's going to hurt terribly to tell Mose goodbye."

"Maybe you won't have to say goodbye," she said with cheery optimism. "Could be he might ask you to stay there with him. Or you might even throw those inhibitions of yours out the door and ask him to go with you to Stone Creek. I imagine Dad and Jack would be happy to hire him on."

Rising to her feet, Bonnie walked over to the windows. Twilight was falling over the desert hills and she couldn't help but think how last night at this time, she was standing on the cliff with Mose and he was kissing her as though she was precious to him. Even if their budding relationship ended tomorrow, she would always remember those moments and how incredible it had felt to have his lips on hers, his arms tight around her.

"Look, Bea, it all seems simple and easy to you because everything worked out great for you and Kipp. But that doesn't mean the same will happen for me. Besides, your idea is way off base. Mose isn't interested in marriage. And even if he was interested in having a wife, he'd never leave Three Rivers. He's already made that clear to me. Working as one of Holt's three horse trainers is a highly prestigious job. It's not something he'd ever give up. Moreover, I wouldn't want him to."

Beatrice didn't immediately reply, and when she did, she sounded thoughtful. "You shouldn't be worrying about these things right now. You need to enjoy this time you have with Mose. I promise everything will work out. I happen to believe in the old saying that love will find a way."

Love. Love. Her sister continued to use the term as though Bonnie's feelings for Mose were already settled. There was so much more she wanted to learn about him. So much she needed to know before she could really open her heart to him.

Or had she already made the dangerous mistake of allowing him to step into her heart?

"Sweet Bea, you're still a hopeless romantic," Bonnie said, then quickly changed the subject. "Now it's time for you to tell me what you've been doing. Has the boutique been busy?"

"Oh my gosh, *busy* isn't the word for it. Once fall arrived, I thought there would be lots of summer markdowns left hanging on the racks, but they've already sold out and women are clamoring for more winter fashions to come in."

"What about the things you've been designing? Are they selling?"

Her soft laugh was laced with disbelief. "Believe it or not, I can't keep enough of them in the boutique. I have two seamstresses working for me now, and fortunately, both of them live in Burley, not far from the boutique. And listen to this, in the past three days I've had two different clothing companies contact me about doing a line of Western fashions for them. Major companies, I might add."

"Oh wow! My sister is going to become famous. But I'm not a bit surprised at this news. You have the eye, the imagination and talent. See, all those years you slugged your way through college is paying off."

"Yes, they're paying off. But honestly, Bonnie, I don't have any intentions of going in with a big company. That isn't what I want. My plans are to keep things simple and design clothing for the women near my home, who frequent my boutique. And of course, for my family. Since my time is limited I want to use my talent for the people I love. Does that sound corny? Or foolish?"

Bonnie answered, "Nothing corny or foolish about it. I think you've grown so much since you and Kipp were married. You don't have to wonder about what you want out of life—you already know. Mom and Dad are proud of you. As we all are."

After a short pause, Beatrice made a sound that was a cross between a giggle and a sob, and suddenly Bonnie realized her sister's call was more than a simple hello.

Turning away from the windows, Bonnie walked over and sank onto the leather couch. "Okay, Bea, out with it. Something is going on with you, so you might as well tell me now."

"Nothing is wrong, sissy! I'm—just bubbly and happy."

Frowning, Bonnie replied, "You're always bubbly and happy. That's not what this is. Why do you sound like you're choking on a chicken bone?"

Beatrice laughed. "Because I want to shout and sing. When I told you I've been very busy, that was an understatement. I've made a couple of trips to the medical clinic in town this week. The last visit was today, and the doctor confirmed I'm two months pregnant!"

Joy rushed through Bonnie. "A baby? Oh my darling sister! This is thrilling news. Have you told Kipp?"

"He was the first one to get the news. As you might guess, we're both over the moon. He or she should be born in early July so Kipp is already hoping for a Fourth of July baby." She laughed. "Firecrackers and sparklers! Barbecues and picnics! Our child won't likely forget his birthday parties."

Bonnie chuckled. "What fun that will be! Have you given Mom and Dad the news?"

"No. Not yet. I wanted to speak with you first. I'm going to call them as soon as I hang up."

Shaking her head, Bonnie said, "Why didn't you tell me this news as soon as I answered the phone? Instead, you let me drone on about Mose and what's been happening down here."

"Because you meeting Mose is also important! Who knows, this time next year you might be pregnant with *his* baby. If he's as great as you make him sound, that would be wonderful."

A pang of sorrow suddenly hit Bonnie smack in the middle of her chest. Mose would never come close to being *that* serious about her. Still, she wasn't going to let that stop her from seeing him as much as she could. Maybe that made her a glutton for punishment, but at least she'd have a few precious memories to take home to Stone Creek. And that was far more than she'd ever had from any other man.

"You're good at dreaming, Bea. And I love you for wanting me to have a family. But you shouldn't be leaping to such conclusions. You have plenty to think about now—you, Kipp and the baby. I'm so happy for you," she told her, then asked, "Remember when we were little girls and all we ever wanted was a baby doll to play with and a horse to ride? Now you're going to have both."

"Oh Bonnie, you're going to make me cry or laugh. I'm not sure which," she said in a choked voice. "These days any little thing makes me overemotional. If the checkout clerk at the grocery store asks if I want paper or plastic bags, I very nearly burst into tears."

Bonnie chuckled. "You can fix that problem by taking your reusable bags. So what did the doctor have to say about your health? Is everything okay so far?"

"Thankfully, he declared me very healthy and he's not expecting any problems. Kipp and I are praying he's right."

"You'll definitely have my prayers, sissy."

"I love you, Bonnie. Now I'd better hang up and call Mom and Dad," she said, then suddenly added, "Before I go, I want to say how proud I am of you."

Bonnie frowned. "Me? I've not done anything."

"Yes, you have. You're shaking off that last bit of shell you wrapped around you seven years ago. So don't let anything stop you now, Bonnie. Reach for what you want and hold on."

Tears unexpectedly stung Bonnie's eyes. "I'll try. More importantly, you take care of yourself and the little one."

The sisters exchanged goodbyes and Bonnie thoughtfully placed the phone on the desktop.

Reach for what you want.

Oh yes, Bonnie wanted to reach for Mose and hold tight. But in the end what would that gain her? A few days of excitement and pleasure? Memories to look back on in her golden days?

Sure a part of her wished that meeting him would lead to more than a brief affair. But temporary pleasure in his arms was okay, she told herself. It had to be.

Chapter Nine

Moments later, Bonnie was rising from the chair to return to the box of photos on the floor, when a light knock sounded on the door.

Glancing around, she saw Jazelle standing in the open doorway.

"Am I interrupting anything important?" the housekeeper asked.

Bonnie's half-hearted laugh held a husky note. "Are you kidding? I've been sifting through old photos. And talking with my twin sister. She gave me some surprising news. She's going to have a baby—in early July."

Smiling, Jazelle took a few steps into the office. "What a nice Christmas surprise! If I remember right, you said your twin didn't have any children yet."

"Right. So it's a pretty exciting time for her and her husband."

"Absolutely." Her smile turned dreamy. "Now that Madison is in preschool, I'm having empty-nest feelings. Another baby would be nice."

"What about Connor? Is he having these empty-nest feelings, too?" Bonnie asked.

Jazelle chuckled. "Connor would have a whole house full of kids if I agreed to have them."

Jazelle's happy face had Bonnie wondering if she'd ever

experience having a family of her own. Falling for a confirmed bachelor was hardly the way to achieve her dream, she thought ruefully.

Bonnie's daydreams were suddenly interrupted by the snap of Jazelle's fingers. "Oh, this talk about babies got me sidetracked. I'm here to give you a message."

Frowning, Bonnie glanced at her phone. "A message? Did I miss someone's text?"

A crafty grin crossed the housekeeper's face. "This is an in-person message. Mose is waiting out on the patio. I tried to get him to come here to the office to speak with you, but he said he was too dirty and would muss up the floors. Hah! As if Blake and Chandler don't walk in with cow manure on their boots."

Mose! Was waiting to see her? Suddenly birds were singing and bells were ringing. "Mose is on the patio? Really?"

Her surprised reaction pulled a chuckle from Jazelle. "Yes, really. Why are you looking so astonished? Don't you think the man might want to see an attractive woman?"

Bonnie glanced down at her jeans and black tank top. She hardly looked her best, but with him waiting, there was nothing she could do about her appearance.

"I'm not wearing any makeup and my hair hasn't been brushed since early this morning."

Jazelle laughed as she followed Bonnie out of the office. "And you know something? None of those things matter."

Bonnie hurried on through the house and out to the kitchen, where Reeva and Sophia were busy getting dinner ready.

"Better get out there before the man runs off," Reeva tossed over her shoulder as Bonnie rushed toward the door leading out to the backyard.

"Gran, you couldn't run Mose off if you sprayed him with the garden hose," Sophia joked, then said to Bonnie, "Tell

Mose to come in and have dinner. We have plenty. It's Mexican night and Gran even made menudo. And no one even has a hangover—yet, that is. They might, after Jazelle makes palomas and margaritas."

"I'll tell him," Bonnie promised, then hurried out the door and down the rock steps.

As she crossed the lawn, she caught sight of Mose sitting at one of the picnic tables. The moment he spotted her approach, he took off his hat and placed it on the table, then walked out to greet her.

"Hello, Bonnie. I hope I didn't interrupt anything important." He held out his hands to her. "Jazelle insisted that you weren't busy."

She placed her hands in his, while the smile on her face was so wide she marveled that her cheeks weren't cracking. "You haven't interrupted anything. I'm so happy you're here," she assured him. "Are you finished up at the horse barn for the day?"

He continued to hold her hands and Bonnie felt a strong urge to step close enough to press the front of her body next to his. But the patio wasn't exactly hidden, and anyone looking out from the house or passing by could see them, and she didn't want to embarrass him, or herself.

Releasing her hands, he glanced at his wristwatch. "Actually, no. I have about ten minutes before I have to get back to the barn. Holt is expecting a buyer this evening and wants me to show a horse for him." He chuckled. "Like I'm the best one to show off this horse. Colt or Luke could do the job just as well or better."

Her smile was full of pride. "Apparently, Holt thinks you're the man for the job. But to be honest, I wish you didn't have to go back to work tonight. I wanted you to have dinner with us."

His brows shot up. "Dinner? Oh Bonnie, look at me. I'm

coated in dust and hay and manure. And by the time I'm finished, I'll look even worse. I couldn't sit at the Hollister dining table like this."

She thought for a second. "Okay, then you and I can eat in the kitchen. There's a spacious booth where Sophia and Colt eat most nights. And sometimes Reeva joins them. We can have our dinner there. It's Mexican-food night. Will you?"

He smiled down at her and she could see in his eyes that he wanted to accept her invitation.

"Okay. I'll be back. What time will you be eating?"

Thrilled at his answer, she said, "Around seven. But don't worry about the time. The food will be on the stove whenever you get here."

He reached for her hands and gave them a squeeze. "I didn't come by to wrangle an invitation for dinner. I wanted to let you know Holt is giving us a couple of hours off tomorrow afternoon. So if you're free, we'd have enough time to ride to the old ranch house."

"Of course, I'll be free! I'd love to go," she told him.

"I've been thinking about you," he said, his voice husky.

She felt her cheeks growing warm. If he only knew the thoughts she'd been having about him. "I've been thinking about you, too, Mose."

He awkwardly cleared his throat, then said, "After I got home last night, I worried that the ride might've been too long for you."

"Not at all. You probably can't tell by looking, but I'm in fairly good shape," she said jokingly. She wasn't about to admit she'd lain awake for hours, her mind whirling with every touch they'd exchanged, each word he'd spoken to her. But she was telling the truth when she said that the ride hadn't left her sore. It had only been her thoughts that were out of control.

His brown eyes glinted as his gaze traveled from her face all the way down to her sandaled feet. "I can tell."

His unexpected reply caused her to draw in a deep breath and she wondered if he could see how being near him filled her with indescribable joy.

He touched his fingertips to her cheek. "I'd better be going."

She nodded. "I'll be watching for you."

Turning, he grabbed up his hat. Cramming it on his head, he strode off to a ranch truck parked beyond the backyard fence. And as she watched him drive away, a swell of emotions filled her chest.

What was he doing, Mose asked himself as nearly two hours later, he parked his truck on the graveled drive in back of the big ranch house. Was he trying to win the biggest-fool-of-the-year award? If so, then he was well on his way to being crowned the champ.

From day one, he'd been telling himself Bonnie was off-limits to a man like him. And yet none of those inner lectures he'd been giving himself had made him see common sense. He couldn't think about the misery he was going to feel when she disappeared from his life. No, all he could focus on was the pleasure of being with her. Even if he was only talking to her or holding her hand.

He was walking toward the yard gate, when he spotted her hurrying down the back steps of the kitchen. She'd changed her jeans for a long skirt printed with red and pink flowers. A pink shirt was tied at the front of her waist, while the long sleeves were rolled up to her elbows. He couldn't imagine her looking any prettier than she did at this moment.

By the time he reached the gate, she was already there holding it open for him.

"Hello, Mose. I'm so happy you could make it."

"So am I."

She latched the gate behind him, then looped her arm through his, and Mose thought how the simple contact made him feel special and wanted.

"Sophia and Colt are just now filling their plates," she said. "So your timing is perfect."

"I would've been here sooner," he explained as they started toward the house. "But the buyer was extremely particular. He wanted to see the horse do everything except serve him a cup of coffee."

"Oh gosh, you must have been under a strain."

Grinning, he gave her a wink. "Only to see you."

She jokingly rolled her eyes. "Has anyone ever accused you of being cheesy?"

"Plenty," he said with a chuckle. "Don't let me get too near a microwave. I might melt."

She gave his arm a playful shake. "I think you're full of nonsense, Mose. But it's nice nonsense."

He patted the hand that was resting on his arm, then opened the door and gestured for her to precede him into the kitchen.

As soon as Mose and Bonnie stepped into the room, Colt called out from his seat at the booth. "Hey, come on, you two! Before Sophia and I eat up everything."

"I see you didn't wait for your buddy," Mose told him, then gave Bonnie a conspiring wink.

"Can I help it if I was starving?" Colt countered. "Besides, I figured you'd probably be at the barn showing horses until midnight."

Mose removed his hat and hung it on a rack near the door. "Holt finally pressed the man for an answer," he said to Colt. "And thankfully, they agreed on a price."

Placing a hand on his arm, Bonnie ushered him toward an industrial-sized cookstove equipped with several gas burners. Several pots and casserole dishes were sitting atop the heavy grates.

"Come on," she said. "The plates and utensils are here on the end of the cabinet."

After their plates were filled with an assortment of spicy Mexican food, they joined Colt and Sophia, who were sitting next to each other, leaving the opposite bench seat empty.

Once the two of them had slid in, Sophia said, "I took the liberty of pouring sweet iced tea in your glasses. But there are some margaritas left if you two had rather have one."

As far as Mose was concerned, he didn't need tequila to give his senses a kick. Having Bonnie sitting close to his side already had his head buzzing.

"This is fine for me," Mose told her. "I'm so tired, the alcohol might make me doze off and fall face forward in my plate. And I don't want to embarrass Bonnie."

Sophia's amused grin was aimed at Bonnie and Mose. "Bonnie wouldn't be embarrassed. If I know her, she'd prop you back up and wash your face for you."

With one brow arched in question, Mose looked over to Bonnie. "Would you?"

A tentative smile bent the corners of her lips. "Of course. You might smother with your face in a plate full of food."

Colt laughed loudly and Mose scowled at his friend. "You're such a nice guy."

"Sophia thinks so. Don't you, honey?"

Sophia leaned over and placed a little kiss on her husband's cheek. "Ninety-eight percent of the time. The other two percent is questionable."

The whole table laughed before Colt leveled an empathetic look at Mose. "You've had a long day."

Mose flexed his shoulders to ease the stiffness before he dug his fork into a cheese-smothered tamale.

"I don't mind," he said, then glanced at Bonnie. "Find anything interesting in your history dig today?"

Bonnie reached for her glass of iced tea. "A photo of Parnell with his name and the year 1936 written on the back. After a little research, I determined the vehicle in the background was fairly new at the time of the photo. And since the pic was snapped in front of the ranch house, Parnell must've been living here at the age of twenty-one. I'm hoping I'll find more as I go along."

"I heard Maureen say they're almost finished with rounding up the late calves," Sophia commented. "Once she gets caught up, she'll be pitching in to help you."

Colt looked doubtful. "Maureen getting caught up? That's unlikely. Not with Christmas coming and all the decorating and shopping not yet finished. Besides, no matter what's going on during the year, she's always busy."

Mose hoped Maureen stayed too busy to help unravel Parnell's life. The longer it took to complete the task, the longer Bonnie would be here on Three Rivers. And for now, that was the most he could wish for.

"Busy and on the go," Sophia said with a nod of agreement. "Tomorrow evening, she and Gil are going over to the Blue Stallion to have dinner with Isabelle and Holt. It's Wes's fourth birthday and they're having a party for him."

"Oh, so that's why Holt is giving us a little time off tomorrow," Mose remarked. "I thought it was for good behavior. Didn't you, Colt?"

Sophia groaned and Colt looked over at his wife. "What's the matter? Don't you think Mose and I can be good guys?"

"If you tried really hard at it, which I'm not sure you ever do," Sophia said, while giving Bonnie a conspiring wink.

Bonnie's glanced at Mose, and the twinkle he saw in her blue eyes made him wonder if she had a naughty side that she'd not yet revealed to him.

"I'm happy Mose is getting a little time off," Bonnie spoke up. "The two of us are going to ride to the original ranch house tomorrow afternoon. I'm excited to see the place."

From the corner of his eye, he could see Sophia and Colt exchange sly glances. Clearly, they had the idea something was beginning to simmer between him and Bonnie.

"How nice of you, Mose," Sophia said. "I've lived here on Three Rivers for four years and Colt has never offered to show the place to me."

"Oh, for Pete's sake, Sophia," Colt said to his wife. "You can't ride a horse for more than five minutes and you're terrified the whole time you're in the saddle. How do you expect to get there without climbing on a horse?"

"A Jeep? A truck?"

Colt leaned over and kissed Sophia's cheek. "You'd be shaken to bits."

She playfully wrinkled her nose at her husband. "Kate told me that before she and Blake got married, he drove her to the cabin in a truck. Obviously, she wasn't shaken up too much. She married Blake a short time later."

"And has since given birth to two sets of twins," Bonnie added slyly.

Colt gave his wife a suggestive grin. "Bonnie has a good point. I should drive you out to the cabin one day."

Her expression tender, she patted his arm. "I don't know about twins, but if the trip was guaranteed to produce one baby, I'd be thrilled."

Bonnie glanced at Mose, but she didn't say anything. He wondered what she was thinking. That the old homeplace was an ideal love nest? A perfect spot to seduce a woman? Hell, no telling what she'd be expecting from him tomorrow.

Colt cast another pointed glance at Mose. "Mighty nice of you, buddy, to take Bonnie riding. Especially when you rarely have time to spend off a horse's back."

Mose focused his gaze on the enchiladas piled next to the tamales. "I'm glad to help Bonnie with her history search."

Colt's wicked little chuckle implied he already knew that Mose was head over heels crazy about Bonnie.

Well, aren't you, Mose? Why don't you have the guts to admit it?

For the remainder of the meal, Mose managed to shut out the jeering questions. But try as he might, he couldn't ignore Bonnie's presence. They were sitting so close together her thigh was pressed against his, causing shafts of heat to rush down his leg. While the subtle scent of flowers emanating from her clothes was a constant reminder of how it had felt when he'd held her tight in the circle of his arms, how she'd tasted when he'd kissed her.

Yeah, Mose could admit he was becoming besotted with Bonnie, but he'd never have enough courage to reveal his feelings to her. No, to do that would be opening himself to rejection. And he couldn't take that risk again. Not now, or ever.

Chapter Ten

The next afternoon, when Bonnie and Mose set out for the old ranch house, the sky was clear and the sun warm enough to forgo heavy jackets. Unlike the desert area they'd ridden through three days ago, this trip led them through patches of forests consisting of golden-leaved cottonwoods and aspen, mixed with green pine and juniper. In other areas, low mountains were covered with tufts of grass and scrubby creosote bushes, while sage and mesquite grew along water-carved banks of meandering arroyos.

The farther they rode, the more shaded the trails grew. The cool air drifting through the woods was pungent with the scent of evergreens. Dinah was as obedient as ever, thankfully. Because most of the pathways were narrow, Bonnie was forced to keep the mare directly behind Bear. Occasionally, the gelding would glance around as if to make sure his girlfriend was keeping up and Bonnie wondered if Mose was thinking about her as much as Bear was thinking about Dinah.

Last night, when Mose declared it was time for him to head home, Bonnie had walked with him as far as the back porch. She'd not been disappointed when he'd pulled her into his arms and kissed her not once, but twice.

But were a few stolen kisses all he wanted from her?

Maybe he'd never be interested in deepening their relationship. The thought was as bleak as a stormy sky.

"We're almost there," Mose called back to her. "Ready for a rest?"

Now that the trail had widened somewhat, she urged Dinah forward until the mare was walking at Bear's side.

"I'm too excited to see the house to think about resting," she answered, then thoughtfully glanced around her. "I'm guessing we've ridden a few miles from the big ranch house. I wonder why Edmond and Helena decided to settle here first?"

"I figure the availability of water was their first concern," he answered, then cast her a sheepish grin. "I hadn't told you yet—I was going to let it be a surprise, but there's a pretty little waterfall and a pool not too far away from the back of the house. According to Gil, the falls comes from a natural spring and never runs dry."

Excitement spread a wide smile across her face. "A waterfall! Oh, you *have* surprised me!"

"Before we start home, we'll take the horses to the water hole and let them have a nice drink," he told her.

She lovingly patted Dinah's neck. "Good. I'd hate to think of Dinah being thirsty while she makes the long trek back to the horse barn."

His expression softened as he watched her comb her fingers through Dinah's mane. "You do love horses, don't you?"

"Very much. If I couldn't be around horses, my life would be—well, half empty."

He reached over and clasped her free hand in his. "I'm glad. Until you—well, none of the women I've dated could make this kind of trip."

She slanted him a pointed look. "Uh—none of the men I've dated could do it, either."

They both laughed and he squeezed her hand.

"Let's go look things over," he said.

They nudged the horses into a walk and a short minute later, emerged from a stand of giant cottonwood trees and into a small grassy area. Halfway across the tiny meadow, Bonnie spotted the old ranch house nestled at the foot of a rock cliff and shrouded on one side by a huge cottonwood with a stand of pines on the other.

"Oh! There's the house!" She exclaimed as she reined Dinah to a stop and stood up in her stirrups to peer at the weathered structure. "This is—"

To her dismay, she was suddenly too choked with emotion to speak. She felt Mose's hand gently grasping her shoulder, and she leaned into the touch gratefully.

"Are you okay?" he asked gently.

Nodding, she swallowed hard, then turned her head toward him. "Sorry, Mose. I didn't expect to—feel so much when I saw this place. It's really a bit overwhelming to actually see where my family began their lives out here in the West."

"I can only imagine." His fingers tightened on the ball of her shoulder.

Nodding, she said, "Come on, let's get closer. I'm anxious to look around."

They rode the horses deeper into the clearing, and after dismounting, Mose hitched both animals to a dead tree limb that had fallen a few yards away from the house.

Bonnie remained at Mose's side as they walked up to the front of the small log structure. Nearly a hundred and eighty years of weather had beaten the logs smooth and faded them to a pale gray color. A wooden planked door sat directly in the center of the building, while to the right side of the entry was a tiny window covered with a board shutter. There was no porch, but the roof provided enough overhang to shield the one flat rock that served as a step up to the door.

"In spite of its age, the cabin is in sturdy condition. Holt says the family keeps a close eye on the house and takes care of patches and repairs whenever something needs it," Mose told her.

"The house is crude. But strangely there's a rustic charm about it." She placed a hand against her chest as it filled with tender emotions she didn't quite understand. "Perhaps I see it that way because at one time it was my ancestors' home."

"I don't think it's just you. The cabin does have lots of character outside," he stated.

She glanced up at him. "Have you seen the inside?"

"I have. Not long after I came to work here, Gil and Maureen wanted me to ride out here with them. I got the impression they wanted to show me a small piece of Three Rivers legacy."

"Hmm. Wonder why they considered it important for you to learn some of the history of the ranch? I don't imagine they go to such lengths with every employee that hires on at Three Rivers."

He shook his head. "No. And I've often wondered why they made such a bother with me. I'm guessing that for some reason Maureen and Gil wanted me to build a deep connection to the ranch and the Hollisters. Maybe because I'd told Holt about my parents' divorce and they knew I came from a broken home—a split family—and felt I needed to see there are families who stick together. Not just for a while, but through centuries."

The weight of emotions swelling in her chest grew heavier as she imagined Mose as a teenager. Seeing his parents divorce and their home torn apart must have left him scarred and wondering if anything in life ever lasted. Especially anything worthwhile.

She said, "I don't know about Gil, because I'm still getting to know him. But there's something about Maureen that I noticed right off. She takes one look at a person and seems to understand their whole psyche. It's a little eerie. But the people she loves, she *really* loves. I think you're one of those people, Mose."

Shrugging, he cast her a sheepish glance. "Either you're misguided, or she is. I'm just a ranch hand."

He was more than that, she thought. So much more. But it was obvious that bragging on his skills or his character as a man made him self-conscious, which caused her to wonder if his attitude about himself stemmed from a woman in his past.

Just like you felt down on yourself for years because Ward rejected you, Bonnie. Surely, some woman likely stomped on Mose's heart. But don't get the idea you can heal it for him. You haven't even been able to heal yourself.

Blocking out the mocking voice in her head, Bonnie reached for his hand. "I'll ask Holt to give me his opinion about you. In the meantime, you're my guide. Aren't we going into the cabin? Or is it locked?"

"It's never locked. Better to let a trespasser walk in rather than have them break down the door," he explained. "In a few minutes, we'll go inside the cabin. I thought we'd explore the falls first."

"The falls! I very nearly forgot about them. Let's go!"

With his hand still wrapped around hers, he urged her past the house and into another wooded area of pines, desert willows and ash trees. The scent of the pines followed them as they walked a narrow trail that led through tangled clumps of briars and patches of prickly pear. Above their heads, birds chirped and fluttered among the limbs, while on the ground, a pair of rabbits scurried into the underbrush. Bonnie felt as if she was strolling into a wonderland of nature.

After they'd walked a few more yards, she tilted her head

to one side and listened closely. "I think I hear tinkling. We must be getting close to the falls."

"We're almost there," he said.

He'd barely had time to speak the words when Bonnie spotted the glimmer of water in the distance. As they drew closer, she saw a pool surrounded by boulders and low-growing bushes, some of which were covered with tiny red-and-white blooms. At the back side of the little pond, a curtain of water was spilling from the side of a steep cliff and trickling over a wall of layered rock.

"Oh Mose! This is like something out of a fairy tale!" Her eyes glistened with moisture as she looked up at him. "I'm so grateful you brought me here to see this incredible spot."

"Believe me, Bonnie. I'm enjoying it as much as you." He placed a hand against her back and gently nudged her forward. "If we look around the pool, we'll probably find some wildlife tracks. One of the best things about this place is it gives the deer and other animals a cool drink anytime they need one."

"Like a little oasis in the desert," she said.

Around the water's edge, they discovered several deer tracks and a few smaller tracks that appeared to belong to raccoons. To one side of the falls, a flat ledge of rock jutted out from the cliff and Bonnie couldn't resist taking a seat on the edge and trailing her fingers through the trickling water.

"Come sit with me, Mose." Her smile inviting, she patted a spot next to her. "I promise not to flip any water on you."

Smiling wryly, he took a seat a few inches away from her and stretched out his long legs to let his boots rest on the ground. "I'm not worried you'll get me wet. I'm more concerned about a rock falling from the top of the cliff and hitting me in the head."

Twisting her upper body around, she peered at the wall of rocky mountain rising up behind them. "I don't think any rocks will fall, but we can keep our hats on just in case," she said with an impish grin.

"I think you like living dangerously," he joked.

"I can't imagine the long dangerous trek Edmond and Helena made to get here to Arizona," she said. "Just imagine, how it must have been for them, carrying endless buckets of water from here to the house. I wonder why he didn't build it closer to the falls."

"He must've had his reasons." He glanced thoughtfully at her. "Has anyone ever talked to you about why Edmond came here to Arizona?"

She shook her head. "I've been trying to piece together the very early beginnings of the family and how the ranch began, but I've not found much about Edmond. Other than he and his wife, Helena, came from somewhere back East."

"What about children? Did they have any children before they first moved here? I can't imagine making such a dangerous trek with a child," he said.

"No, their first child, Joseph, was born about three years after they arrived here. Later, they had another son, George, and after him a girl, Cynthia. Unfortunately, George died in a mining accident when he was twenty. And Cynthia died at age four from diphtheria. I've been told that Joseph was the Hollister who really turned Three Rivers into a massive, productive ranch. He was my great-great-grandfather."

He said, "So it's fairly obvious that Maureen's son Joe is named after him."

"Yes. Joseph is Joe's great-great-grandfather, also. But back to your earlier question, I don't know what initially brought Edmond out here to Arizona. Has anyone told you the story?"

He shook his head. "Holt says his family has different ideas about Edmond. Gil and his late brother, Joel, believed

Edmond's plan all along was to start a ranch and build a herd of cattle. But Blake thinks otherwise. He believes Edmond came here in search of gold. He says it stands to reason the man had to have funds to construct a house and barns and purchase livestock. His idea is that Edmond found gold and used it later to build the ranch."

"Hmm. Sounds logical. But wouldn't there be old records of where Edmond filed a claim?"

"Not necessarily," he answered. "He probably kept the strike a secret to avoid thieves killing him for his gold."

Amazed by the whole idea, she said, "If that truly was the case, then there could be gold somewhere here on Three Rivers Ranch. Maybe even around the old house or this waterfall!"

"Hah! I didn't think to bring a pick and shovel with me," he teased. "But I would've if I'd known you would want to start digging."

She wrapped her hands around his arm and gave it a playful tug. "I'm not a fortune seeker. So we'll put off the gold digging for another day."

He slipped an arm around the back of her waist and helped her off the ledge. "Let's go," he said.

When they reached the cabin, Mose guided her to the back of the structure where a wide porch sheltered another heavy wooden door.

"This leads straight into the kitchen," he told her. "We should find an oil lamp on the table. I'll need to light it. Otherwise, it'll be too dark to see much of anything."

"I'll stay behind you," she told him.

Mose opened the door and pushed it wide enough to allow the late evening sun to filter into the opening. The light was enough for them to locate a small wooden table jammed against the wall. A hurricane lamp full of oil and a box of matches were sitting on top, waiting to be put to use.

"The place is a bit dusty," he said as he picked up the matchbox. "But for the most part it's usually kept tidy. A couple of ranch hands come out here fairly often and sweep up."

Bonnie stood at his side while he lit the lamp and adjusted the flame so that it was bright enough to illuminate the room without smoking up the globe.

Once he was finished with the lamp, he looked around to see Bonnie was turning in a slow circle to survey the room.

"Oh my, it's amazing to see this. On Stone Creek, there's a cabin on the mountaintop that Grandfather Lionel built back in the 1960s. Compared to this, it's practically new," Bonnie said in an awed voice.

There was a look of wonder on her face as she studied the walls of chinked logs and the low ceiling made of rough-hewn timbers.

"It does have a solid wood floor," he commented. "I expect back in those days having a real floor was considered fancy."

"Yes, I imagine Helena appreciated not having dirt floors," she replied.

At one end of the small space, there were several shelves attached to the wall to serve as cabinets, a few steps over sat a cast-iron wood-burning cookstove and, next to it, a small table with a white granite pitcher and matching wash pan.

"I can't imagine preparing a meal in this kitchen." She walked over to the cookstove and lifted one of the burner plates. "First of all, I wouldn't know how to cook on a wood-burning stove. I can build a fire, but I wouldn't know how to adjust the heat. I'd have burned everything to a crisp."

As he watched her inspect the stove, he realized there was so much about her he didn't know about. And even more he wanted to learn.

"Do you know how to cook?" he asked. "In a normal kitchen, I mean."

She glanced at him, her expression comical. "I do. I started helping Mom in the kitchen when I was barely old enough to see over the cabinet counter."

Surprised, he asked, "Your Mom cooks, too?"

"Why yes, Mom cooks for the whole bunch of us. Naturally I help her. And so does Clementine. But Clem would be the first to tell you that she doesn't know all that much about putting big meals together. Her skill is making simple meals at the sheep camp."

Needing to be near her, he walked over to where she stood. "So, on Stone Creek you don't have a cook like Reeva or Sophia?"

Her laugh in response was full of humor. "Oh my gosh, no. We're not that well-to-do."

More than curious, he had to ask, "Is Stone Creek ranch house very big?"

"I guess you'd call it fairly large. There are two stories and five bedrooms."

So she'd always lived with a certain amount of luxury, he thought. "Then, you must have a housekeeper."

Her short laugh was dry. "Not hardly. We all pitch in to keep the house tidy and the laundry caught up. Why? Did you think my family has the same standards of living as Maureen and Gil?"

Shrugging, he was glad the room was filled with enough shadows to hide the embarrassment on his face. "I wasn't sure. Sorry for asking personal questions. It's just that I'm trying to picture your life in Utah."

"I don't mind. Ask all the questions you'd like. But I think I recall telling you that Stone Creek didn't begin to compare in size and wealth of Three Rivers."

He grimaced. "You did tell me. But most places aren't that grand. Just because your family's ranch is smaller doesn't mean you're on the poverty list."

"True, we aren't. We've always been comfortable. But we don't have excess funds like Maureen and Gil. A large portion of the ranch's profit goes to maintaining and expanding it."

"I see." The Utah Hollisters apparently had money, but they believed in saving and investing it into their work. That was quite a bit different than Nicole and her family back in Texas. Because her mother had always done the household chores, she'd held the idea that she shouldn't have to lift a hand to do manual tasks. "Have your parents ever considered coming down here to Three Rivers for a visit? Surely your dad must be curious about where his grandfather once lived."

"He's very curious. But he's very busy, which makes it hard for him to get away from the ranch for any length of time. But my parents are planning on making the trip down here later in the summer, when both ranches aren't so busy with haying and roundup."

Her answer lifted Mose's spirits somewhat. Surely if her parents came down for a visit, Bonnie would come with them and he'd have a chance to see her again. But he didn't want to think that far into the future. Especially today when they were having this private time together.

Picking up the lamp, he gestured toward the open doorway leading into the other parts of the house. "Come on. Let's look at the other two rooms."

When they entered the adjoining room, Mose placed the lamp on an overturned wooden crate serving as a coffee table, then stepped over to the front wall and unlatched the window. The open square allowed fresh air inside, along with a shaft of sunlight and cacophony of birdsong.

"This must have been their living room. I wonder if they

cut down a cedar or pine and decorated it for Christmas," she mused aloud. "I don't imagine Helena had any fancy ornaments or garland. But those things aren't needed to celebrate Christ's birth."

"You're right about that," he said.

She moved closer to a couch and chair, which was upholstered in dark green fabric and, compared to the cabin, looked only a few years old. "I'm sure Edmond and Helena didn't have these back when they called the place home," she joked.

Mose chuckled. "No, but I wonder if the Hollisters brought furniture with them from back East, or if Edmond might've built something for them to sit and sleep on."

"Or found something at the nearest trading post," she suggested. "One thing appears obvious, he hadn't made a gold strike before he built this cabin. And I'm beginning to think Blake has the right idea about Edmond's motive for coming to Arizona. Think about it, Mose. The grand ranch house where the Hollisters live now couldn't have been built only from cattle-sale profits. He'd not been here long enough to have that huge of a herd. No, he made quick cash some other way."

"Yeah, this cabin is quite a contrast to the ranch house the family lives in now," Mose commented.

Nodding, she said, "The whole idea of how the ranch got started is intriguing. But I can't let myself get sidetracked with Edmond's life. I'm here to find out about Parnell."

Mose's gaze traveled over her soft features, and he realized her face, hair, voice, even her touch had all become incredibly dear to him. Strange, he thought, how his relationship with her had begun, and would most likely draw to an end, because of a man who'd died more than eighty years ago.

"I don't have any doubts that you'll uncover Parnell past life," he told her, then determined to end his worrisome thoughts, he inclined his head toward a doorway at the back of the room. "The bedroom is through there. Want to have a look?"

She flashed him a smile. "Sure."

Mose followed her into the next room and then realized he'd made a big mistake. Most of the space was taken up with a standard-sized bed with an iron-railed head and footboard and a colorful patchwork quilt covering the mattress. All it took was one look at the bed to send his mind on an erotic fantasy of him and her together, naked and making love.

He tried to shut off the image, but it only worsened as she moved to the side of the bed and ran a hand over the cover.

"What a pretty quilt. And there are pillows, too." She sat down on the edge of the mattress. "This feels great. Does anyone ever stay here overnight?"

Hoping to clear his mind, he drew in a deep breath and blew it out. "I honestly can't answer your question. I'm guessing they probably do. It's quiet and—secluded. Even the phone signal is zero out here, so a person wouldn't be interrupted with calls or texts."

She looked at him and he noticed a tentative smile quivering the corners of her lips. "So when you say this is a getaway from everything it's *really* a getaway."

He couldn't stop himself from sitting down next to her, or wrapping an arm around the back of her shoulders. "We shouldn't have come in here," he muttered.

Her gaze connected with his and he could see questions swimming in her blue eyes. Along with something he could only interpret as desire. The idea that she might want him, even half as much as he wanted her, was more than his brain could absorb.

"Why?" she asked.

Her one word question made him groan. "Because I've been fighting all afternoon to keep my hands off you. Now that we've stepped into this bedroom, it's getting even harder to hold back."

"And what is so wrong with that?" she asked. "I'm not going to break if you touch me."

Sultry shadows mixed with the innocent light in her blue eyes, and it was all he could do to keep from pulling her into his arms and fastening his mouth over hers. Yes, she would welcome his kisses, but they were so completely alone he feared they might be tempted to go beyond just kissing.

He let out a rueful sigh. "You don't understand, Bonnie. I might not be able to stop touching you."

"Have you ever thought that I might not want you to stop?"

"Bonnie. Bonnie."

Whispering her name was the only answer he could give her and then, before he could change his mind, he twisted his upper body toward her and pulled her into his arms. The moment she landed against his chest, her head fell back to give him perfect access to her lips.

As soon as their lips met, her arms wrapped around his neck and she pressed herself so tightly against him, he was amazed that either of them could breathe. But the closeness felt perfect and right and so did the taste of her kiss.

Chapter Eleven

Only a few seconds passed before Bonnie decided she'd truly walked into a wonderland. It was a place she never wanted to leave. Mose was kissing her with a fervor that robbed her of her breath and spun a wild kaleidoscope of colors behind her closed eyes. And with everything inside her, she clung to him.

When he lowered them both onto the bed, she hardly recognized the fact that her shoulder was sinking into the mattress. She was only aware of hot desire flashing through her like streaks of jagged lightning. The taste of his lips was like gulping down dark wine. The sensation went straight to her head and blocked out everything but him.

As his lips continued to feast on hers, she ran her hands over his shoulders, down his arms and across his back. His muscles were like bands of iron and the heat from his body was adding to the simmering sensations swirling somewhere deep within her.

Was this how it felt to make love to a man, she wondered. The feelings coursing through her were wild and shocking and completely glorious. And she never wanted it to end. It couldn't end, she thought. Not until this needy ache in her womanhood had been sated and her mind was capable of thinking clearly.

And then, suddenly, the euphoria she was experiencing was fractured as he tore his mouth from hers and pressed his face against her neck. "Bonnie—I must be losing my mind! I shouldn't be doing this. But you taste so good—feel so good."

Somehow her arms managed to tighten around him. "Oh Mose. I didn't know this would feel so—fantastic. I never thought kissing could be like this. And you should be kissing me—now—again," she whispered urgently.

A groan sounded in his throat before he moved his head just enough to fasten his lips over hers.

This time when he kissed her, Bonnie ceased to think. All she knew was that she was in Mose's arms and he was turning her body into one molten piece of flesh.

It wasn't until his hand cupped the mound of one breast and she wrapped her leg over his that he reared his head back and stared at her with dark, worried eyes.

"Mose—what—"

Before she could ask him what was wrong, he sat up and eased slightly away from her. Dazed and confused, Bonnie stared at his back and waited for him to explain.

"I didn't plan this, Bonnie," he said, his voice low and husky. "When we kissed I—wasn't expecting either of us to—lose control."

He made it sound as though they'd very nearly committed a crime, and the idea cut her deeply. Every moment she'd been in his arms, each second his lips had been on hers, had been an incredible journey for her. And maybe that's what he was trying to tell her, she thought. He just hadn't liked it enough to want to continue.

"I'm sorry you weren't feeling it, Mose," she said quietly. "And I sure wouldn't want you to do something that would cause you regrets later on."

He twisted around to look at her, and Bonnie couldn't decide whether she was seeing disbelief or humor, or a mixture of both on his face.

"Weren't feeling it? Regrets?" he repeated as though her words had been spoken in a foreign language. "Is that what you think?"

Pushing herself to a sitting position, she faced him. "There's not much else I can think, Mose. You're the one who put an end to things."

With a helpless groan, he looked up at the ceiling. "I had to, Bonnie! Otherwise, we might have ended up having sex and—well, that's something we, uh, can't just jump into."

"Oh. So you've never had spontaneous sex with a woman?" she asked in a dry tone. "Somehow I can't believe that."

Groaning again, he raked a hand through his hair, then looked at her. "This isn't about me and other women. It's about you and me. And I— It's all different with you, Bonnie."

She was trying not to feel rejected, but it was very hard when she could see he was obviously struggling to make excuses for ending the heated exchange between them.

"You mean, because I'm not very experienced?"

"No! That has nothing to do with anything!" He released a frustrated breath and then reached for her hand. "I'm thinking—you're special to me, Bonnie. And I don't want us to ruin things between us by jumping into something as serious as—"

"Making love?" she finished for him. "Why can't you just come out and say it, Mose? Or if the word *love* makes you that uncomfortable, just think of it as having sex."

His lips stretched to a thin line of disapproval before he turned his head and looked away from her. "I can't call it *making love*, Bonnie. I don't think— We, uh, need to know each other better before we reach that stage. And I can't call it *sex* because that image just doesn't fit you."

Her heart felt as heavy as a rock as she stood. "You're right. It doesn't fit me. At least that's what I've been told by other men. It was stupid of me to think you were any different from them."

She hurriedly left the bedroom and was striding through the kitchen with intentions of going outside to the porch, when Mose caught up to her.

With a hand on her shoulder, he spun her around to face him, and her heart ached when she saw regret twisting his features.

"Bonnie, wait a minute. You're misunderstanding everything I've been trying to say."

"Really? It all sounded very clear to me." She shook her head. "Don't worry about it, Mose. I'm not angry with you. I'm just a little upset with myself. I—lost control and I shouldn't have. You're not interested in me. Not seriously. And just having sex with a man who isn't even sure he wants it isn't me. So you were right to stop things when you did."

With a tiny growl in his throat, he pulled her into his arms and, after tucking her head beneath his chin, pressed his cheek against her hair. "Sweet Bonnie, you're still wrong. I stopped us because you're *too* special to me. Our relationship is something I want you to be sure about. I don't want us to end up in bed together because the chemistry between us boiled over. I want it to mean more than that."

Her eyes misted over as she tilted her head back and looked up at him. "Are you trying to say you want me, but you want it to be at the right time and at the right place?"

A faint smile quirked the corners of his mouth. "Exactly. I just couldn't say it as well as you." He lowered his head and pressed several light kisses along her cheekbone. "I want you, Bonnie. Probably more than you realize. And these feelings I have for you are all new to me. I need to sort them out and decide what they mean—for me and for you. And I'm thinking you need to do some sorting, too. Okay?"

Wrapping her arms around his waist, she hugged him tightly. She believed he was being sincere. She also knew he was right. They did need to think and sort out their feelings. But at this very moment, she had to admit she was disappointed. "Okay," she whispered.

They stood that way for a long moment before he finally eased her out of his arms.

"We'd better be going," he said huskily. "I'll shut the window and blow out the lamp."

After the two of them left the little house, they unhitched the horses and led them down to the waterfalls. Once the animals had drunk their fill, Mose helped her into the saddle.

As they rode away from the falls and past the little log house, Bonnie couldn't help but feel a pang of regret. She'd probably never have the chance to visit this homeplace again. Even worse, she'd lost her opportunity to make love to Mose there.

Reach for what you want and hold on.

Bonnie sighed as her sister's words drifted through her thoughts. She'd reached for Mose and she'd held on tight, but he'd still slipped away. So what kind of advice would Beatrice give her now? To reach again, only hold on tighter the next time? Or to simply accept the fact that Mose wasn't meant to be in her life?

The questions haunted her throughout the long ride back to the ranch house.

The next evening, as Mose drove home from a hard day in the training pen, he told himself he should be a happy man. He had a dream job, a nice house, plenty of good friends and a view beyond his living room window that was right out of a Western magazine. The Hollisters treated him like family and he had no doubts that if he ever had a serious problem, they'd always be there to back him up. For the first time ever, he had a real home. A permanent home.

Then, there was Bonnie. She was a lovely young woman inside and out. Until he'd met her, he'd not known he could derive so much pleasure from simply being in a woman's company. Just seeing her smile, hearing her voice made everything around him seem brighter and more beautiful. And that was the major reason he wasn't happy. He was downright depressed at the idea he could be falling in love with Bonnie.

For a few minutes yesterday at the old Hollister ranch house, he'd totally forgotten himself. He'd been gripped with the desire to make love to her to the point where he'd nearly forgotten about everything else. Even today, he was still amazed that he'd found the willpower to pull away from her.

Make love. Make love.

Mose had felt sort of sick inside when Bonnie had suggested that he'd prefer to think of it as sex rather than lovemaking. He'd also felt like the biggest fraud in Yavapai County. Because deep down, a little voice had been saying if he took her to bed, it truly would be an act of love. And that scared the hell right out of him.

Saying goodbye to a loved one was torture. As a teenager, he'd never forget the empty helplessness he'd felt when, after his parents' divorce, he and Mitch had told their mother goodbye and watched her walk out the door and go live in another town. Since then, he'd vowed to never put himself in such a vulnerable position again. And he hadn't. Even when Nicole had ended their relationship, the only thing that had really hurt was his pride. But things were different with Bonnie. He feared his heart was already involved.

He was doing his best to push the thoughts aside when he finally parked the truck in front of the house. He was tired and hungry. A cold beer and a plate of food would hopefully lift his dark mood.

Just as he was about to climb to the ground, the phone in his pocket vibrated and with a heavy sigh, he paused long enough to check the ID.

Colt's name beneath the number had him quickly punching the accept button. "What's the matter? Already missing me?" he asked dryly.

Colt chuckled. "With my boots off and Sophia handing me a plate full of Hollister beef, I'm not missing anything. But I am a little worried."

Not bothering to climb out of the truck, Mose settled back in the seat. "Why? What's happened?"

"Nothing has happened. I'm just concerned about you."

"About me? I don't know why. I'm fine," Mose insisted, then frowned. "Did I forget to do something important today?"

"Mose, are you kidding? You never do anything wrong at work. I just happened to notice you seemed a little subdued today. Is your family back in Texas okay?"

Mose pushed back the brim of his hat and wiped a weary hand across his forehead. Obviously, he'd not done a very good job of masking his dispirited mood. "Last time I spoke with them, everyone was fine. Dad is probably working too hard. But that's standard for him."

"Yeah. So my and Luke's dad is the same way, but he doesn't listen to our advice about slowing down," Colt replied. "Then, are you feeling blue because Christmas is coming and you won't be seeing your family through the holidays? You know, Holt will give you time off to go visit them."

"My family is scattered from here to there. I'd have to travel over half of Texas to see them. No. I'm fine with visiting with them over the phone."

"Well, if it's not your family, then, I'll just come straight out and ask you what's your problem," Colt said.

Mose muttered a curse word under his breath. "What makes you think I have one?" he asked crossly. "You think I'm supposed to be laughing and joking all day long? Hell, what's wrong with being quiet for a while?"

His outburst was so out of character that Colt went silent for a long stretch. Finally, he said, "Nothing. If you're normally a quiet kind of guy. Which you aren't."

Mose felt awful. Not just because he was torn over Bonnie but because Colt was the best friend he'd ever had and Mose had snapped his head off when the guy was only trying to help.

"Sorry, Colt. I'm being a jerk. I've sorta been a jerk all day, haven't I?"

"Sort of. But that's okay. We all have bad days," Colt said, then asked, "Did something go wrong with you and Bonnie yesterday? I know you were looking forward to the ride to the cabin. But today—well, other than your family, she's the only thing I can think of that might have put such a crease in your forehead."

"Wrong? No. Everything went great," Mose answered. "The whole ride was—too good, actually."

"How can something be too good?"

With the phone still jammed to his ear, Mose climbed out of the truck and started up the stone walkway to the house. "Like too much beer on a weeknight," Mose said flatly. "It's good while it's going down. But the next day you feel like hell."

"Oh, so you're telling me you enjoyed your time with Bonnie too much," Colt replied in a calculating voice. "I'm beginning to get the picture now. You're worried that you're falling for Bonnie. You think you're setting yourself up for a heartache. Right?"

Mose let himself into the house. "Sort of."

Colt snorted. "There's no *sort of* about it. So what happened between the two of you to put you in such a foul mood?"

Trying not to let his mind dwell on the image of the two of them lying tangled in each other's arms on the bed, Mose took off in a quick stride to the kitchen. "Look, Colt, what happened is—I realized how much I like Bonnie's company. I realized I feel differently about her than any other woman. And I—okay, I'll just come out and admit it. I don't want to think about her leaving Three Rivers."

There was a long pause and Mose used the break in the conversation to pull a long-necked beer from the fridge. Then, holding the phone to his ear with the aid of his shoulder, twisted off the lid.

"Have you told Bonnie how you feel?"

Mose grimaced. "She knows I'm fond of her."

Colt snorted a second time. "*Fond!* Hell, Mose, you can do better than that! You need to tell her you *love* her!"

The bottle in Colt's hand froze before it could reach his lips. "*Love?* I never mentioned anything about loving Bonnie!" Mose shot back at him.

"You didn't have to. I can read between the lines," Colt stated smugly. "So it won't do you any good to argue the point with me. Bonnie is the one who needs to hear the truth from you."

Mose gulped a large swallow of beer before he said, "Look, Colt, you're going way too fast. I've not known Bonnie long enough. It takes time for something as serious as you're talking about to develop. And we've not had that time together—yet!"

Colt chuckled knowingly. "Yeah, sure. I took one look at Sophia and knew she was the one."

Mose swallowed another mouthful of beer. "You also knew Sophia was on Three Rivers Ranch to stay. While it's clear as the Arizona sky that Bonnie will be leaving soon—probably before Christmas. Big difference, buddy."

"Okay, I see where you're coming from. But you can't give up. Anything might happen to change things."

Mose could already picture what was eventually going to happen. Bonnie would say goodbye with a smile and a kiss. She might even shed a tear, simply because she was softhearted. But that wouldn't stop her from flying back to Stone Creek Ranch. The home she loved. The home she'd said she'd never leave.

Closing his eyes, Mose massaged his tired, gritty eyes, then blew out a heavy breath. "This isn't going to end well, Colt. But even knowing that, I can't stay away from her. And what makes it worse, she doesn't understand why I'm trying to keep my distance."

"Neither would I."

"It's a moot point anyway, because I couldn't stay away from her even if I tried," Mose admitted ruefully.

"I'm glad to hear it."

Not yet bothering to switch on a light, Mose stared across the shadowy kitchen. He didn't need a light to see Bonnie's beautiful face floating before his eyes.

After blowing out a heavy breath, he said, "Even if her leaving wasn't an issue, I can't forget she's a ranching heiress, Colt. She's a Hollister. And I'm just Mose Martel."

"I've seen the way the ranching heiress looks at *just* Mose Martel. Don't sell yourself short, my friend. And that's enough pep talk from me for the time being. Anyway, Sophia has dessert ready. I'll see you in the morning."

Even though Colt ended the call, Mose continued to stand by the refrigerator, staring blindly across the room.

Was he selling himself short? True, he hadn't been able to hold on to Nicole. But Bonnie wasn't Nicole and he needed to remember that fact. He also needed to follow Colt's advice and not catastrophize about the future until it arrived.

Carrying the beer and his phone over to the kitchen table, he sank into one of the wooden chairs, then lifted off his hat and hung it on the back of the adjacent chair. A quick glance at the time told him the Hollisters were probably finished with dinner, so with any luck, Bonnie might be free to answer his call.

After three rings, he was beginning to have his doubts she was going to pick up the phone, but then her voice was in his ear and the sound of it filled him with a sweet sort of contentment.

"Hello, Mose. I'm so glad you called."

"Am I interrupting your dinner? By this time, I thought the Hollisters would probably be finished with the evening meal, but I couldn't be sure."

"Actually, I think they're all still in the dining room. I ate here in the kitchen with Reeva."

So that meant Colt and Sophia were already home when he called a few minutes ago, Mose thought. Which was a little unusual for the couple. They usually ate in the kitchen of the big house.

"What about Colt and Sophia?" he asked. "Why didn't they hang around and eat with you two?"

"Sophia was feeling a bit tired, so they took their food home where she could rest," she explained. "Once the family finishes eating, I'm going to help Reeva and Jazelle clean up."

"I see. Well, I'm sure you're wondering why I'm calling."

He shifted around on the chair, feeling like a teenager asking the prom queen for a dance.

"I was hoping you called because you were missing me and wanted to hear my voice."

He couldn't stop a grin from spreading across his face and he wondered why he'd been in such a funk all day.

"I have missed you today and it does me good to hear your voice."

"I'm glad," she murmured.

He sucked in a bracing breath. "Actually, I'm calling to see if you'd like to have dinner with me tomorrow night. My intentions were to take you to a nice restaurant in town. But I just remembered, I'll be working a little too late to make the trip into Wickenburg. Do you think you could manage to eat my cooking? It would give me a chance to show you my place, too."

When she didn't answer immediately, Mose figured she was trying to come up with a polite excuse. "Uh—Bonnie, if you'd rather not come—"

"No! I mean, I'd love to have dinner and see your home!" she said in a happy rush. "You just took me by surprise, that's all. But are you sure you want to go to the trouble of cooking? I'm just as happy to eat a sandwich or something out of a can."

She wanted to make things easy for him, which underscored the obvious difference between her and Nicole, who'd often demanded he take her to fancy restaurants. Suddenly Colt's advice came back to him.

Don't sell yourself short, Mose.

His friend was right, Mose thought. He wasn't that same young man who'd traveled from one ranch to another, seeking out daywork or breaking horses for whatever bit of wage he could make.

Smiling to himself, he said, "If I end up opening cans. I promise to spice up whatever comes out of them."

She laughed. "What time should I show up?"

"With any luck I'll be home by six thirty. So come anytime after that. Do you know how to get here?"

"I'm sure Sophia can give me directions. I'll find you."

"Great! Then I'll see tomorrow evening," he said.

"Yes. Tomorrow evening. Good night, Mose."

"Good night, Bonnie."

He hung up the phone and as he rose from the chair, he was struck with a happy burst of energy. Bonnie would be here tomorrow night! As soon as he chucked down a couple of sandwiches, he had some sprucing up to do.

At the double sink, he washed his hands and face and was pulling a loaf of bread from a bread box on the cabinet when he heard scratching and loud meows at the back door.

Flipping on an overhead light, he walked across the room and opened the door to find his two cats, the claws of their front paws latched into the screen of the storm door.

"Okay, you two, you don't have to destroy the screen to tell me you want your supper." He let the cats into the kitchen, then shut the door behind them. "Come on."

The tabby cats, a gray male named Seymour and an orange female he called Margo, trotted after him as he crossed over to a cabinet counter. While he put their feed bowls on the floor and filled them with dry morsels, the cats meowed loudly and wove around and through his legs.

"Listen you two, we're going to have company tomorrow night. A pretty lady is going to come see us and I expect you to behave. And if you're good cats, I might give you a can of sardines as a reward. Got it?"

Both cats meowed as if they understood every word Mose had said to them, then dropped their heads and dug into their bowls. Mose gave each one a stroke down the back, then went about making himself a pair of sandwiches out of cheese and cold cuts.

He sat down with the sandwiches and a bag of potato chips and began to eat. After downing a couple of bites, his phone pinged with an incoming message from Bonnie.

What should I bring tomorrow night?

With a wide smile on his face, he typed out one word.

Yourself.

The next day after lunch, Bonnie was at work in the ranch house office, slowly sifting through a container filled with old newspapers and photographs. So far, she'd found a few articles listing Parnell's name, but none of them had offered any clues as to his character or his life once he'd left Three Rivers.

However, after days of looking at pictures, one thing had clearly stood out to her. In the latter half of the 1930s, Parnell was abruptly absent from all of the family images. And the few society articles she'd found in local newspaper clippings hadn't mentioned the young man joining the family at charity events or other local gatherings. No question about it, Parnell had been the black sheep of the family. Bonnie just couldn't find out why he'd been disowned by his father, Joseph. Unfortunately, the lawyer who'd handled Joseph's will and testament had passed on many years ago. He'd surely been aware of the reasons behind Joseph disinheriting his son, but he didn't seem to have shared any of those secrets in print before ending up in his grave.

She was wondering if there was a chance she might run

across more of the lawyer's documents or letters when a light knock sounded on the door. Maureen stepped into the room wearing her cowboy hat and work jeans. With roundup still going on, Bonnie couldn't imagine Maureen leaving the ranch yard for any reason.

"Maureen, has something happened? I thought fall roundup wouldn't be wrapped up until tomorrow."

Walking over to a far corner of the room, Maureen pulled off her hat and hung it on a hall tree. "We managed to get the last of the cow/calf pairs rounded up this morning. Those calves are being branded as I speak. So now that things are winding down, Gil insisted I come on to the house. He's feeling guilty because we haven't been much help to you."

Rising from the desk chair, Bonnie walked over to her. "Gil shouldn't be concerning himself about me. You two are busy enough without trying to solve a family saga. Besides, there isn't any hurry about this, is there?"

Maureen smoothed a hand over her ponytail, as she leveled a guarded look at Bonnie. "Have you talked with your father lately?"

The question caught Bonnie by surprise. "Dad? No. Not in a few days. Why? Have you?"

Nodding, Maureen said, "He called yesterday. Of course, he asked if we'd been making any headway on Parnell's life story. I told him we hadn't really learned much, other than Parnell was a black sheep."

Bonnie darted a suspecting look at Maureen. "Is Dad getting impatient for me to come home? He's probably missing my work in the office. And my help with Mom, getting things ready for the holiday. It's only a couple of weeks until Christmas."

The notion of packing up and leaving Three Rivers was something Bonnie didn't want to ponder. She needed more time with Mose. And not just a few more days, or weeks. Her feelings for Mose had grown to such a point, she wasn't sure a lifetime with him would be enough. But having a future with Mose would depend on whether she could convince him that the two of them were meant to be together.

"I could tell by the sound of his voice that he's missing you." Maureen reached out and gave Bonnie's shoulder a squeeze. "I hope you're not cross with me, but I took the liberty of telling him that you're seeing a young man. And most likely, you'd want to stay here on the ranch longer—I think I used the word *indefinitely*."

Bonnie stared at her in shock. "Oh my! You told him that?"

Her expression smug, Maureen gave her shoulder another squeeze. "I did. And I wasn't wrong about your feelings for Mose, was I?"

Bonnie could feel her cheeks turning pink. "I guess when it comes to Mose, I'm as clear as a piece of plastic wrap. But still, you really said I'd be staying indefinitely? Maureen, that's—" Pausing, she shook her head. "Mose likes me, but he's not into anything long-term. His interest in me is only temporary."

A shrewd smile crossed Maureen's face. "Right now, I expect Mose doesn't know what he wants. But he'll see the light. And when that happens you need to be ready."

Bonnie awkwardly cleared her throat. "Uh—I should probably tell you I'm going to have dinner with Mose tonight. He's invited me over to his place. He's cooking."

Maureen's little laugh was triumphant. "Sounds to me like Mose is already beginning to figure out what he wants."

"I hope—well—I'm looking forward to going." Turning, Bonnie thoughtfully walked over to the computer desk where she'd placed a stack of photos and old letters she'd not yet looked through. "So what did Dad say when you told him I was interested in a man? I imagine his head was reeling."

"He was a bit surprised," Maureen admitted. "But overall he seemed pleased. Especially after I explained how Mose is a great, hardworking guy."

More heat rushed back into Bonnie's cheeks as she picked up a handful of the photos and turned to face Maureen. "I imagine someone in my family has probably told you I've—never been much on dating. They all believe I'm going to end up an old spinster."

Shaking her head, Maureen moved across the room until she reached a closet door located on the back. "When I first met your mother and we were discussing our children—like mothers do—she mentioned how years ago you'd had a rotten experience and basically lost trust in men and yourself. Is this true?"

Bonnie absently placed the photos back to the desktop. "You've summed up my social life in college and beyond pretty well, Maureen. For a long time, I didn't want to venture off the ranch for any reason," she said ruefully. "And then Jack married Van and—well, you know Van. She has a way about her that makes people see the best in themselves. Through her, I began to realize it was time I faced the world again."

"Yes, Van has always been special to all of us. Now that she lives on Stone Creek, we miss her. But we're glad she's happy with Jack, and now they have a son. Finding love and being happy is what it's all about, Bonnie. And you shouldn't be worrying about getting back to Utah for Christmas. Or what your parents are thinking, or your siblings. Make sure you're happy, that's the main thing." She grinned at Bonnie. "And from what I see, Mose puts a rosy glow on your cheeks."

Mose gave her more than rosy cheeks, Bonnie thought. He made her feel like a desirable woman. Something she'd never thought possible. Something she'd believed was a feeling reserved for other women, not her.

"To be honest, Maureen, when Dad told me he wanted me to travel down here to Three Rivers, I never thought I'd be meeting anyone like Mose. He's—uh, not like any man I've ever known."

"Nice surprise, huh?" Maureen asked with a knowing smile.

"The nicest."

At the back of the room, Maureen opened the closet and motioned for Bonnie to join her. "Come over here and help me lift this box. It's big and filled to the brim."

"With what? I thought you'd already found all of the ranch's old papers."

"I thought so, too. But Blake pulled this from an old safe up in the attic and carted it down last night," Maureen replied. "Three Rivers Ranch originated a hundred and eighty years ago and a lot of Hollisters have been born between then and now. So tons of paperwork pertaining to the ranch and the family has been collected over the years. We might get lucky and stumble on to something important."

Curious now, Bonnie quickly joined her at the closet. "Maureen, I was thinking earlier about the idea of Joseph disinheriting his son. Obviously, he had his will altered, which means legal letters and documents had to be written and signed. If we could find some of the legal writings of the family lawyer, there might be explanations attached."

"It's very possible," she agreed. "So let's get this box over to the desk and start digging."

Together they lifted the large box from the floor of the closet and placed it near the larger of the two desks.

While Bonnie untaped the flaps on the top, Maureen picked up the phone and rang Jazelle's number.

"Jazelle, if you're not too busy, could you bring a pot of coffee to my office. Bonnie and I need a pick-me-up." After a short pause, she said, "No. Nothing to eat. I don't want to ruin my appetite for the lasagna Reeva is making. And Bonnie doesn't want to spoil her appetite because she's eating Mose's cooking tonight."

Jazelle apparently made a comical reply because Maureen suddenly laughed. "Okay, I'll tell her."

She hung up the phone and looked over at Bonnie. "Jazelle says your head will be in the clouds and you won't know whether you have an appetite or not."

Blushing again, Bonnie let out a good-natured groan. "Jazelle is a hopeless romantic."

Her smile shrewd, Maureen said, "So are you, Bonnie."

Romantic? No. Bonnie had always considered herself a practical woman. Not the dreamy-eyed swooning type who longed for the touch of a man. But after meeting Mose something had happened to her. Now she could hardly wait until tonight to show him she'd thought long and hard about the two of them making love, or having sex.

No matter which way he wanted to view the connection, this time she was determined not to let him slip away.

Chapter Twelve

Even though Mose's house had a little dining area furnished with a nice maple table and chairs and a matching china hutch, he usually ate in the kitchen. Being alone and wolfing down sandwiches or leftovers didn't exactly make for a dining room type of meal. But tonight he wanted to have everything as nice as he could make it for Bonnie.

He'd set the table with his best plates and glasses and even dug some linen napkins, which had apparently belonged to Maureen's mother, from a drawer in the china hutch. He didn't have any idea of how to fold them correctly, but he figured just having them next to the plates would be a step above a paper towel. On his way home from the ranch yard, he'd stopped and picked a few wildflowers for a centerpiece for the table. He only hoped the pickling jar he'd been forced to use as a vase wouldn't ruin the effect.

He was in the kitchen, dumping an ice tray into a plastic container when he heard Bonnie drive up in the front of the house. The reality that she'd arrived caused his hands to tremble as he quickly shoved the container of ice into the freezer and hurried out to the front of the house to greet her.

She'd already departed the truck and was halfway down the rock walkway by the time Mose stepped onto the porch. As soon as she spotted him, she smiled and waved.

"Hi, Mose! Am I late?"

Smiling back at her, he didn't bother glancing at his watch before he stepped off the porch and walked out to meet her. And all the while he moved toward her, his gaze was riveted on the white blouse and the V neck that dipped to a point between her breasts. The sleeves were rolled up past her elbows and the tail tucked into the tiny waist of a red-flowered skirt that swished around her calves. On her feet were a pair of black cowboy boots with red-and-white-flowered inlays, and Mose was experienced enough with boots to know they'd cost more than a pretty penny.

When he reached her side, he promptly planted a kiss of greeting on her cheek. "Your timing is perfect," he told her. "And I need to add, you look very beautiful this evening."

She reached for his hand and slid her fingers through his. "Thank you, Mose. I left the ranch house a little early. I wasn't sure how long it would take me to get here."

He squeezed her soft little fingers and marveled at how happy it made him to see her again. "You made it just in time to have enough daylight to look around outside. Unless you're in a hurry to go in and eat."

"I'm in no hurry. I'd like to see everything." Her gaze moved beyond his shoulder to the front of the house. "This is all so lovely, Mose. And the cottonwood next to the house still has nearly all its golden leaves."

"Once the leaves fall, it makes a thick carpet. 'Cause I don't rake them." Chuckling, he gestured helplessly to the ground beneath their feet. "I let Mother Nature blow them away. Besides, they cover up the sparse grass. If I fertilized and watered the lawn it would flourish, but water is too scarce for that sort of thing."

"The yard goes perfectly with the stucco house. I like the tan color trimmed with dark brown. And the terra-cotta-tiled roof just sets it off," she told him. "Plus you have a saguaro in your yard. It makes me feel like I'm really out West."

He laughed. "You *are* really out West, Bonnie."

She looked at him and smiled a bit sheepishly. "Yes, I am. And I should tell you what I thought when I first saw you at the airport."

"Let me guess. You were wishing Maureen or someone else had come to taxi you back to the ranch?" he asked jokingly.

Laughing softly, she slipped her arm around the back of his waist and gave him an affectionate squeeze. "No. I was thinking you looked like a gunslinger who just stepped out of the Red Dog Saloon."

With a comical frown, he asked, "Where's the Red Dog Saloon? I might need to look this place over."

"It's only in my imagination."

They both laughed and then Mose said, "A gunslinger, eh? I guess you could say I'm like your brother Flint. I've hung up my holsters."

Following her example, he slipped his arm around the back of her waist. "Come on and I'll show you the backyard."

With their arms anchored at the back of each other's waist, they strolled around the east end of the house, where a little patio extended from the back door. The square was shaded by two tall junipers.

He said, "The creek is just beyond those trees. You might enjoy looking at it. Sometimes there are mule deer hanging around there or a squadron of javelinas. Have you seen any of those wild animals since you've come to Three Rivers?"

"You mean the animals that look like feral hogs but aren't really hogs at all?" she asked. "I've heard about the critters, but haven't seen one yet."

Her question caused him to chuckle. "Yeah, they look like hogs that aren't really hogs. They're a peccary, an animal that originated in South America, but I only learned about javelinas after I moved here. Even though some of them live in West Texas."

"I imagine you've learned about lots of different things since you moved here," she said. "I have and I've only been here a short time."

"What have you learned, other than the fact that I'm not a gunslinger?" he teased.

She thoughtfully tapped a finger against her chin. "Oh, that I like living in the desert. I like the wide blue skies and all the different kinds of cacti and chaparral. And I like the people. Especially one tall cowboy," she said.

There was a playful tone to her voice yet he heard sincerity in her words. For a woman of Bonnie's caliber to have feelings for him filled Mose with a mixture of awe and pride.

"Lucky me," he murmured.

"No. Lucky us," she said with an impish grin.

He was thinking about lowering his head and kissing the patches of sunlight flickering upon her cheeks when she suddenly dropped her arm from his back and moved over to the patio.

Standing in the middle of the rock floor, she turned a full circle. "Oh, this patio floor is just like the one at the big ranch house! It's beautiful!"

Mose was always amazed that Bonnie found pleasure in things he'd not expected her to even notice. "It's small, but it serves the purpose."

She stepped over to a wooden Adirondack chair and trailed her finger over the armrest. "Do you sit out here often? Drinking coffee here early in the morning would be nice. Especially if you had a bird feeder hanging in one of the junipers."

Was she asking in a roundabout way if he sat on the patio

with other women? The idea was laughable. He didn't share his home with female friends. At least, he hadn't until her.

"It sounds like it would be nice," he agreed. "But during the summer months, I get to the horse barn earlier in the mornings so the horses can be worked in the cooler hours. And in the winter months, I'm usually hooked up helping Holt with the foaling mares."

"You're like my Dad and brothers. They never have much leisure time."

He smiled at her. "I've had more leisure time since you've been here than I've ever had since I came to work for Three Rivers. I think Holt is being extra good to me because he—uh, wants me to have time with you before you—go back home to Stone Creek."

When she didn't immediately reply, he glanced over to see she was gazing off at the thick stand of trees bordering the creek. Her expression was a mixture of emotions he couldn't begin to read and he could only wonder what was going through her thoughts. Was she looking forward to returning to her family in Utah? Or was it bothering her to think of telling him goodbye? Either way, he wasn't going to ask her those pointed questions. He didn't want to ruin this night with her.

She walked over to him and reached for his hand. "I want to have time with you, too," she murmured, then squeezing his hand, asked, "Ready to walk down to the creek?"

Glad she wasn't going to dwell on the awkward moment, he smiled and nodded. "Sure. Maybe we'll see a javelina. Or a mountain lion. Some of the ranch hands have spotted them, but I don't get away from the training arena enough to see some of the wildlife here on Three Rivers. Heck, there are still miles of land on this ranch that I've not seen yet."

As they began walking toward the tree line, Bonnie said,

"Maybe we should take another ride and look over a different area of the ranch. I'd like that. Would you?"

Mose would like anything that put the two of them together. Even if the togetherness was only temporary. "I'd like it a whole lot," he said. "We'll plan to go soon."

A few minutes later, Bonnie stood on the edge of the creek bank and watched the clear water move swiftly over the boulders jutting up from the riverbed. Blooming desert willow trees blotted out the waning sunlight and cooled the air around them.

Rubbing the chill from her upper arms, she sidled closer to Mose and sighed with appreciation as his warm arm wrapped around her shoulders. "This is an enchanting spot, Mose. Do you ever fish here?"

"Never was much for the sport. Guess that's because where I lived, you had to travel for miles and miles just to find a hole of water big enough to fish in," he said wryly.

Smiling faintly, she looked up at him. "And as a kid you were probably too busy riding horses. I wish I could've known you back then."

His expression turned wry. "I don't believe you would've been interested in me. I was an awkward skinny teenager. And anyway, when I was in junior high you were only in first grade. In case you haven't noticed, there's a definite age gap between us."

"We're grown adults now. The gap doesn't matter. Not to me."

She thought he was going to argue the point, but he must've decided their age difference wasn't a problem, because suddenly his head was lowering toward hers.

The kiss he placed on her lips was the first real kiss he'd given her since their trip to the old ranch house. Though he kept the contract brief, it was enough to send her heart into a hard thud.

"I—uh, think we'd better head back to the house and have dinner," he suggested in a husky voice. "You're getting cold and I'm getting hungry."

She could've told him his kiss had made her forget all about being chilled or hungry, and that she would be happy to keep standing on the creek bank wrapped in his arms. But it was clear the tender moment was past for him.

She said, "Yes. I'm ready to go to the house."

Once they reached the rock patio, he let them in at the back door, and as they walked through the small kitchen, Bonnie sniffed with appreciation. "Something smells yummy. Are you sure you did the cooking?" she teased. "Or did you finagle Sophia into fixing something for you?"

He shook a chastising finger at her. "Once you taste my cooking, you're going to apologize for misjudging my skills as a chef."

She laughed. "Okay, we'll see."

He wrapped a hand beneath her elbow and was about to guide her out of the kitchen, when two cats came trotting into the room. The tabbies took one look at her, then dashed for cover under the table.

Bonnie laughed. "Very friendly cats, Mose. Have you taught them to chase off company?"

"That's Seymour and Margo. She's the redhead. And I warned them about being good cats tonight. But since I never have visitors, they're not accustomed to strangers."

"Did you bring them with you from Texas?" she asked, a bit surprised that he was a cat owner.

"No. They were a part of a litter that was born in the horse barn. I brought them home shortly after their mother weaned them. Most of the time, they're outside cats. But when I'm home they like to be in here with me."

"No doubt. They want your company," she said. "To be honest, I would've guessed you to be a dog man."

He shrugged. "Oh, I like dogs, too. But if I tried to keep a dog here, he'd just trot right back to the ranch yard to be with his buddies. Besides, cats are soft and snuggly and—"

When he paused, she finished for him. "I think the word you're looking for is *independent*."

Chuckling, he said, "Exactly. And I like that about them. They think they know more than I do. And the heck of it is, they probably do." He urged her toward the doorway leading out of the kitchen. "Come on. You can take a look at the rest of the house and then we'll eat."

The inside of the house was much larger than Bonnie had expected it to be. The three bedrooms were all roomy and beautifully furnished with carved wood furniture, including beds with posts that stood halfway to the ceiling. There was one main bathroom, and a half bath in the master bedroom. The living room was a long rectangle with a gorgeous view of the distant desert mountains.

A long couch covered in brown hairy cowhide was flanked by two stuffed armchairs done in butterscotch-colored leather. At one end of the room was a small fireplace with a stone hearth, and she noticed the rocks were the same as those that made up the patio floor outside. Three framed photographs were sitting on the mantel, along with a pair of worn jingle bob spurs and a big chunk of lapis lazuli.

Bonnie walked over to inspect the photos and Mose followed.

"This must be you and your brother," she said as she peered at the first of the pictures. The two men were standing next to a truck loaded down with hay bales. They appeared to be somewhere in their early twenties, and from what she could see beneath the brims of their cowboy hats, they both had wide smiles on their faces. "You two look very much alike in this photo. Do you still resemble each other?"

"Somewhat. Mitch is a little heavier than me. Not fat, just more muscle."

She shot him a pointed grin. "You look like you have plenty of muscle to me."

He cleared his throat. "You've not seen me with my clothes off."

She drew in a deep breath and let it out before she turned to the next photo. A dark-haired, slender woman was sitting in a lawn chair. She was dressed in worn jeans, a T-shirt and huaraches. Her thick wavy hair was pulled back on both sides and anchored with barrettes, while a pair of sunglasses covered her eyes. Even with her face partially hidden by the eyewear, Bonnie could see she was an attractive woman.

"Who is this lady? Your mother?"

"Yes. Her name is Elizabeth, but everyone calls her Lizzy. In the next photo, the man standing with me is my dad. His name is Duncan, but he goes by Dunn. They're both in their late fifties now."

Dunn Martel was a tall man like Mose but he appeared to be whipcord thin. A wide-brimmed hat was on his head, but Bonnie could see enough to tell his skin was leathery brown. No doubt the man had worked out in the elements all of his life and his two sons had followed in the business of training equines.

"It's sad that your parents are divorced," she said thoughtfully. "Do they ever see each other now? Or is that a stupid question?"

When he'd walked up behind her at the fireplace, he'd

placed a hand on the back of her shoulder and now he gave her a gentle squeeze.

"It's not a stupid question. Surprisingly, they do see each other when Mom visits Hereford to see Mitch and her old friends. And Dad."

"You said surprisingly. Does that mean they parted on bad terms?"

She twisted her head around just enough to see a grimace on his face.

"I guess you could say my parents had a tumultuous marriage. Even in the beginning, they loved a lot but they also fought a lot. Eventually, the squabbles and arguments overcame the special feelings they had for each other. At least, that's the way Mitch and I saw their relationship. I think they parted just because they didn't want to hurt each other anymore. Does that make sense?"

She swallowed as a lump of emotion filled her throat. She'd never met Mose's parents, yet it seemed they were two people who'd been in love and had children together. Now they were apart and that was a great loss. Not just for Lizzy and Dunn, but for their sons, too.

"Yes. Unfortunately, it does," she said.

"Anyway, I'm not sure how Mom's second marriage is working out for her. The last time Mitch talked with her on the phone, she made the comment several times that *Nelson isn't your dad.* I guess she still thinks of our dad." With a hand on the side of her waist, he guided her away from the fireplace and the memories. "Let's go eat. Everything is ready except for putting it on the table."

She flashed him a teasing grin. "I'm ready to see if you're a real cook or just all talk."

Chuckling, he ushered her into a small dining area located

just off the living room. When Bonnie spotted the table all set for two and the centerpiece of wildflowers, she was stunned.

"Mose! You did all this? For me?"

"Sure. Why not?"

"Because you're a busy man. And I don't need special treatment."

"*Special?* You deserve five star-treatment. Besides," he teased, "don't you think I do this every day?" With a proud grin on his face, he pulled out a chair and helped her into it. "Now, stay put and I'll bring everything in."

Once he had the food and drinks on the table and had taken his seat next to her, she reached over and placed a hand on his arm.

"Thank you, Mose. You've gone above and beyond."

"You're welcome, but maybe you should wait about the thanks until you taste the food," he told her.

He pulled the lid off a huge serving dish to reveal a perfectly browned beef roast, small golden potatoes, baby carrots and onions all resting in a bath of brown gravy.

"I am properly impressed. But I want to know how you got all of this cooked so fast. You couldn't have left the horse barn early enough to prepare roast!"

With an unassuming shrug of one shoulder, he said, "Easy. I got up early enough to throw it all into the Crock-Pot. See, I know my way around the kitchen."

She shot him a provocative little smile. "You've surprised me, Mr. Martel."

"Yeah. I'm just full of them," he replied.

They filled their plates, and as they began to eat, Mose asked whether she'd been making any progress in the ancestry work.

"Not much. We can't find any sort of document or letter that explains why Joseph disinherited his son. Gil has decided to call his Aunt Sarah out in California to see if she might be willing to come for a visit and stay for the holidays. Her father, Hamilton, was Parnell's brother, so he thinks she might be able to give us some insight into the mystery."

"Why hasn't Gil thought about calling her before now?" he asked.

"He's been waiting for a better time. Sarah's husband passed away not too long ago and then she's been dealing with some serious health issues of her own. But Gil recently talked to one of her sons and he says his mother has recovered now. So hopefully, she'll be willing to fly here for a visit. If nothing else, Gil and the rest of the family would love to see her. From what I understand, Sarah doesn't get back here to the ranch very often."

"I see. Well, it sounds like things are moving forward for you. Is Sarah the only Hollister left of that generation?"

"No. Avril is still living, but she's in assisted living now and her health is failing. There was another older sister, Lorena, but she was killed in a car accident when she was in her forties. Their older brother, Axel, was Gil and Joel's father. He passed away several years ago."

"Yes, I've heard Holt speak of his Grandfather Axel. To hear him tell it, he was a hard-boiled kind of guy—until you got to know him."

"Hmm. Well, keeping a ranch the magnitude of Three Rivers in the black would tend to make a man ruthless at times," she commented as she lifted a piece of beef to her mouth.

Smiling, he said, "I'll be sure and tell Blake he's not nearly ruthless enough to manage Three Rivers."

Laughing, she exclaimed, "Don't you dare!"

During the rest of the meal, the conversation moved on to other things. Mose told her stories about some of his horse-breaking experiences and she told him of some of the more interesting things that had happened on Stone Creek.

By the time she finished the beef and vegetables on her plate, she was too stuffed for dessert, but she didn't want to disappoint him by declining.

"I honestly don't know if I can hold anything else," she told him. "But I'll try. What did you make?"

His smile was sheepish as he rose from his chair. "I confess. I didn't make the dessert. Sophia did. It's some sort of cake-looking thing. She called it a *torte*. She was making several for the Hollisters' evening meal, so she made an extra for me."

Standing, Bonnie said, "Sophia is too good for her own good."

"Colt knows he's a blessed man. I only wish he and Sophia could have a child, or two or three."

She looked at him with surprise. "You honestly want that for them?"

He grimaced. "Why should that surprise you? They want children and they'd make great parents."

Shrugging, she said, "Well, you've made it clear you're not a family man. So I just didn't expect you to understand Colt's desire to be a father."

He looked away from her. "It's not that I have anything against kids. But in my case, I know that I don't have the makings to be a father. Better for a man to realize his shortcomings before he tries to take on such an important job as raising children."

Bonnie wanted to ask him why he thought he didn't have the makings to be a father. Had his own father failed him in some way? Or was he simply too afraid to be a dad? No. She couldn't imagine him being afraid. So what was his reason?

"I don't believe anyone knows what sort of parent they'll be until they actually become one. And even then it's a learning experience," she said. "One that repeats itself with each child, because no two kids are the same. Dad is sixty-three now and I've heard him say he's still trying to figure out fatherhood. However, Mom never seems to second-guess her parenting. But then, mothers are different."

A wan grin on his face, he glanced at her. "Yeah. Mothers are different."

He started toward the kitchen and she followed directly behind him. "If you have coffee, I'll make some to go with the torte," she suggested.

"Sure. I have plenty of coffee. I'll show you where everything is."

While she made the coffee, sliced two portions of the torte and placed them on small paper plates, he cleared the table of the leftover food and stacked the dirty dishes into the dishwasher.

"This dessert smells so delicious I've forgotten about being too full." She looked over to see him drying his hands on a paper towel. "I think the coffee is finished. If you're ready, I'll pour us a cup."

He joined her at the end of the cabinet, where she was waiting for the coffee to finish dripping into a glass carafe. With his arm nearly close enough to brush her shoulders, she couldn't help but notice the heat radiating from his body and his masculine scent settling around her like a soft blanket.

"I'm ready," he said. "Would you like to take our dessert into the living room? It would be more comfortable."

Now that they'd finished dinner, they could spend the remainder of the evening simply being together—without any chance of being interrupted. And going to the living room meant they could sit close together. The idea left her trembling with anticipation. "Sounds good," she said softly.

"I'll get a tray," he said.

While he placed the coffee and the servings of torte on the

tray, she peered under the table in search of the cats. "Aww, Margo and Seymour are gone. Did you let them outside?"

"No. They're in the utility room." He jerked a thumb toward an open doorway on the back side of the kitchen. "They have a bed in there. After they get to know you, they'll get friendly."

She laughed. "How will they get to know me if they run off and hide?"

"Are you saying my cats are causing a catch-22?" he asked with amusement.

"I am. But I won't give up. Before the evening is over, I'll bet you I'll manage to pet both of them."

"If you manage to get within a foot of my cats tonight, I'll be duly impressed." He picked up the tray and motioned with his head for her to follow. "Come on. Before our coffee gets cold."

Out in the living room, Mose placed the tray on a coffee table in front of the couch. They sat down together and Bonnie was thrilled when he didn't put a measurable distance between them. Instead, he was close enough for his arm to press against her shoulder and his thigh to push against her leg. She doubted he had any idea of the wild upheaval his nearness caused her or how much she wanted to show him the fiery attraction he sparked in her.

"I apologize for not having a TV," he said. "The trees around the house block out any chance for a satellite system or antenna. And, in my opinion, choosing between the trees or a set is no choice. Colt says I should get a TV set anyway and watch DVDs, but there's nothing I want to see."

"I'm not much for it, either. Bea always had her favorite programs, but I'd much rather read a book," she said as she sliced the fork into the rich chocolate torte. "So what do you do here at night?"

"Not much. Here lately I've been digging postholes to build a corral a little farther east of the house. Just in case I want to ride Bear over and keep him here for the night. But most of the time, I just kick back and enjoy the quiet." He glanced at her, his grin a bit wicked. "That is, unless some of the guys want to go to the Fandango. But usually, we only go there on the weekends."

"What and where is the Fandango? I've not heard any of the Hollisters mention it."

"The Fandango used to be one of Holt's favorite hangouts. But that was before he married Isabelle. It's a big nightclub/dance hall out on the western edge of town. It—uh, gets kind of rowdy out there at times, if you know what I mean. But they have great live bands and—"

"Plenty of girls to dance with," she finished for him.

He chuckled guiltily. "How did you guess?"

"Even if I've never really been one to enjoy the nightlife, I still know it exists, Mose. My brothers, particularly Cord, liked to have a good time. But Maggie and their little daughter, Bridget, have changed his lifestyle." She bit back a sigh and took a careful sip of coffee. "But even though it's been amazing for Cord, I realize family life isn't for everyone. And I understand you don't want it for yourself. You like being free and not having to answer to anyone. Right?"

He looked down at the piece of torte as though it needed a thorough inspection before he took a bite. After a moment, he said, "I guess you could put it that way. At least this way, I'm not responsible for anyone but me."

His attitude should have Bonnie quickly swallowing down the dessert and telling him good-night. But it wasn't that simple. Even though her mind was telling her he'd never be her lifelong partner, her heart was telling her to follow Beatrice's advice. Hang on and not let go.

"And you'll save yourself a lot of worries that way," she murmured.

He didn't reply and she remained quiet as she finished the last bite of the torte. When she placed her plate on the coffee table, she said, "I'll have to tell Sophia her dessert was sinfully delicious."

"She's outdone herself with this one," he agreed.

Sipping her coffee, she lifted her gaze to the wide picture window. "It's gotten dark outside."

His gaze followed hers. "Yes, it has. Are you thinking you should be going?"

Her head whipped around to stare at him in wonder. "It's still early. I don't want to leave. Unless, you'd like for me to go."

This time, he was the one who looked stunned. "Bonnie, no! I don't want you to be anywhere except right here by me."

Warm joy poured through her as she quickly set her coffee down and turned to him. "Oh Mose, I thought—" Pausing, she snuggled her head against his shoulder. "I was afraid I'd made you angry."

He placed his cup and plate on the coffee table, then reached for her hand and pressed it between the two of his. "Sweet Bonnie, how could you make me angry?"

"By talking too much."

Groaning, he looked into her eyes. "You haven't said anything to make me angry. If I'm quiet, it's because I'm thinking."

"About what?"

"You. And how much I want you in my arms."

Tilting her head back, she smiled at him. "I want to be in your arms just as much, Mose."

He gently touched his fingertips to her cheek and whispered, "Bonnie. Sweet Bonnie."

Sighing, she curled her hands over the ridges of his shoulders and proceeded to plant kisses along his jaw and down the side of his neck. He tasted salty and totally male and she was struck with the urge to slide her lips and hands over his body. She wanted to taste the other parts of him, to feel his hard muscles beneath her fingers. The desire was so heady it caused her voice to come out rough and raspy when she spoke.

Lifting her head, she looked into his brown eyes. "At the old ranch house you told me you wanted me to sort out my feelings. Well, I've had time to think and sort. And I know for certain you're the only man I've ever wanted to make love to me."

For a split second, doubt shadowed his eyes, but the darkness was instantly replaced with sparks of raw desire.

"I need you to be sure," he said thickly.

"Let me show you how sure I am, Mose. Let me love you."

His groan was close to being a sound of pain as he cradled her head in his hands and tilted her face up to his. When he kissed her, she could feel the same hunger as before, only this time he wasn't holding his desire on a tight rein. His eagerness fueled the flames licking deep within her.

Her arms still around his neck, she twisted around and pressed her body closer to his. At the same time, his tongue delved past her teeth and into the open cavity of her mouth. The contact caused her senses to fly off in all directions, and by the time he finally lifted his head, she was clinging to him, aching to feel him inside her.

Between ragged breaths, he muttered, "I think it's time we showed each other. Don't you?"

To answer, she placed her hand in his. He quickly stood and drew her up from the couch. Neither of them spoke a word as they walked out of the living room and down a short hallway to his bedroom.

Chapter Thirteen

The room was full of shadows, but there was enough light filtering down the hallway from the kitchen to shed a shaft of light over the stretch of floor that led from the doorway to the bed. A digital clock on the nightstand glowed red numbers, and beyond the parted curtains at the window, she glimpsed a patch of starlit sky.

But the chance for Bonnie to further observe her surroundings ended abruptly when they reached the side of the bed and Mose pulled her close to him. She slid her arms around his waist and tilted her face upward to receive his kiss. A thrill rushed through her as his mouth crushed hungrily down on hers. For long moments, their tongues mated, and all the while their mouths were connected, she felt his hands roaming her back and shoulders, then farther down until they were cupping the rounded mounds of her buttocks.

The need to touch his bare flesh was so intense she couldn't bear to wait for him to shed his shirt. Instead, she wedged her hands between them and began to pull apart the pearl snaps. As soon as the fabric parted, she flattened palms against his chest and slowly slid them up and down his heated skin.

With a guttural groan, he lifted his head and buried his face in the curve of her neck. "Oh Bonnie, do you know what you're doing to me? Do you know what it means to me to have you here in my arms, like this?"

"I hope it means something good," she murmured.

His choked laughter was a sound of disbelief. "*Good?*" he repeated. "That's like saying the desert is kind of warm in the middle of July. It's so much better than good, my sweet Bonnie."

He lifted his head and as her eyes met his, her heart felt so full of emotions, she figured it had to be close to bursting.

"I thought you might not want me, Mose. I was afraid you might turn me away and I—couldn't bear that. Not now." Not ever, she thought. But she didn't say the words aloud. Everything between them was too fragile and new to test with words like *forever*.

"There's no danger of that happening," he said on a rough breath.

To emphasize his promise, he stepped back and reached for the buttons on her shirt. And soon, but not nearly soon enough to suit her, she was standing in front of him with nothing on but her lacy undergarments. Next to her bare feet, her boots and clothes lay in a pile on the floor.

He allowed her just enough time to push his shirt off his shoulders, before he placed his hands on each side of her waist and lifted her onto the bed. She lay back against the mattress, and as she watched him undress, she kept wondering why she wasn't embarrassed for him to see her in nothing but her underwear. And how she was unabashedly staring at his beautiful male body and glorious manhood.

Somehow, Mose had managed to chase away the timid Bonnie. And this new version of her couldn't wait to become completely his.

When he stretched out beside her on the mattress, she promptly reached for him. As their bodies rolled together, she was overcome with the sensation of his skin touching hers, his hands moving against her flesh. Until Mose, she'd not realized what it was to have her body needing and wanting, but she understood it now.

One of his hands moved to her hair, where he pulled the scarf loose from her ponytail and delved his fingers into the loose, wavy strands.

"Your hair is beautiful, Bonnie." He pressed his lips to her forehead, then moved on to her eyes and nose and finally her lips. "But so is everything else about you. How did I manage to get you here in my bed? Lying close to me? Please don't tell me I'm dreaming. Because if I'm dreaming, I'll have to wake up, and I don't want that to happen."

Snaking an arm around his back, she snugged herself so close to him her breasts were flattened against his chest and the juncture of her thighs was pressed against his hard erection.

"If you're dreaming, then so am I. But this is real, Mose. Incredibly, deliciously real."

"Yes, so delicious." He brushed his lips against hers and the delicate contact caused goose bumps to erupt on her arms and down her back.

After a kiss that literally robbed her of her breath, he reached around to middle of her back and unclasped her bra. Once the garment slipped downward, he dipped his head to her breasts. The sensation of his tongue laving her nipple had her fingers curling into his back and a growl vibrating deep in her throat. Was this the way she was supposed to be feeling? Like she'd lost all control? She didn't know. She couldn't have guessed.

While his mouth focused its attention on her breasts, his hand slid along her inner thigh until he reached the crotch of her panties. As soon as his fingers touched the lace barrier, she expected him to ease away from her long enough to remove the undergarment. But he didn't bother putting distance between them. Instead, he slipped his finger beneath the strip of fabric and touched that part of her that was already wet and aching for him.

When his finger pushed into the folds of her womanhood, she groaned and arched her hips toward the erotic pleasure.

"Mose! This is— I can't wait!"

He slowly moved his finger deeper into the heat of her. "You don't have to wait, sweetheart. Let loose and enjoy."

With both her hands, she clutched a tight hold on his upper arms. "Oh Mose—you're making me—oh, oh, please—"

The rest of her words trailed away as she lost control, her whole body feeling as if she was spinning off into space. In the back of her mind, she recognized his lips had latched over hers and his hand was still between her thighs, but that was all she knew until her flight among the stars ended and she landed breathlessly back on the bed.

When she opened her eyes, his face was hovering over hers, and the smug grin on his lips made her want to laugh and cry at the same time. But instead of doing either, she gasped out the question, "Why did you do that?"

"Because I wanted to give you pleasure."

"But I—we should—it should have happened together."

"It will happen, my sweet." He pressed a row of kisses up and down the side of her neck. "We have plenty of time, don't we?"

Closing her eyes, she thrust her fingers into his hair and absently combed the waves away from his face. She didn't want to think about ever leaving his bed. She didn't want to think of anything, except him. "We have all night."

"So we'll make that be enough." He eased back from her. "But I think—before we go any further, I'd better put on some protection."

She bit down on her bottom lip as his suggestion reminded her of just how inexperienced she was at this sort of thing. "I'd not thought of birth control. But you don't need to worry about protection, Mose."

His expression turned to one of confusion. "I don't? Wouldn't we be risking a pregnancy?"

Her cheeks were suddenly burning. "No. I, um, I take the Pill. The doctor prescribed them to get my period regulated—understand? So as far as birth control goes, I'm covered."

He looked relieved. "Oh. I wasn't thinking along those lines. I mean—I know you're not the promiscuous sort. And I've not been with a woman—well, in a long time. I've just had a health checkup, too."

If the exchange between them hadn't been so awkward, she would have laughed. Instead, she glanced away from him.

"*Promiscuous*," she said wryly. "I'm sure it's pretty obvious to you how inexperienced I am. But I—"

Before she could finish, he said, "I don't care about that, Bonnie. All I care about is you being here with me now." Pausing, he ducked his head and peered into her eyes. "Unless—are you trying to tell me you're a virgin?"

She released a heavy breath. "No. But you could say I'm close to it. I've only been with one guy, one time. And it was—uh, not an experience to remember. If you get what I mean. To make things worse, later on, he turned out to be a real bastard."

"Hmm. You know what I'm thinking right now?"

Her lips were quivering as she looked back at him. "I can't imagine."

A tender smile curved his lips as he leaned forward and kissed her forehead. "I'm going to do my best to make you forget about that one time."

Her eyes misted over as she wrapped her arms across his back and whispered, "You already have, Mose."

As Mose peeled the tiny black panties from Bonnie's hips, he was amazed that he was managing to find a thread of self-control. The desire coursing through him was like nothing he'd ever felt before. He was gripped with a hot ache that was growing with each passing second. And it wasn't just her lovely curves, or pale, smooth-as-silk skin that were spinning his senses and heating his loins. Nor was it her sweet plump lips, soft arms, and tender hands urging him closer. No, he wanted her simply because she was Bonnie. *His* Bonnie.

And that was a terrifying reality.

Even so, he wasn't going to allow the fear to creep into his brain. She wanted him and he wanted her. Tonight nothing else could matter.

He tossed her panties onto the pile of clothes he'd already made on the floor, then climbed back onto the bed with her. As he reached for her, she shivered and he brushed his hands up and down her arms and over her back.

"If you're cold, we can get under the covers," he said, rubbing his cheek against her hair.

"I'm not cold. I'm just—wanting you, Mose."

Her admission stoked the hot coals in his loins, and as he gathered her against him, he kissed her cheeks and nose and finally her lips. "Don't be worried, sweetheart. This will all be on your terms. Not mine."

"I'm not worried. Not with you," she whispered.

She drew her mouth around to his and as Mose kissed her she eased back against the mattress and he anchored his weight above her. He entered her slowly, and as her warmth surrounded him, indescribable pleasure rushed from his loins to his head and before he could move his hips, even a fraction, it was a fight for him to keep from climaxing.

Beneath him, her hands were sliding over the parts of his body she could reach, and each track of her fingers left a trail of fire upon his skin. The moist kisses she was planting across his chest and around each flat nipple were teasing his senses to the point of agony, while the tiny moans in her throat added fuel to the flames.

As soon as he managed to settle his hips into a steady rhythm, she began to meet each thrust with eager abandon. And in a matter of a few brief moments, he forgot everything except her soft warm body yielding to his and the frantic exploration of her hands setting his flesh on fire.

Time ceased, as over and over their bodies moved together, each of them straining to find relief from a desire so intense they couldn't slow the frantic pace.

It should have happened together.

Her earlier remark drifted through the back of his mind as he heard her whimpers and felt her hands on his buttocks, tugging him deeper.

Together. Together.

The word was his last thought before his loud grunt joined her soft mews. And then he fell straight off a cliff and tumbled over and over until he was seeing stars against a black velvet sky.

He couldn't comprehend how long he floated through the brilliant lights. Wasn't sure if he was even breathing during the journey. He only recognized Bonnie's hands were digging into his back and her ragged breaths fanned the side of his face.

When he finally collapsed, returned to Earth, part of his weight fell onto the mattress while the remainder was draped over her. Moments passed before he could collect himself enough to roll off her, but even then, the room continued to spin around him.

She rolled into the curve of his body and snuggled her cheek against his shoulder. Her breasts were rapidly rising and falling as she worked to regain her breath, and he realized with some amazement that she'd been just as totally consumed with their lovemaking as he'd been.

Lovemaking.

Yes, Mose could call it that now. To himself, at least. But not to her. No, the last time he'd declared his feelings to a woman, she'd turned her back on him. Now to even form the word *love* on his tongue would choke him. As long as Bonnie didn't realize she was holding his heart in her hands, the easier it would be to tell her goodbye.

But Bonnie isn't that kind of woman, Mose. She's kind and gentle and she cares about you. What makes you think she'll walk away?

She was a Hollister, he thought, as he absently smoothed his fingertips up and down her arm. From what Holt had told him about the Utah Hollisters, he understood she had a fancy home, a big family and financial security to go back to. He couldn't compete with those things. He'd always be just Mose, a horse trainer.

Her hand slipped across his abdomen and anchored a hold on the side of his waist. "I'm afraid to let go of you," she murmured. "I might float away and you'd have to scrape me off the ceiling."

His lips curved into a faint smile. "No chance of that happening. Because I have no intentions of letting you go."

She didn't reply and he glanced down to see she'd closed her eyes and her breathing had slowed. Her long lashes formed crescent shadows on her cheeks and he thought how he'd never seen skin so smooth it actually looked poreless. Nor had he encountered such a tempting pair of strawberry-pink lips. They curled up at the corners and possessed enough power to wipe every thought from his mind.

"Are you going to sleep?" he asked gently.

"Hmm." Opening her eyes, she rubbed her cheek against

his shoulder. "I'm not about to go to sleep yet. I want to be awake and enjoy every moment here with you."

He thoughtfully stroked his fingers through a long strand of hair lying against her breast. "Are Maureen and Gil expecting you back at the ranch house tonight?"

Tilting her head back, she studied his face and Mose suddenly wondered if he looked different now that they'd made love. How could he not look different when everything inside him felt as if it had been shaken and turned upside down?

"I saw them just before I left to come over here," she said. "They didn't ask when to look for me. And I didn't volunteer a certain time. I'm twenty-seven, Mose. A grown woman."

"Are you telling me you don't have to hurry back to the ranch house tonight?" he asked.

"Not unless you want me to."

If Mose had any sense, he'd make some sort of excuse about having to get up early in the morning. He'd tell her how Holt had a hard day planned for them tomorrow and he needed his rest. But when it came to Bonnie, he was totally losing all common sense. Not to mention his heart.

His sigh was a sound of helpless surrender as he rested his chin on the top of her head. "I don't want you to move from this bed," he told her.

She suddenly chuckled. "But, Mose, if I don't get out of bed, how am I going to make friends with Margo and Seymour?"

Growling, he tugged her up from the mattress and onto his chest. "Right now you need to quit thinking about those darned cats and concentrate on making friends with me," he muttered in a low, suggestive voice.

Her blue eyes met his at the same time her lips tilted into a sexy smile. "I thought we were already friends. But I'm willing to work on making us *really good* friends."

Pulling her head down to his, he fastened his lips over hers and after a few moments of drinking in the sweetness of her mouth, he felt himself growing hard again. And when he positioned her over him and entered her a second time, he had to accept the fact that he was a lost man.

The next morning over breakfast, Maureen informed Bonnie that Aunt Sarah would be arriving in two days. Which meant Bonnie needed to speed up the process of searching through the papers and photos so that anything pertinent she might find could be shown to the woman. So much for having much free time to spend with Mose.

Not that he'd asked Bonnie to spend another night with him. In fact, when she'd left his house early this morning, he'd not mentioned anything about seeing her again. However, he had promised to call her and she'd been content to leave things at that. No doubt Beatrice would've scolded her for not pushing the issue with him. But it wasn't Bonnie's style to be pushy. If Mose wanted to be with her again, he'd contact her.

Yet she had to admit she'd been a bit disappointed last night when he'd not mentioned having any kind of meaningful feelings for her. Could a man touch her the way he'd touched her, kiss her with such hunger, and not feel something, she wondered. And maybe their time together had touched him deeply, but he'd been wary to tell her so. After all, she'd not confessed her feelings to him.

All through the day, Bonnie had been telling herself she was probably expecting too much, too soon from Mose. Even though she was inexperienced in the romance department, she knew enough to understand a man hardly needed to love a woman to have sex with her. Ward had been proof of that, she thought ruefully. But as for Mose, she had to look at things realistically. Just because her heart had flipped head over heels for him, she couldn't expect him to automatically fall in love with her in return.

Now, as the afternoon grew late, Bonnie was in Maureen's office, scanning through a folder of legal documents, when a light knock sounded on the door. A moment later, Jazelle walked in carrying a tray of coffee, along with a few pieces of divinity and fudge candy.

"Break time," she declared in a singsong voice. "Reeva made the candy this morning and I talked her into letting me have a few pieces."

"I could certainly use the coffee." Bonnie left the desk and walked over to where Jazelle was pouring the beverage into a cup. "I'm losing what little steam I had earlier in the day."

Jazelle handed her a cup. "You should try the candy. It's full of nuts—protein to help you power on."

Bonnie sighed. "Maybe later. I'm trying to get through this stack of documents before dinner tonight. And at the rate I'm going, it's not going to happen."

"Where's Maureen? I thought she was helping you?"

"She was. But about an hour ago, Blake called her down to his office for some sort of meeting. Something about him and Tag shipping a herd of cattle down to Red Bluff. I got the impression Maureen would like to make the trip so she could visit Camille and Matthew and their little boy, Harry, but she can't leave the ranch now with Gil's Aunt Sarah coming."

Jazelle nodded. "Well, Camille and Matthew and little Harry will be here for Christmas, so Maureen will get to visit with her daughter then. You're going to enjoy that family. Camille is a lot like her mother."

"Uh, Jazelle, I'm not sure I'll be here for Christmas," Bonnie told her.

Frowning at her, Jazelle said, "You have to be! You can't leave without enjoying all the partying and gift giving."

Not to mention being with Mose on Christmas Day, she thought longingly. But she didn't want to bring that up now.

"Well, we'll see," Bonnie hedged. "Maybe I'll find a way to stick around through the holidays."

"Now you're talking." Jazelle reached for a piece of the divinity, and after enjoying a bite, said, "I've been getting one of the downstairs bedrooms ready for Sarah's arrival. Since the woman's had hip replacement recently, Maureen didn't want her to have to struggle with the stairs."

"I'm looking forward to meeting Sarah," Bonnie replied. "Maureen tells me she's a lovely woman."

"She is. She and her husband came for a visit back when I first started to work here on the ranch eleven years ago. At that time, I was pregnant with Raine. She was very kind and wanted to do things to make me comfortable, rather than me serving her."

Wouldn't we be risking a pregnancy?

Jazelle's mention of being pregnant triggered the memory of Mose's words last night. Of course he wouldn't want Bonnie to experience an unplanned pregnancy. But the mere idea of having his child had filled her with deep longing.

Trying not to let her thoughts go there, Bonnie said, "I was sad to hear she lost her husband a couple of years ago."

"Yes. They'd been married since they were teenagers. I don't know how anyone survives that kind of loss."

Bonnie didn't know either because she was already wondering how she was going to survive without Mose. And there was little doubt in her mind that she would be spending her life without him. Because he clearly had no intentions of turning into a family man.

Purposely shaking away the somber thought, Bonnie took a grateful sip of the coffee. "This is a lifeline, Jazelle. Thank you for bringing it here to the office."

Smiling, she sank onto one of the wooden chairs, sitting at an angle to Bonnie. "No problem. I love making people feel a bit pampered. And at lunch I could see you were kind of draggy."

Heat rushed to Bonnie's cheeks and she quickly glanced away from her friend. "I—uh, didn't get much sleep. I ended up staying late at Mose's."

At the very least, Jazelle's short laugh was suggestive. "Late? I'd say getting home at breakfast time is early. Not late."

Bonnie groaned with embarrassment. "I've never done anything like this before. Now, you and Sophia must think I'm being reckless or foolish. Or that I've lost my mind."

"We don't think anything of the sort. If you want to know how we're really feeling about the situation, we're thrilled."

Grimacing, Bonnie said, "Yes, it's rather amazing that a guy as sexy as Mose took a second look at me."

Jazelle laughed again. "Bonnie, you're so funny. I don't know what you see when you look in the mirror, but I'm sure Mose sees a heck of a beautiful, desirable woman."

Shaking her head, Bonnie said, "Looks aren't everything, Jazelle. Compared to his other girlfriends, I imagine I'm plenty boring."

Rolling her eyes, Jazelle said, "You're underestimating yourself. And from what Colt tells Sophia, Mose doesn't have any steady girlfriends."

"I'm fairly sure he doesn't. Steady would mean serious and he's not—uh, ready for that." At least, he didn't appear to be ready, Bonnie thought regretfully.

"That's too bad," Jazelle said. "Sophia and I believe he'd make some woman a dandy husband."

The notion of Mose having some other woman in the same

bed where she'd lain in his arms was so dreadfully painful, her mind quickly blocked out the image.

"Mose has said that he doesn't want to be a husband," Bonnie told her.

Jazelle grinned. "Maybe he doesn't right now. But later on, you could change his mind."

Bonnie stared down at the brown liquid in her cup. Last night when he'd made love to her, she'd believed everything between them had changed. She'd hoped it was the turning point of their relationship. But when he'd not said a thing about wanting to be with her in the future—well, she needed to accept she was just a *very temporary* girlfriend to him.

"What's wrong, Bonnie? You're not saying a word. Didn't you and Mose have an enjoyable evening together?"

"The night was wonderful, Jazelle. Really. Mose is a great cook. Who would've thought it?"

Jazelle's mouth dropped open and then she laughed loudly. "You spent the night with the man and all you can say is he's a great cook? Bonnie, if you ever decide you don't want to be a ranch secretary, you can do stand-up comedy. You'd have the audience roaring."

Bonnie was trying to think of a suitable reply when Jazelle's phone rang and she quickly pulled it out of a pocket on the bib apron she was wearing.

She answered, and after a few seconds, said, "Yes. I can do that. I'll drive the truck." Then, after a short pause, added, "Okay. I'll be down in two."

Slipping the phone back into her pocket, she headed toward the door. "Sandwiches wanted at Blake's office," she explained. "I'll see you later. In the meantime, you need to smile."

Bonnie plastered a wide smile on her face. "Okay. I'll do my best."

Jazelle gave her a thumbs-up before hurrying out the door.

Once the housekeeper was out of sight, Bonnie refilled her cup with more coffee and carried it over to the desk, where she tried to pick up where she'd stopped when Jazelle had walked into the room.

But her mind just wasn't ready to leave Mose and the incredible night they'd shared. And she could only wonder if their lovemaking had tilted his world the way it had jolted hers.

The day had turned out to have nearly record-setting heat for December standards, and for most of the afternoon Mose's shirt and the waistband of his jeans had remained wet with sweat. In between training sessions, he'd downed several bottles of water, along with a few sports drinks, but nothing had helped to restore his energy. He was dragging, and though he wanted to blame his lethargic condition on the unusual weather, he knew exactly why he felt sapped... Bonnie.

He'd only slept a few short minutes last night. But how was a man supposed to sleep with a woman like Bonnie lying next to him? It had been impossible to quit wanting her and each time he'd reached for her, she'd fallen willingly into his arms.

Last night, he'd realized he was in trouble, but now, in the light of day, he recognized he'd made the fatal mistake in making love to her. It hadn't just come from his body. It had come from his heart. Now he didn't know what to do. Every cell in him wanted to tell her how important she'd become to him. Every thought he had was about her and the desire to see her again. But to do that would only be diving deeper into a hopeless pit.

No, he needed to cut off all ties with her. He needed to get on with his life and pretend she was already gone. Because very soon, she really would be gone.

"Are you okay, Mose? You look a little green around the gills."

Mose glanced around to see Dex had walked up to where he was standing in the shade of a mesquite tree, drinking yet another bottle of water.

"I'm okay. I just thought I'd take a little break under the tree. The breeze is better here than it is over by the barn. It's damned hot today."

"Yeah. I've been hosing the horses a little longer than usual," the young groom told him. "You plan on doing much more today?"

Mose darted a curious glance at him. "It's only four o'clock, Dex. Of course, I'm going to do plenty more. Why? Are you wanting off for some reason?"

"No. I'm just thinking you need to go home and go to bed. You must be coming down with something."

He was definitely coming down with something, Mose thought ruefully, but what should he call it? A virus that specifically targeted fools? A lovesick fever? Whatever the malady, he'd definitely caught it.

"I'm okay, Dex. Haven't you ever heard of a guy just being tired?"

"Sure. But you don't ever get that way. You're kind of a man of steel around here."

If he didn't feel so miserable, he would've laughed. "Dex, even a piece of steel bends when it's heated to a certain point. Now go saddle the yellow filly. I'll be there to get her in a few minutes."

Dex decided he'd said enough, and turning away, strode quickly back to the barn. Mose finished his water, then walked over to a holding pen where several more horses were waiting to be put through their training exercises.

Watching the young animals mill around the dusty pen, he

thought how Bonnie was so at home on a horse. The reality had surprised him greatly. But not nearly as stunned as he'd been last night when she'd made love to him with such passionate abandon. Even thinking of how it had felt to be inside her, to feel his hands cupped around her plump little breasts was enough to make him shiver on this blistering-hot day.

"Hey, Mose. Think we're going to work our way through this little herd before the end of the day?"

He glanced around as Colt walked up to him. His friend was mopping the sweat from his face with a handkerchief, while carrying a large bottle of lime-colored sports drink.

"I think so. Unless we melt first. We're in the third week of December! What's this summer going to be like? A roaring furnace?"

Colt chuckled. "Wishing you were back in Hereford?"

No. There wasn't anything he needed back in Texas, Mose thought. Bonnie wasn't there.

She won't be here for much longer either, Mose. So get over it and move on.

Silently cursing the tormenting voice in his head, he leaned his shoulder against the nearest fence post. "Not hardly. It's damned cold there now. Besides, Three Rivers will always be my home."

"I'm relieved to hear it. I was beginning to feel a little uneasy about you."

He frowned at Colt. "I've told you plenty of times that my roots are here."

"So you say. But when a man gets serious about a woman—well, anything can happen."

Mose stared at him in stunned fascination. "*Serious?* Guess you're talking about Bonnie now?"

Colt impatiently rolled his eyes. "Well, hell, you know I'm talking about Bonnie. Who else have you been seeing?"

"No one!" Mose barked. The idea of being with any woman other than Bonnie literally made him sick. "And I don't get why you're even bringing Bonnie, or any of this up now!"

Colt studied him for a long moment, and from the man's knowing expression, Mose realized his outburst had been telling.

Slapping a friendly hand to the back of Mose's shoulder, Colt said, "Sorry, buddy. I have a habit of forgetting your personal life is none of my business. It's just that I'm happy. And I want you to be happy with me."

Feeling two inches tall, Mose said, "Don't pay any mind to me, Colt. I'm feeling wrung out today. I think the heat is getting to me."

Colt slanted him a skeptical glance, but he didn't make a comment about Mose's rough appearance. Instead, he took a long swig of his drink, then flashed him a smug smile. "I didn't come over here to tell you that you look like something your cats dragged up. I just got some news I wanted to share."

Mose wearily lifted his hat and raked fingers through his sweat-flattened hair. "I think I've already heard the news. Holt is sending several horses down to Red Bluff. Matthew and TooTall are trying to build a larger remuda."

"Yeah. Eight horses are going down to Red Bluff. But that's not my news. Sophia called me a few minutes ago. She's just learned she's pregnant."

It took a moment for Colt's words to enter Mose's sleep-deprived brain, and when the announcement finally registered, a wash of unexpected emotions poured through him. His best friend ever was finally going to get the child he'd been longing for. It was stupendous news. And yet there was a part of him that felt empty and envious.

You don't need to worry about protection.... I take the Pill.

Last night, when Bonnie had assured him she was protected from pregnancy, Mose had been relieved. And yet afterward, when she'd lain curled next to his body and his hand had rested on her lower belly, he'd imagined her waistline swollen with their baby and the image had brought a sweet ache to his chest.

"Sophia is going to have a baby? You're not joshing me, are you?" Mose asked.

Colt's laughter was a sound of pure joy. "Not this time. This is for real. She's on her way home from the doctor's office in Wickenburg. She's going to surprise her grandmother with the news as soon as she gets here. This has to be the most wonderful Christmas gift ever!"

"Is Sophia okay? What did the doctor say?"

A beaming smile seemed like it might become a permanent fixture on Colt's face. "That she couldn't be healthier. He doesn't anticipate her or the baby having any problems. It's great, isn't it?"

Mose reached to shake his friend's hand. "Congratulations, Colt. I'm really happy for both of you."

"Thanks, Mose. I only hope that one of these days you're going to feel like I do right now—on top of the world!" He turned and, as he jogged away, yelled over his shoulder. "I've got to tell Holt. He'll say I have my work cut out for me to catch up to his three boys!"

Mose thoughtfully watched Colt trot off before he clapped his hat back on his head and slowly followed his friend to the barn.

On top of the world.

No, Mose thought ruefully. He'd never be able to make that much of a climb.

Chapter Fourteen

During the next two days, the ranch house was a flurry of activity. Not only was everyone celebrating Sophia's pregnancy announcement, but more last-minute decorations were being erected in both the front and backyard and dozens of gifts were beginning to mound up beneath the huge tree in the den. Colt was getting the Christmas sleigh as the family called it, which was pulled by horses and sat on wagon wheels instead of skids, ready to haul the children over a south range trail where Santa would supposedly drive his reindeer through the Joshua trees.

Along with the Christmas preparations, the family was anticipating the arrival of Sarah. And Jazelle was making last-minute checks to make sure the woman's bedroom had everything Sarah could possibly want. For the most part, Bonnie had been stuck in the office, reading documents and letters until she thought her eyes were going to go on strike. But yesterday the hard work had managed to produce Joseph's revised will and testament.

The document was proof positive that Parnell had been left out of inheriting any of Joseph's fortune, including the ranch and all its holdings. Unfortunately, there'd been no codicil or letters of explanation attached to the document. However, it was clear the legal documents had been authorized by a notary public in 1938. Six years before Parnell had been killed on a Normandy beach.

Bonnie had been pleased over the discovery, but finding the document was hardly enough to chase away her glum mood. Three days had passed since she'd left Mose's house after their night of lovemaking, and she'd not heard one word from him. His silence not only confused her, it hurt her deeply. Sure, he was a busy man. As far as she could tell, there was never a quiet time at the horse barn. But it would only take a few seconds for him to type a text message, or a minute to call and give her a quick hello. And the more time that slipped by without him making contact, the more it was becoming obvious that either he regretted taking her to bed, or she'd been nothing more to him than a one-night stand.

Now, as she made her way to the den to meet with Maureen and Gil and Aunt Sarah, she did her best to push thoughts of Mose from her mind. There'd be time enough later to think about the sexy horse trainer, she thought sadly. Like the rest of her lonely life.

"Oh Bonnie, there you are. We're just having a martini. And Jazelle mixed them with a heavy hand," Gil said with a laugh. "Want to risk one or drink something else?"

"Thank you, Gil. The martini sounds good."

Bonnie followed him over to the wet bar located in a corner of the large room. Across the wide expanse of the den, the giant Christmas tree was ablaze with twinkling lights. The pile of gifts beneath the heavily decorated limbs was growing higher with each passing day. So far, Bonnie had been forced to do all her shopping online, but the delivery truck hadn't delivered any of her orders yet. She was keeping her fingers crossed the things would get here before the holiday arrived. Or her father called and requested her to come home.

Gil poured the drink from a shaker and handed it to Bonnie. She carried the cocktail over to where Maureen was seated on a couch, while opposite from her, Sarah sat on a love seat.

Her smile inviting, Gil's aunt patted the cushion next to her. "Come sit next to me, Bonnie. So I can get a close-up look at your pretty face."

Yesterday, Bonnie had been a bit amazed when she'd met Sarah Hollister Rhodes. Before the woman had arrived, Bonnie hadn't asked anyone to describe her appearance. She'd simply pictured Sarah as a tottery gray-haired lady with a wrinkled face and wearing practical clothing. Instead, the seventy-seven-year-old woman possessed an exceptionally smooth complexion, beautiful iron-gray hair that fell in waves to her shoulders, and a slender figure dressed in very feminine clothing. And this evening was no exception. Wearing a midnight-blue dress that swished against her legs, and with diamonds glittering on her ears and fingers, the graceful woman reminded Bonnie of a 1940s movie queen.

"I'd love to sit by you, Sarah," Bonnie said with a smile. "But don't look too closely at my face. I'm afraid this Arizona sun is adding more freckles to my cheeks and nose."

Sarah tenderly patted the back of Bonnie's hand. "Those are angel kisses. They're beautiful."

Yes, Bonnie had heard the old saying. But she'd also heard that freckles were left by kisses from a lover in a past life. Mose had kissed her cheeks and nose and plenty of other places, she thought. Had they been together in life a long time ago? Would they be together in this one?

Reach for what you want and hold on.

Yes, Beatrice's motto had worked for Beatrice. That didn't mean it would be effective for everyone else. Her twin had loads of personality. She brought sparks to a room. Compared to Beatrice's sunny demeanor, Bonnie was a cool gray sky.

Even if she reached out to Mose again, she wasn't sure she had what it took to hang on to him.

She sipped her martini and hoped the alcohol would burn the negative thought from her mind.

"Are you getting rested up from your travels yesterday, Aunt Sarah?" Gil asked as he took a seat next to Maureen. "Commuter flights aren't always comfortable."

Sarah waved a dismissive hand at him. "I couldn't feel better. You've all been spoiling me like a princess. And seeing the ranch again has lifted my heart. Especially with everything decorated so beautifully for Christmas."

"We're glad you're enjoying your stay," Maureen told her. "Does everything look the way you remembered?"

"Before I married James and moved away, this house and land were my home. That was many years ago, when I was only eighteen, but I've not forgotten anything about this place. Before I leave, I'd like to take a ride around the ranch and look a bit of it over."

"A ride?" Bonnie asked curiously. "You mean in a four-wheel-drive truck?"

Sarah let out a tinkling laugh. "Why no, honey, I meant on a horse. I do still ride. I live on my and my late husband's little ranch. Before he passed, we rode together practically every day. I had to take off to recuperate from hip replacement, but I'm back on my horses. They keep me young, you see."

"Aunt Sarah, we're not about to let you leave anytime soon," Gil told her. "We want you to stay well past the holidays. Actually, we'd like for you to stay with us for a few months. Your sons will see after your ranch in California. And you know we have plenty of room. You're the only family I have left from Dad's generation and family needs to be together as much as they can be."

"You know, Gil, I think you've talked me into it. And you

didn't even need to twist my arm. I didn't bring many things with me, but I can always go to town and buy what I need," Sarah told him, then gave Bonnie a sideways wink.

Gil glanced at his wife. "I'm sure Maureen would be happy to take you on a shopping excursion."

"More than happy," Maureen told her. "And Bonnie loves to ride horses. I'm sure she'd enjoy showing you around the ranch."

"I'd love to go riding with you, Sarah," Bonnie said eagerly. "But you'll need a hat and plenty of sunscreen. Or you'll end up with angel kisses of your own."

They all laughed at that, and then Sarah cast a somewhat regretful look at Bonnie.

"I realize you've all been waiting on me to talk about Uncle Parnell. But after meeting Bonnie—you're just too nice and sweet for me to have to tell you such awful things about your great-grandfather."

"*Awful?*" Gil repeated. "Was he really that bad of a guy, Aunt Sarah? We know Joseph disinherited him, but Joel and I used to think that was probably over some sort of father/son disagreement. Lots of families have disagreements. It doesn't mean one of them is bad."

Maureen looked over at her husband. "But there's more to it than the will, darling. Parnell left the ranch and never returned. He changed his name, or at least used an alias."

Gil grimaced. "I've not forgotten any of that. I'm just holding out hope that Aunt Sarah might say the man had some redeeming qualities."

Sarah sighed. "I'm afraid I'd have to use my imagination if you wanted me to say something nice. But you need to keep in mind that everything I know about Parnell was told to me and my siblings by our parents."

"Your father, Hamilton, was Parnell's older brother. If anyone should've known the facts, it would've been him," Gil told her.

"Yes," Sarah said with an affirming nod. "And I believe Father told us how it really was with his younger brother. He said that Parnell had always been a wild child. Even when they were in elementary school, he was constantly getting into trouble."

"Did he make failing grades?" Bonnie asked. "Could be he had a learning disability and acted out because of it."

"Oh no. Father said Parnell was extremely smart. His grades were even better than Father's. And he graduated high school at the top of his class. It was his behavior that was problematic. Anything he could do to anger his father, he'd do it. Like tearing down a fence just because he didn't want to ride around it. Or letting a pen of bulls loose into a herd of heifers just because he thought it was funny."

"A prank like that isn't funny!" Bonnie exclaimed. "It's dangerous. Not to mention it could create devastating effects later on!"

Sarah said, "From what I gathered about him, he didn't care if he caused anyone misery. And his attitude only worsened as he got older. He loved to drink and carouse, and he slept around with scores of women. That isn't uncommon for some men. But Parnell took it to extremes. Eventually, he started talking to my father about wanting to do a little moonlighting. Just for kicks. And wanted Hamilton to join him."

Bonnie glanced blankly at Gil and Maureen, then to Sarah. "I'm sorry, what is moonlighting? Making moonshine whiskey?"

Sarah shook her head. "No. But it wouldn't surprise me if he tried a hand at that, too."

"*Moonlighting* is cattle rustling in the dark of night," Gil explained to Bonnie. "Of course it's a major felony."

"Father told him he was crazy and he'd soon end up in the penitentiary. But before that happened, Parnell was arrested for public drunkenness and street brawling. If I remember correctly, Father said Joseph bailed him out on those occasions but warned him he was finished helping him out of scrapes."

"So you believe it was just a culmination of things that made Joseph finally disown Parnell and kick him off the ranch?" Maureen asked.

"There was a final straw," Sarah said grimly. "Parnell was involved in a drunk-driving car accident that resulted in him injuring innocent motorists. Joseph paid off the injured folks and somehow got the charges dismissed, but after that, he sent Parnell packing once and for all."

"Is it true Joseph ordered the entire family to never speak his son's name again?" Gil asked. "Dad never would talk about Parnell to us, other than to say he'd been banished from the Hollister family. As kids, we didn't understand exactly what he meant. To us, *banished* sounded like something really bad. Later, after we were grown, we didn't dare bring up our uncle's name. Not unless we wanted a hard glare from Dad."

"How awful," Bonnie said in a hushed voice. "And how weirdly parallel to my family. Grandfather Lionel would get angry if any of us spoke his ex-wife's name. And he tore up all her photos, except the one my dad managed to sneak away and hide."

Sarah shook her head with regret. "Sounds like your grandfather had some of his father's ways."

"Unfortunately," Bonnie agreed.

"Do you have any idea what happened to Parnell from the time he left the ranch and went into the military?" Gil asked. "You read the letters Bonnie brought with her that were written by Parnell's in-laws. They revealed he was deployed to England where he married and had a child."

Sarah sipped the last of her drink and placed the glass on an end table next to her armrest. "Yes, I read through everything Bonnie gave me. Actually, once I started, I couldn't stop. It said so much about my uncle—an uncle I'd only heard of through the gossip that went on behind closed doors. Parnell's story is sad and tragic and makes me so proud my son is a good, responsible man," she said, then joked, "I mean, after all, he is half Hollister. There's a wild streak in there somewhere, but thankfully it doesn't dominate him."

"According to everything we've learned, the wild streak ruled my Grandfather Lionel," Bonnie said wryly.

Sarah reached over and laid a comforting hand over Bonnie's. "We can't pick and choose our relatives, honey." She looked over to Gil. "But as to your question, Gil, I'm afraid I don't know anything about Parnell's years between the time he left Three Rivers and entered the military. I only remember Father saying he received a letter from his brother saying he'd joined the army. It was the first and only time anyone in the family heard from him. Then, in 1944, Joseph received word from the defense department that Parnell had been killed during the France invasion."

Maureen frowned thoughtfully. "Well, I still can't figure out why he used the alias Peter. And why he told his in-laws that the Hollisters weren't to be trusted. It wasn't like any of the family was going after him in any way. They simply shut him out."

Sarah shrugged. "I think it was simply his way of hiding from his past transgressions. He wanted his wife and in-laws to believe he was an upstanding man who'd been terribly wronged by his family back in Arizona. After all, he told them the Hollisters had stolen his wealth from him."

"You're right about that, Aunt Sarah," Gil said. "When you look at the whole picture of things, he wanted everyone to think he was a golden boy."

"How sad to know his wife died thinking her husband had been Peter Hollister, a loving man who'd given his life for his country," Bonnie said.

"As far as that goes, he *did* give his life for his country. And we should give him credit for that," Gil spoke up. "It was one redeeming thing he did in his life."

"Actually, he did do something we can be grateful for." Sarah reached over and patted Bonnie's arm. "He had a great-granddaughter who's a wonderful part of the Hollister family. Just as I'm sure her whole immediate family is."

Bonnie gave the woman's hand a grateful squeeze. "Thank you, Aunt Sarah, but don't speak too soon. You might find out I'm really a bad girl living under an alias."

Maureen laughed, while Sarah clapped her hands with glee.

"Oh Bonnie," Maureen said between chuckles, "there are times I'm shocked at what comes out of your mouth."

"I think living here in Arizona has loosened my tongue." Among other things, Bonnie thought. Where Mose was concerned, she'd definitely let loose. But what good had that done her? All it had accomplished was to leave her with a pile of bittersweet memories. "And speaking of loosening my tongue, I think I'll go call Dad and let him know how Aunt Sarah has filled in the gaps. He's been waiting for a long time to learn about his father and grandfather. At least, he'll know part of the story now."

"Of course, Bonnie. Go on and make your call," Gil told her, then looked over at his aunt and winked. "In the meantime, I think Aunt Sarah could use another martini."

Sarah smiled at her nephew. "How did you ever guess?"

* * *

Later that night, Bonnie went down to the kitchen to have dinner with Sophia and Colt, but discovered the couple had already gone home for the night. But the sight of Reeva lifted her spirits somewhat. Sophia's grandmother had become the grandmother she'd missed having in her life.

Standing at the cookstove filling herself a plate, the older woman motioned for Bonnie to join her. "Get yourself a plate, sweetie. It's grilled salmon tonight with stir-fried vegetables. And I put a big bowl of tossed salad on the table. You need to help me eat it."

Bonnie picked up a plate from the cabinet counter and joined Reeva at the stove. "Sounds delicious. I love salmon." She darted an anxious glance at Reeva. "Is Sophia feeling okay?"

"She's feeling great. But now that she's carrying a little Crawford, Colt wants her to rest as much as possible," Reeva answered. "He's going to drive her crazy before the baby is ever born."

"It's because he loves them so much," Bonnie told her.

Reeva sighed. "I know. And I'm sure it worries him because she miscarried several years ago. But he needs to have faith that everything will turn out for the best."

Faith. Yes, Bonnie needed to trust that she didn't meet Mose just to get her heart broken. She had to believe they'd been brought together for a meaningful reason.

"Sophia will be fine, Reeva. But I hope you don't overwork yourself just so she can rest."

"No chance of that. Jazelle is already stepping up and pitching in to help me."

The two women carried their plates to the booth and Bonnie motioned for Reeva to sit. "I'll get our drinks. You want iced tea, or something else?"

"Tea will do for me."

Bonnie placed the drinks on the table, then took a seat across from the cook.

As the two women started to eat, Reeva asked, "How are things going with Aunt Sarah? Has she helped with your family-tree work?"

"Oh yes. She's been great. She had a long talk with me and Maureen and Gil a little earlier this evening. And she was able to tell us all sorts of information that we hadn't heard before. I think most of the mystery about Parnell Hollister has finally come together."

Reeva looked at her. "Does that mean you're not going to be doing any more work on the project?"

"There are still some things I'm going to search through, just in case there might be some important information we weren't aware of. But for the most part, I believe we've found out everything we can about Parnell. No one seems to know where he went or what he was doing those few years after he left the ranch and before he entered the army. I suppose that part of the man's life will always be a mystery."

"Who knows? You might accidentally run into someone who was acquainted with his wife. And there had to be people who knew Lionel before he left England. Didn't you say he was about nineteen when he came to the United States? Surely he had teenaged friends over there."

Bonnie's eyes widened. "Reeva, you're a genius. I hadn't thought about that possibility. Not that I'd take off to Great Britian to do a search. But I could dig around on the internet."

"Have you talked to your father yet and told him what Sarah had to say?"

Oh yes, she'd talked at length to her father. He'd not been surprised to hear Parnell had been a rogue who'd deserved to be written out of the Hollister will. However, Bonnie could tell it saddened him to learn his grandfather hadn't been a stand-up guy.

"I have. I'm getting the feeling that he's finally ready to put all this behind him. At least, this interest in his grandfather. I think now he's just eager to get to know his half sister and her daughters." She looked down at her plate and drew in a deep breath. "And I haven't told Maureen yet, but he wanted to know if I'd be coming home for Christmas. To tell you the truth, Reeva, I don't understand why he's pushing for me to fly back to Utah so soon. He and Mom were so anxious for me to come down here. Not just because of the family-tree thing, but so I could take a break from the ranch."

"Did he say outright that he expects you to come home? Or was he just asking casually? There's a difference, you know."

"He didn't demand it. But I got to thinking he and Mom might be struggling to keep up with all the office work. Our ranch has grown quite a bit in the past few years. The paperwork, phone calls, billing and that sort of thing have all increased. He probably didn't want to say right out that they need me. And then, there's the holidays. I've never been away from the family at Christmas."

Picking up her glass, Reeva leaned back in the booth and eyed Bonnie closely. "What did you tell him?"

Bonnie swallowed hard as emotions balled in her throat. "I told him I need to wrap up a few things here before I leave. But, Reeva, I... I'm just not ready to go back to Utah. I feel like I have family around me. I'm loving Three Rivers and... everything about living here. I wanted to spend this Christmas with you folks."

Reeva's expression was filled with gentle understanding. "And with Mose?" she suggested. "Everyone knows you've grown close to him."

A pain squeezed the middle of her chest. "Oh Reeva. I don't

think Mose is as close to me as I am to him. So maybe for the sake of that situation, it would be best if I did go home."

Reaching across the table, Reeva gave Bonnie's forearm a gentle pat. "Don't you think Mose should have a say in this?"

Bonnie groaned. "I'm not sure he cares to have a say. I haven't heard from him since—since the night he cooked dinner for me."

"All the more reason you should give him a call. Sometimes men need to be nudged. You need to know where Mose stands before you say any more to your father. That's the way I see things." She gave Bonnie one of her rare smiles. "But I'm just an old woman. What do I know?"

Touched that the woman was trying to encourage her, Bonnie went around to the other side of the table and gave her a tight hug. "Reeva, I love you."

The woman's eyes suddenly misted over. "I love you, too, sweetie," she said gruffly. "Now eat your dinner and go call that man of yours."

Bonnie finished the meal with Reeva, then helped her and Jazelle clean the kitchen before she retired to her bedroom. However, once she was in the privacy of her room, she didn't call Mose. Instead, she picked up her phone and texted him a message.

Will you be home tomorrow night? I'd like to come see you and talk.

Several minutes passed without any response, and she was about to decide he was going to ignore her completely when her phone dinged with an incoming message.

I'll be here.

The three words was all he said, and Bonnie's first urge was to fall across the bed and weep. But she'd always been the strong, practical twin. She wasn't going to give in to tears, she told herself. She'd gone into this relationship with Mose with her eyes open. She'd known from the very start he wasn't in the market for love, or anything close to it. Now she had to bear up and face the reality of moving on with her life without Mose at her side.

I'll come by at 6:30.

She tapped out the reply, then placed the phone on the nightstand. It wasn't likely Mose would call just to say he'd be glad to see her. But she'd keep the phone near, just in case.

The next day it was pretty nigh impossible for Mose to think of anything except Bonnie. The idea of seeing her again was shaking the ground beneath his feet. If Colt or Luke or any of the grooms noticed he was distracted, they didn't mention it, which was a relief to Mose. He couldn't talk to anyone about Bonnie. And he didn't know how he was going to manage to talk to her tonight.

But when he'd read her text saying she wanted to see him, he'd not been able to refuse her. Where she was concerned, he was a big coward, but on the other hand, he'd not wanted to come off as an unfeeling jerk.

Unfeeling, hell! Bonnie made him feel things he'd never felt before in his life. They'd left him vulnerable and running scared. For the past four days, he'd been aching and longing to hear her voice and have her wrapped in his arms. But the fear of jumping into deep water and never being able to swim out was terrifying. Better to ache now, he kept telling himself, than to drown in sorrow later.

Now, at the kitchen table, as he finished a bowl of chili and swigged down the last of his beer, he realized his nerves were jumping. Even his cats must have sensed he was in a bad state of mind. Both were sitting on their haunches a few feet from his chair, staring up at him as if they expected him to explode.

"What are you two looking at?" he barked at the cats. "Haven't you ever seen a man have a meltdown?"

Margo and Seymour exchanged confused looks, then turned expectant eyes back on Mose.

With a helpless groan, Mose rose from the table, and after scraping his bowl and placing it in the dishwasher, he pulled another beer from the refrigerator and carried it out to the porch to wait.

Ten minutes later, Bonnie pulled to a stop in front of the house and as she climbed out of the work truck, Mose put down his beer and walked out to greet her.

"Hello, Mose. How are you?"

The smile on her face was just as sweet and warm as he remembered, and it amazed him that she didn't appear to be annoyed or angry with him. She *should* be angry. He'd not followed through on his promise to call her. He'd not been a gentleman, period.

"I'm okay. And you?"

She leaned up and kissed his cheek, and for one second, Mose thought about circling his arms around her and crushing her to his chest. He wanted to kiss her. He wanted to carry her into the house and make love to her over and over.

Oh Lord, how was he going to get through this? How was he going to keep from breaking down in front of her?

She gave him another smile. "I've been very busy. Gil's Aunt Sarah arrived a couple of days ago and she's been helping me get things wrapped up with the family tree. At least, the parts we could wrap up."

He tore his eyes off her beautiful face to glance back at the house. "Would you like to come in? I don't have anything cooked for supper, but I can offer you a sandwich or something to drink."

"No, thanks. Before I left the ranch, I ate some of the appetizers Sophia made for dinner tonight, so I'm not hungry."

With a hand beneath her elbow, he ushered her into the house, then gestured awkwardly toward the couch. "Make yourself comfortable, Bonnie."

She sat on the end cushion and after smoothing the folds of her skirt, folded her hands in her lap. Mose sat down on the cushion next to her, but was careful to keep a few inches between them.

Glancing around the room, she said, "You don't have a Christmas tree. Aren't you going to put one up? There aren't that many days left until Santa comes."

"There's no reason to put up a tree just for myself. Besides, Santa doesn't come to my house."

His voice not only sounded brittle, it was lost and empty. And her spirits plummeted. Had she done this to him? Had taking her to bed changed him from the Mose she knew and loved into a shell?

"He might. If you invited him," she said.

He didn't reply and she turned a quizzical look on him. "Am I interrupting anything?"

"Why would you think you're interrupting?"

"I get the feeling you're just waiting for me to leave. If you're not in the mood for company, you should've sent me a message and told me not come. I would've understood."

Mose took off his hat and after tossing it onto the coffee table, raked both hands through his hair. Too bad he couldn't wipe away the agonizing thoughts in his brain, he thought.

"You would have? You must be a saint, Bonnie. Because if I was you, I sure as hell wouldn't be putting up with me."

Her brows shot straight up and he realized his harsh comment had shocked her. Well, better to do it now, than later, he thought.

"What does that mean? I don't understand."

His groan was a sound of pure frustration. "It means I'm a jerk and you should know it!"

"Mose!" Her expression full of concern, she scooted close to his side and reached for his hand. "You shouldn't say such a thing about yourself. That's terrible!"

He couldn't resist enfolding her hand in his and soaking in the feel of her skin against his. "No, it's the truth, Bonnie. I've not treated you right and I'm sorry about that. I should've had the guts to call you—"

Her short laugh was a sound of dismay. "You need guts to call me? Why? You've called me before. It's not like I'd be able to bite you through the phone."

He drew in a deep breath and slowly blew it out. "Bonnie, you know I think you're wonderful and special. You're those things and more to me."

Her expression turned sober as she shook her head. "No. I don't exactly know what you're thinking. After I spent the night here with you, I thought we, uh, had something very special between us. Didn't you?"

He swallowed hard as a burning ball of emotion threatened to choke him. "Yes. It was something—I'll never forget."

She squeezed his hand. "Neither will I. That's why I—I've been a little confused as to why I haven't heard from you. Have you been super busy or something? You look very tired."

He could've told her his problem was fatigue. He felt empty. There was no light or joy left in him. All he could feel was loss and pain. Colt, or anyone who knew him, would say he'd brought the misery on himself. And perhaps his buddy would be right.

No one was forcing Mose to keep his distance from Bonnie. He could tell her he was crazy about her. He could tell her he'd be willing to spend the rest of his life trying to make her happy. But what good would that do when he knew from experience that trying wouldn't be enough? She was used to a standard of living he couldn't give her, and she lived in a community hundreds of miles away. Those unchangeable facts were a torment he couldn't shake.

"We've been loaded with extra work. But that's just part of the job. I'll get rested." He forced his eyes to meet hers. "So what happened when you finally got to speak with Sarah? Was she able to fill in the missing parts about Parnell?"

"She's been great. Like a walking encyclopedia where family history is concerned. And she's a lovely woman on top of that. I can tell Gil is really enjoying having her here."

"I'm sure. And it's good she was able to help you with the genealogy thing. I know you've been working hard to figure out everything."

"I have worked hard on the project, but I've enjoyed every minute of it. And I'm glad Sarah has come for a visit. She's my relative, too. Her uncle was my great-grandfather, so this is giving me a chance to be with her. And guess what? She loves riding horses, so she and I are going on a ride together in the next couple of days. Before I—"

When she didn't continue, he looked at her. "Before what?"

She glanced away from him and blew out a heavy breath. "Before I leave to go back to Stone Creek. My father is urging me to come home for Christmas and—well, I told him I'd be there."

If someone had whammed him in the chest with a sledgehammer, he wouldn't have felt any more pain than he did at this moment. "I see. When will you be leaving?"

"Maureen has purchased a plane ticket for me for a flight this coming Saturday. She seemed to think it would be better to get home before Christmas Eve and avoid the congested flights and the highways clogged with holiday travelers."

For long moments, his mind went blank. Yes, he'd known all along that she'd eventually be leaving Three Rivers. But a part of him had hoped against hope she'd tell him she loved him too much to leave. Now he could mark off that slim chance of happening. She'd never mentioned the word *love* to him. And obviously she wasn't going to bring it up now. He'd been a fool to think, even for one second, that she'd be willing to give up her life on Stone Creek for a more modest existence with him.

You'll survive, Mose. On your own.

"I'm going to miss your company, Bonnie. The horseback rides we took together and just being with you. But I—think it's probably for the best that we'll not be seeing each other again."

Bonnie felt as if someone had stomped the air out of her. She'd come here tonight hoping and praying that Mose would welcome her into his arms. That he'd kiss her and carry her to his bed and tell her how much he'd missed her. And most of all, she'd prayed he would say he loved her too much to ever let her leave Three Rivers.

Oh Lord, she'd been so wrong about his feelings for her. She'd seen what she'd wanted to see, so she was the only one to blame for the pain she was going through now.

Tears swam in her eyes, but she did her best to blink them back. "Oh—I thought—we'd make the most of these last few nights together."

He didn't look at her and Bonnie thought it was just as well. She didn't want him to see the shock and pain that was undoubtedly on her face.

"Like I said, I'm going to miss you. But I never did enjoy long goodbyes. And that's exactly what us being together would be," he said bluntly. "A long, miserable goodbye."

She wanted to throw herself into his arms. She wanted to ask him why he was hell-bent on refusing her. Most of all, she wanted to tell him how much she loved him. But he was clearly blocking her out of his heart and his life. All she had left now was her pride, and if she didn't leave now, it was going to be shredded into pieces.

Even though her lips were quivering, she managed to smile and give his hands a squeeze. "I want you to know you've made my time here on the ranch very special, Mose. I'll always remember you. And I hope your Christmas is the best ever."

She leaned in and kissed his cheek, then hurried out of the house before the tears in her eyes rolled onto her cheeks.

So much for being strong, she thought. And so much for trying to hold on to something she never had in the first place.

Chapter Fifteen

By the time Friday afternoon arrived, Mose had sunk into a dark haze of misery. The memory of Bonnie's face when she walked out of his house for the last time continued to play over and over in his mind. And that tiny little kiss she'd placed on his cheek—the spot still burned. His lips ached to kiss hers. His whole body ached to touch her and make love to her.

Oh yes, Mose loved her deeply. More than he ever would have thought he could ever love anything, or anyone. But what good would he ever get from the all-consuming emotion, except never-ending pain? His love wasn't enough to give her the kind of life she needed and deserved.

"Mose! Watch out!"

Dex's shout of warning came too late to penetrate Mose's fuzzy brain. The stallion's teeth sank into his shoulder before he realized the animal had walked up behind him.

"Oww—damn!"

Mose yelled and jerked away from the horse's bite at the same time Dex rushed up and grabbed a secure hold on the lead rope dangling from the animal's halter.

"Are you okay, Mose? Did he get you bad?" Dex asked Mose, while keeping a careful eye on the rowdy stallion.

Muttering another curse, Mose rolled his shoulder as fiery pain raced up the side of his neck and down his back. "I don't think it's that bad. It just hurts like hell."

"What's going on here?"

Both men looked around to see Holt striding up to them. A look of concern furrowed his brow as he glanced from Dex to Mose.

"Possum nabbed Mose on the shoulder."

"Go take care of the horse," Holt ordered the groom, then turned to Mose and gave his shoulder a cursory inspection. "Your shirt is torn and blood is already soaking through. Better come to the office and let me take a look at the damage."

"I'll be fine, Holt. It's not that bad," Mose insisted.

"Don't argue!" Holt snapped. "And why the hell weren't you watching him? You know Possum bites. You can't just lead him off like you're on a stroll in the park!"

Before Mose could defend himself, Holt was pushing him through the arena gate and down the shedrow.

"You don't have to remind me that Possum bites," Mose told him. "He's nipped me before. He just managed to get a deeper bite this time."

"I wonder why," Holt said with a heavy dose of sarcasm.

Mose bristled. "What does that mean?"

"Later. Right now we're going to take care of that wound," Holt told him.

Halfway down the shedrow, they entered an alleyway that would take them inside the barn and down to Holt's office. Once they were inside the room, he sat Mose down in a chair in front of his desk.

"Take off your shirt," he ordered, while gathering antiseptic and bandages from a cabinet at the back of the room. "When was the last time you had a tetanus shot?"

"Last month. So you don't need to jab me with another one of those."

"Lucky you," Holt said as he placed the medical supplies on the corner of his desk.

"Yeah, lucky me," Mose muttered. "I should've been watching closer. I'd just finished with Possum and was taking him over to Dex. Guess the stallion wanted to get back at me for making him trot in his right lead. He hates doing that."

Holt grunted. "He probably hates being called Possum, too. But that has nothing to do with you not paying attention to your work. I—"

"Who says I haven't been paying attention? Have you been out in the arena keeping tabs on me?" Mose asked crossly, then blew out a heavy breath. "Sorry, Holt. Go ahead and fire me. I deserve it."

Chuckling, Holt poured antiseptic onto the wound. The reddish-yellow liquid rolled down Mose's back and beneath the waistband of his jeans, but he didn't care. A pair of stained jeans was the least of his problems.

"Hell, Mose, you'd have to commit murder for me to ever fire you, so get that out of your mind. Right now, I'm more concerned about you getting hurt."

"The bite isn't that bad, is it? Does it need stitches?"

"I don't think so. And as for you getting hurt, I'm not talking about these teeth marks on your shoulder. You're going to get your head kicked off or a few bones broken if you don't get your mind on your business. Now, tell me what's going on. Are you unhappy here on Three Rivers? Is that it?"

Stunned by Holt's question, he twisted around to stare at him. "I don't want to live anywhere but here. I love working for you. I don't ever want that to change. Why would you doubt that?"

Holt placed a pad of gauze against the wounded flesh. "Because the past few days, you've been acting like a zombie around here. Something is wrong with you, and if you don't get it straightened out you're going to get yourself seriously hurt or maybe even killed. And then I'd have to stop work for a funeral and I can't spare the time. Not to mention it'd mess up everyone's holidays."

Mose let out a rueful groan, while Holt tore off a piece of adhesive tape and plastered it over the gauze.

"You don't understand, Holt. My problem is—impossible to straighten out. It's just something I'll have to get over eventually. I expect it might take a while."

"And in the meantime, Possum can take a bite out of your other shoulder? Won't work, Mose. You might as well tell me what's wrong. I'll help you fix it."

He plastered two more pieces of tape onto the bandage, then stepped back and folded his arms against his chest.

Mose glanced up at him. "Guess you're waiting for me to talk," he muttered.

Holt rocked back on his heels. "We don't have all day."

"All right, dammit! Since you want to know, I'll tell you. Bonnie is leaving tomorrow morning. She's going home to Stone Creek Ranch—where she belongs."

"Oh. How do you know she's leaving tomorrow? Did she tell you?"

Mose looked away from him. "Yes, she came over to the house and told me Maureen purchased her a plane ticket for Saturday. And Colt found out through Sophia that her flight would be leaving in the morning."

"And you don't want her to go?"

Mose groaned. "It's killing me to think of her leaving."

Holt said, "You've told her that you want her to stay, but she's going anyway? I'm surprised. I got the impression Bonnie loves it here. So am I to believe she just doesn't love you enough to stay? Is that your problem?"

Holt's blunt question was like a knife blade to his already aching shoulder. "I don't know," he mumbled. "I mean, I don't know if she loves me or not. She gave me the impression she did, but she never said so. Besides, her parents need her to come home—to run the office."

"Hah! Bonnie is a grown woman. She can choose what kind of life she wants, and she can decide where she wants to live it. Her parents are perfectly capable of hiring another secretary." Holt pulled up a nearby chair, and after taking a seat directly in front of Mose, said, "Listen, my friend, if you really care about Bonnie, you get your rear in gear and go see her! Tell her you love her and want her to stay with you."

"But, Holt, how can I ask her to make a life with me? She's a Hollister."

Wry amusement twisted Holt's features. "I'm a Hollister, too. What has that got to do with anything?"

"You have money. I don't."

"Bonnie doesn't want money. I'm betting she'd rather have you." He leaned forward to emphasize his point. "If I'd had to depend on my wealth to persuade Isabelle to marry me, I would've been out of luck. If a woman really loves you, money, or the lack of it, doesn't matter. She'll just want to know you love her back."

"I had a woman before who wasn't satisfied with just me," Mose said flatly. "I don't want to go through that humiliation again."

"Mose, if you ask me, you made a great escape. That woman, whoever she was, didn't love you."

"I'm not sure Bonnie does, either."

Grinning now, Holt reached over and slapped Mose's knee. "You won't know until you ask her."

The next morning, Bonnie made her rounds telling all the children goodbye. She'd also said an emotional farewell to Jazelle, Reeva and Aunt Sarah before she'd carried her bags down the stairs to be loaded into the truck that Maureen would be using to drive her to the airport.

Last night, before Bonnie had retired to her room, Maureen had pulled her aside and cautioned her to think hard and deep before she made the decision to go back to Utah. Especially after she'd talked to her parents on the phone and they assured her she had their blessings if she wanted to stay at Three Rivers. But Bonnie had argued that her parents needed her and it would be best if she returned to Stone Creek.

Maureen had understood Bonnie was merely using her parents as an excuse. She was actually running from Mose. But thankfully, Maureen didn't press Bonnie on the matter. But now, as Bonnie took one last look over her bedroom, Sophia walked in and from the determined look on her pretty face, she knew her friend wouldn't be so tactful about keeping Mose from the conversation.

"Okay, Bonnie, I'll just come out and say that what you're doing is ridiculous. Furthermore, I hate you because you're doing it."

Bonnie arched a brow at her. "*Hate?* Your heart is too soft to hate anyone. Especially me. I happen to know you love me."

Which was far more than she could say about Mose, Bonnie thought sadly.

Sophia sniffed. "I can't help it. I have to say something to shock you to your senses."

"My senses don't need to be shocked, Sophia. You knew, like everyone else, that I was here temporarily and sooner or later I'd have to go home."

"Not now! It's almost Christmas. You need to celebrate with all of us! Besides, Three Rivers is your home now," Sophia argued. "You have to stay because of Mose. You have to speak with him, Bonnie. You have to let him know you've fallen in love with him."

Just hearing Sophia say the words caused a pain to rifle through Bonnie's heart. "Mose isn't blind. He knows I have feelings for him. But where he's concerned, that doesn't change anything." She walked over and gave her friend a tight hug. "Anyway, you need to be concentrating on you and Colt and the coming baby. You're a blessed woman, Sophia. Never take your family for granted. Now, come on. Walk with me to the bottom of the stairs. But that's as far as you go. I don't want either of us to start crying."

Once the two women said their final goodbyes, Bonnie started down the hallway, but before she could reach the front of the house, Maureen stepped out of her office to intercept her.

"Bonnie, I'm glad I caught you here," she said. "I needed to let you know I won't be driving you into Wickenburg this morning like I'd promised. I'm expecting an important phone call from the president of the women's ranching committee to come through at any time, and since it will be on the landline, I can't leave. But don't worry, I already have a driver ready to take you."

"No problem. As long as I get to the airport on time." She stepped forward and gave the woman a tight hug. "Thank you, Maureen. You're wonderful. You and Gil and the whole family. I'm going to miss you all so much. I hope everyone has a wonderful Christmas. I'll be thinking of all of you."

Smiling gently, Maureen patted her cheek. "Merry Christmas to you, honey. And just remember, if you have a change of heart, you can come back. You'll always be welcome to make your home here."

Bonnie swallowed hard as she fought to keep from crying in front of the woman. Maureen had a heart bigger than Texas, but she was also an iron lady and she expected others to be equally strong.

"Thank you, Maureen. I'll remember your open invitation."

She kissed Maureen's cheek, then walked briskly out to the waiting truck. Along the way, she did her best not to look at the beautiful nativity scene displayed on the front yard and the decorative wreath hanging on the gate. The same gate where Mose had first kissed her cheek. It was all too heartbreaking.

Since her bags were already loaded in the back seat, all she needed to do was climb in and wait for her driver to appear. But after five minutes passed and he still hadn't shown up, she started wondering if the ranch hand Maureen had picked had forgotten about driving her.

She was about to pull out her phone and call Maureen when she spotted a tall, familiar-looking cowboy walking up the driveway toward the truck.

Was that *Mose*? How could Maureen be so cruel? Why would she deliberately rub salt in Bonnie's wounded heart?

When he opened the truck door and climbed into the driver's seat, Bonnie could barely force herself to glance in his direction.

"Hello, Bonnie."

"Hello," she said curtly.

"Ready to leave?" he asked.

The question made her want to scream at him. Which only proved just how much she'd changed since she'd left Utah. She'd never wanted to scream at anyone in her entire life. But Mose had a way of building a fire in her.

In a stiff voice, she said, "Yes. My bags are loaded."

Without saying a word, he started the truck and began to drive. As the ranch house slowly disappeared behind them, Bonnie yearned to look over her shoulder and take one last mental snapshot of the place. But she didn't want to give Mose the idea that she had regrets about leaving.

From the corner of her eye, she allowed her gaze to run over his rugged form. He was dressed as he usually was in a colorful Western shirt with black cuffs and yokes against a striped background. His worn jeans were stuffed into a pair of tall, butterscotch-colored cowboy boots, while his brown hat was pulled low on his forehead. And suddenly she was remembering the first time she saw him at the airport. She'd been struck with his flamboyant appearance and intimidated by his intensely masculine presence. And never once that day had she imagined she'd end up falling in love with him.

A few minutes passed, and as the silence in the cab continued, the tension in the cab was so thick Bonnie felt like a bomb was about to explode. Finally, the pressure became too much for her and she looked pointedly over at him.

"I don't understand this, Mose. You distinctly told me you didn't like long goodbyes. It's a forty minute trip to the airport. So why are you driving me there?"

"Because I'm a glutton for punishment, I suppose."

Before she could make any kind of sensible reply, he yanked the wheel, turning the truck onto a dim trail on the left side of the road that led into a thick stand of Joshua trees.

Bonnie looked around her in dazed confusion. "What are you doing? You're going to make me miss my flight!"

"That's my intention, Bonnie." He braked the truck to a stop, then killed the engine and turned to her. "Did you honestly think I could let you go?"

She stared at him with a mixture of confusion and pain. "Yes, I did! I still do! What reason do I have to think any differently? You told me we shouldn't be together, or have you forgotten?"

Groaning with regret, he reached for her and Bonnie went willingly into the circle of his strong arms.

"I wish I could forget those things I said to you, Bonnie. Because everything that came out of my mouth was wrong."

"Then, why did you say it?" she asked, her voice choked with emotion.

He sighed. "After we made love, I felt like I was drowning. I realized I loved you. Not only that, but I loved you more than I believed any human was capable of loving. And that scared me, Bonnie. That's why I didn't call or ask to see you again. I thought it best to let the fire between us die."

"But why, Mose? If you love me—"

"Because I don't have enough to offer you, Bonnie. I've gone through this before. When I was much younger I considered getting married, but the woman's family didn't approve of me, and in the end, she wasn't willing to give up her family's wealth. Not for me. It hadn't bothered her to end things and walk away. In the end, I'm just glad I didn't love her."

Surprised by his confession, she leaned her head back and studied his face. "How do you know you didn't love her? If you were considering marriage, you must have felt something for her."

"Oh, at the time I believed it was love. Then gradually, after we parted, I could see I'd had a case of infatuation. But when I met you—oh, Bonnie, you've opened my eyes to what real love is, and yeah, I'm still scared, but you have to know how much I want you in my life—forever. As my wife and the mother of our children."

In spite of her determination not to cry, she couldn't stop tears of joy from sliding down her cheeks. "Oh Mose, I thought— I didn't think I was woman enough to hold on to you. I didn't believe I was woman enough for you to love me."

He pressed kisses across her forehead and onto her cheeks. "Bonnie, Bonnie. Why would you believe such a thing?

You're sexy and desirable and more woman than I'd ever dreamed of having in my life."

She blinked her eyes. "You remember I told you about having one bad experience? Well, the guy had been promising his undying love to me. And then he took one look at Beatrice and made a play for her."

"Your twin? He threw you over for your twin sister?" he asked with disbelief.

"Not exactly. He tried to convince her to go out with him, but Bea didn't waste any time telling him to get lost and never come near me or her ever again."

He shook his head. "So because of him, you've thought you weren't woman enough to attract a man? Bonnie, that's so ridiculous."

Her mouth twisted to a wry slant. "About as ridiculous as you to think I'd choose wealth over you. And just in case you're wondering, even after we get married I'll still get a yearly dividend for my share of the ranch. I just won't get my secretary salary. But I won't need that income. I don't need anything, but you, Mose."

Groaning, he pulled her head against his shoulder and meshed his fingers in her hair. "I guess we were both too insecure to trust our feelings to each other. But now—are you willing to marry me?"

She leaned her head back and gazed into his brown eyes. "It will be an honor to be your wife and the mother of your children, Mose. And just to be clear, I love living on Three Rivers Ranch, but not nearly as much as I love you. I can't wait to make my home with you. That is, if the cats are willing to share their space with me," she added teasingly.

Chuckling, he nuzzled his nose against hers. "The cats are willing and so am I."

She slipped her arms around his neck and rubbed her cheek

against his. "Bea told me to grab you and hang tight, so you might as well know I'm never going to let you go."

"A tight rein, huh?" A smile was in his voice as he held her close. "Don't worry. No chance I'll ever strain against the bit."

Laughing, she leaned her head back and looked at him. "Does that mean you're giving up going to the Fandango?"

Quizzical humor spread across his face. "What's the Fandango?"

He kissed her then and Bonnie could feel the promise of forever on his lips. Her heart was dazzled with love as bright as the Arizona sun.

Once their lips finally parted, he eased her far enough away to pull a phone from his pocket. When she arched a questioning brow at him, he said, "Holt is expecting me back in a couple of hours and I need to let him know I'm going to be late."

She looked at him with comical confusion. "Mose, we're only ten minutes from the ranch yard. Why will you be late?"

"Give me a minute and you'll find out." He punched the phone and stuck it to his ear. After moment he said, "Holt… Yeah, we're on our way," he said, then after a pause went on, "I thought you ought to know I'll be late getting back to work."

Bonnie decided Holt was saying something amusing because a wide smile spread across Mose's face as he listened to his boss.

"No. I'm not expecting trouble," Mose said with a low chuckle. "And we won't be going to the airport. I'm taking Bonnie to town to buy her an early Christmas present." He paused, then added smugly, "No. It's nothing to do with a horse. We're going to the jewelers. I'm giving her an engagement ring."

A ring! Only ten minutes ago, she'd thought she was going

back to Utah and would probably never see him again. She'd been wondering how she was going to live the rest of her life without him. Now her heart was so full she was close to crying.

"Thanks, Holt. And by the way, is your mother always right?"

After a laugh and another short exchange of words, he put the phone away and grinned at her. It was the same suggestive grin she'd seen on his face the first day she'd met him at the airport. At that time she hadn't recognized what was happening to her, but now she realized she'd fallen in love with him right then and there.

She slanted him a sly look. "Okay, Mose, I'm just now beginning to put two and two together. That first day I arrived, Maureen sent you to the airport to pick me up. Now, she somehow finagled you into driving me back to the airport. Am I crazy to think she deliberately threw us together?"

His grin deepened. "No. But you'd be crazy to think anything will ever pull us apart."

With her arms around his neck and her lips against his, she whispered, "Let's go get the ring."

Epilogue

Four days later, on the night of Christmas Eve, Bonnie and Mose were lying in his bed, their arms and legs still tangled from a session of lovemaking. As she rested her cheek against his shoulder, Mose stroked his fingers through her hair and down the bumps of her backbone.

On top of the world.

At the time Colt had made the remark to Mose, he'd never thought he'd experience such a feeling. And he'd sure never believed he'd be marrying into the Hollister family. But here he was with Bonnie's loving arm draped across his chest and her promises of forever still warm on his lips.

This evening, shortly after supper, they'd exchanged their personal gifts. Bonnie had given him a fancy Western shirt with diamond-shaped pearl snaps, while the fabric pattern was tiny red roses on a black background. Along with the shirt, he'd been stunned to find a pair of jingle bob spurs hand made by a well-known spur and bit maker. Because he'd already given a small fortune for her engagement ring, she'd insisted he not spend more money on a Christmas gift for her. But he'd surprised her with a sterling necklace with a horse pendent fashioned from silver and turquoise. And to see the way her eyes had lit up at the simple gift had filled his heart.

Tomorrow the two of them would be celebrating Christmas with the Hollisters at the big ranch house. Even though

Mose had attended several of their celebrations since he'd come to work for Three Rivers, this one would be different for him. Yes, they'd always treated him as family, but now, for the first time in his life, he felt as if he genuinely was a part of the Hollister clan.

Shortly after he'd placed the diamond solitaire ring on Bonnie's finger, he'd called his father and brother back in Texas to give them the news. They'd been stunned to hear the family known for having the richest ranch in Arizona was going to be Mose's in-laws, but they'd also expressed how happy they were that he'd found what he wanted in life. In turn, she'd called her family up in Utah and Mose had enjoyed a long talk with her parents. And he'd made Hadley very happy by asking his future-father-in-law for his blessing.

"What are you thinking about?" she asked, while nuzzling her nose against the side of his neck.

Her voice pulled him out of his deep thoughts and prompted him to glance down at her. "About Dad. I'm still shocked about him and Mom getting married again. Mitch and I both knew her second marriage had never worked. But we weren't aware she'd divorced the man and rekindled a romance with Dad."

She sighed. "I think it's wonderful."

"So do me and Mitch. To think of our parents back together again sort of sets the world right for us. You know, I asked Dad how he could put all the bad behind him and marry Mom again."

"And how did he explain it?"

"In the same way it's been explained down through the years. Nothing can kill true love."

"Hmm. Dunn Martel sounds like my kind of man," she said. "I hope I get to meet your parents soon. Do you think they'll come to our wedding this spring?"

Even though he and Bonnie had only been engaged for a few days, Maureen had already jumped into action to plan a huge wedding for them, which would take place on Three Rivers in April.

"For sure, my parents and brother will be here," he said. "And what about your family? Do you think they'll drive down from Utah for the wedding? Or do you think your parents resent the fact that you're getting married here on Three Rivers, rather than Stone Creek?"

She angled her head against his shoulder in order to see his face. "I've already talked to Mom and Dad about the wedding. They're thrilled actually. They think our wedding will be a special way for both families to come together on a ranch where all of us Hollisters first originated. And Mom is going to make a special trip down to Three Rivers so she can help Maureen with the wedding plans."

He stroked a hand over her hair. "I'm glad your parents feel that way. Because from now on, this will be our home. You won't become homesick on me, will you?"

She raised her head just enough to place a soft kiss on his lips. "That will never happen. My home is where you are, my darling. But—"

He raised up on one elbow and, with an impish but loving grin, gazed down at her. "Don't tell me you're going to back out on marrying me!"

She held up her hand and gazed at the diamond ring glittering in the semidarkness of the room. "And give this beautiful ring back to you? Not a chance," she joked, then planted a kiss on his jaw. "But I have learned something interesting about my family that I think you ought to know."

Curious now, he asked, "Why am I just now hearing about this?"

Her smile alluring, she traced a fingertip down the slope

of his shoulder and across his chest. "Because after I hung up the phone from talking with Jack, you and I had other things on our mind."

"Okay, now that we have those *other things* taken care of, what is this interesting news Jack gave you?"

She said, "It seems as though my brothers have decided they need to make a search of their own into Grandfather Lionel's double life."

His brows pulled together. "What do they want to uncover about his double life? Isn't it enough to know he deceived all of you? Including his ex-wife?"

"According to Jack, it's not enough. All my brothers are thinking—and in my opinion, rightly so—that with Lionel having mistresses, he might have sired other children. Relatives that none of us know about."

Mose's brown eyes widened. "I guess there is a possibility that Lionel's philandering behavior might have produced other children. But, Bonnie, do you think it's wise to dig into things that might be better off dead and buried?"

Her sigh was helpless. "I can't say. Neither can they—that's why they're not going to tell Dad about their intentions. At least, not until they run into something pertinent. And I'm glad about that. Dad has been through so much disappointment over his father and grandfather. He doesn't need more to deal with. But that's enough about the past Hollisters, I'm thinking about tomorrow and all the fun we're going to have celebrating Christmas."

A thought suddenly struck Mose and he darted a glance to the foot of the bed. "The cats have disappeared! If those two are in the living room tearing up the Christmas tree, I'm hauling them straight back to the horse barn and letting their mother corral them!"

Bonnie laughed. "You aren't going to haul Margo and Seymour anywhere. This is their home, too."

Mose let out a good-natured groan. "You have that right. They think it's theirs, not ours."

They both climbed out of bed, and after Mose pulled on his jeans and she threw on a robe, they walked out to the living room where the decorated tree was centered in front of the big picture window. There was just enough light from the starry sky for them to see both cats were asleep and curled up together among the brightly wrapped packages piled on the floor beneath the tree.

"Aww, Mose, look how sweet!" She walked over and knelt down to stroke a loving hand over each cat. "Now, these two are real gifts of the season."

Mose squatted down next to her and, wrapping an arm around her shoulder, tugged her close to his side.

"You are my Christmas gift, Bonnie," he said softly. "For this year and all our years to come."

Her face glowing with starlight, she pressed her cheek next to his. "Merry Christmas, darling."

* * * * *

Get up to 4 Free Books!

We'll send you 2 free books from each series you try PLUS a free Mystery Gift.

FREE Value Over $25

Both the **Harlequin® Special Edition** and **Harlequin® Heartwarming™** series feature compelling novels filled with stories of love and strength where the bonds of friendship, family and community unite.

YES! Please send me 2 FREE novels from the Harlequin Special Edition or Harlequin Heartwarming series and my FREE Gift (gift is worth about $10 retail). After receiving them, if I don't wish to receive any more books, I can return the shipping statement marked "cancel." If I don't cancel, I will receive 6 brand-new Harlequin Special Edition books every month and be billed just $6.39 each in the U.S. or $7.19 each in Canada, or 4 brand-new Harlequin Heartwarming Larger-Print books every month and be billed just $7.19 each in the U.S. or $7.99 each in Canada, a savings of 20% off the cover price. It's quite a bargain! Shipping and handling is just 50¢ per book in the U.S. and $1.25 per book in Canada.* I understand that accepting the 2 free books and gift places me under no obligation to buy anything. I can always return a shipment and cancel at any time by calling the number below. The free books and gift are mine to keep no matter what I decide.

Choose one: ☐ **Harlequin Special Edition** (235/335 BPA G36Y)   ☐ **Harlequin Heartwarming Larger-Print** (161/361 BPA G36Y)   ☐ **Or Try Both!** (235/335 & 161/361 BPA G36Z)

Name (please print)

Address   Apt. #

City   State/Province   Zip/Postal Code

Email: Please check this box ☐ if you would like to receive newsletters and promotional emails from Harlequin Enterprises ULC and its affiliates. You can unsubscribe anytime.

Mail to the Harlequin Reader Service:
IN U.S.A.: P.O. Box 1341, Buffalo, NY 14240-8531
IN CANADA: P.O. Box 603, Fort Erie, Ontario L2A 5X3

Want to explore our other series or interested in ebooks? Visit www.ReaderService.com or call 1-800-873-8635.

---

*Terms and prices subject to change without notice. Prices do not include sales taxes, which will be charged (if applicable) based on your state or country of residence. Canadian residents will be charged applicable taxes. Offer not valid in Quebec. This offer is limited to one order per household. Books received may not be as shown. Not valid for current subscribers to the Harlequin Special Edition or Harlequin Heartwarming series. All orders subject to approval. Credit or debit balances in a customer's account(s) may be offset by any other outstanding balance owed by or to the customer. Please allow 4 to 6 weeks for delivery. Offer available while quantities last.

Your Privacy—Your information is being collected by Harlequin Enterprises ULC, operating as Harlequin Reader Service. For a complete summary of the information we collect, how we use this information and to whom it is disclosed, please visit our privacy notice located at https://corporate.harlequin.com/privacy-notice. Notice to California Residents – Under California law, you have specific rights to control and access your data. For more information on these rights and how to exercise them, visit https://corporate.harlequin.com/california-privacy. For additional information for residents of other U.S. states that provide their residents with certain rights with respect to personal data, visit https://corporate.harlequin.com/other-state-residents-privacy-rights/.

HSEHW25